The 17th Airborne Division was one of five Airborne divisions activated by the United States during World War II. The "Golden Talon" Division first saw combat during the Battle of the Bulge in December and January of 1944-45. Late, in March of 1945, the Division made the Airborne assault over the Rhine River and fought on until Hitler's Germany collapsed.

World War II came to a sudden end with the dropping of the atomic bombs on Japan. At that time, the 17th Airborne was in mid-Atlantic Ocean on its way back to the States to refit and then ship to the Pacific for an Airborne assault on the Japanese mainland. With peace at last, the division was deactivated and quietly passed into American military history.

The 17th Airborne participated in three major campaigns in the European Theatre and in only 65 days of active combat, suffered 1,314 killed and 4,904 wounded in action. Today, the esprit de corps of the Airborne soldier lives on in the hearts and minds of nearly 10,000 veterans of the 17th Airborne Division.

Cover: *The author in December, 1944, Chiseldon, England. Photo by S/Sgt. Richard Lacefield, 17th Airborne Division Headquarters.*

GRANDDADDY WAS AIRBORNE!

BART HAGERMAN

TURNER PUBLISHING COMPANY

Turner Publishing Company

Turner Publishing Staff:
Editor: Herbert C. Banks II
Designer: Heather R. Warren

ISBN: 978-1-68162-222-4
Liabrary of Congress Catalog Card No.:
97-62515

Limited Edition

CONTENTS

PART IV   COMBAT

PART V   HOSPITALS AND HOME

PART VI   REFLECTIONS

INTRODUCTION

Like many other young men of my generation, my time in the military stands out as the most exciting days of my life. I recall and cherish many other exciting times, such my marriage, the births of my children and grandchildren, my 118 parachute jumps, and others. But, for sheer excitement and thrills galore, it's pretty tough to top World War II and life in the Airborne!

My children and grandchildren still beg me to tell them about my military experiences. It has been well over 52 years now since the end of World War II and my memories have begun to fade. So, before they are lost completely, this book is an attempt to record some of those events and experiences for those who may wonder "what did Granddaddy do in the war?"

Let me assure you that this is not a story of wild combat and a dashing, young "war hero". Far be it from that! It is nothing more than the day-to-day story and impressions of an ordinary young man, caught up in the hysteria and patriotic fervor of the 1940s. Rather than being a hero, I was only trying to do my duty as best I could, survive the mess that I found myself in, and get home in one piece.

Understanding the attitude of young men in those days is important to this story. Few were looking for a way to avoid military service. Those who were denied the chance to join the military frequently suffered shattering consequences to their morale and self esteem. It was a blow to their macho and it was a social stigma that was tough to live with. In those days, there was nothing worse than to be classified as 4-F: unfit for military service.

By early 1943, most of my close friends already had left for the service, or were soon to leave. I was eager to join myself. I wanted a taste of the excitement before the war was over. The Airborne, I soon learned, provided all the thrills and excitement I could have ever wanted! Combat, however, was something else. No one is ever prepared to see his friends blown apart and to live in constant fear for his own life.

This book documents some of the experiences I had when as a teen-ager I left home for the first time, joined the army, and went to war. There were good times and there were bad times. My days in the military service remain as the greatest adventure of my life, but it's one I would hope none of my descendants will ever have to experience.

This book is lovingly dedicated to my family that always showed great patience in listening to most of these experiences time and again. It is, however, especially dedicated to my eight wonderful grandchildren who continually asked me, "What did you do in the army, Granddaddy?"

PART I:
THE ARMY AND CAMP MACKALL

CHAPTER 1

YOU'RE IN THE ARMY NOW!

E ver since I could remember, I had known Joe Bailey Orr. As a young lad I had admired him as an outstanding football player at Bowling Green High School. Then, when I was playing football I knew him as a great fan of mine as well as a prominent lawyer in my home town. It was weird as to how he suddenly "turned" on me!

It was April 13, 1943, and I had volunteered for military service through the draft board. Actually, because I had volunteered, I ended up taking the place of someone who would have otherwise been drafted. Whoever he was, I guess they got him the next month!

Two of my friends, Bob Pearce and Robert "Izzie" Isbell, also volunteered with me and of course, we hoped to all be stationed together, wherever that might be. That worked out as we received consecutive serial numbers and ended up starting our military careers together.

I remember very well the morning we left Bowling Green aboard a charter Greyhound bus. The local draft board would ship their inductees to Louisville where they took a physical. Those that passed were given seven days to wind up their personal affairs and then to report back to Louisville. Those that failed were either real sad or real happy as they were returned to Bowling Green and were classified as unfit for service.

All three of us were confident of passing our physical and we were full of the enthusiasm that prevailed in those days. We were ready to serve. So ready were we, that we had decided to decline the seven-day delay in reporting. We were ready to go that very day!

We bid our parents and friends good-bye that morning and assembled outside the old armory building at 10th and Chestnut Streets. We laughed and joked all the way to Louisville and were delighted when we got to the armory which was being used as an Induction Center.

When we got off the bus, the first person I saw was Joe Bailey Orr. He wore the gold leaf insignia of a major and looked real sharp to us in his army suntans. Joe had been in the local unit of the Kentucky National Guard which had been activated earlier. Apparently, he had temporarily drawn this duty of meeting the new inductees and getting them started through the examination process.

"Hey, Joe," I called out to him, "the war won't last much longer after we get into it!"

He smiled and came over and shook hands with all three of us. He agreed it was only a matter of days until Hitler and the Japs would be on the run now that Bowling Green was sending its finest!

We were all in good spirits as he showed us where to go and wished us well. From there on it was a matter of being punched and pinched, weighed and quizzed and we had all passed with flying colors. We had all been marked for the Army. It didn't surprise me as I had tried to get in both the Marines and the Navy and neither would have me because of my bad eyes.

Finally, we were all herded into a big room and told to hold up our right hand. We were administered the oath and then told we were now in the Army! We congratulated each other and filed out toward a waiting bus that was to take us to Fort Ben Harrison in Indiana.

In the area where the bus was parked, there was my old friend, Joe Bailey Orr. Proud of our new accomplishment of passing our physical and now being a fellow-soldier, I yelled, "Hey Joe, I passed! I made it!"

I'll never forget the look Joe gave me. His face turned red and he boiled with anger. It was plain he was anything but the good friend he had always been. He squared his shoulders and came at me almost on the run.

"Who the hell do you think you are, soldier?" he screamed in my face. "Do you see this leaf on my collar? If you have anything to say to me you stand at attention and address me as Major Orr!"

I was completely taken back at this sudden change that seemed to have come over my old friend. I stammered something and froze at attention.

With his face about six inches from mine, he then yelled, "You don't have any business with me, soldier. Get your butt on that bus and get the hell out of here!"

Dumbfounded, I answered, "Yes, Sir!" and climbed on the bus. All the other guys, including Pearce and Izzie who had observed what had happened, roared with laughter. They thought it was great fun!

It took me a few minutes to gather my wits and realize just what had happened. It really wasn't all that complicated. I had just got my first of many "chewing outs". Major Orr had just let me know that after I took that oath, I was definitely a private in U. S. Army and no longer a carefree civilian!

CHAPTER 2
CARROTS FOR LUNCH

I t was a relatively short trip from the Induction Center at Louisville to Fort Benjamin Harrison, Indiana, our Reception Center, but it sure was a gigantic leap in our young lives. We definitely departed civilian life there and began our army careers. I was eager for it but a lot of the guys we met there were reluctantly being dragged headfirst into a life they knew they would hate.

We got there in the early morning hours, were issued blankets, led to a barracks and told to sack out. We didn't have to be told twice—we were tired. Although I remember being excited, I guess I slept well enough that first night.

Early the next day—April 14, 1943—the sergeant who had been put in charge of our barracks, got us up and we had our first army instruction. It was a lesson in how to make up our bunks—the army way! Then we went to chow, got our skinhead haircuts and were issued a stack of clothes that didn't fit very well.

We spent the rest of the morning learning how to "fall in" and do the various facing movements and the basics of close order drill. Pearce and I, having had ROTC at Western, knew these movements so we were singled out as demonstrators. We marched up and down, faced front, rear, left and right and won the compliments of our instructor. I think both of us thought that it was just a matter of time until we were each given corporal stripes!

Reality finally came as I learned I was to be on KP the next day. Two days in the Army and already I had drawn the most despised detail in the Army. I caught quite a bit of heat from Pearce and Izzie on this, but I guess I looked at it as another new experience. In any event, I reported for duty the next day loaded with enthusiasm.

Things weren't too bad at the mess hall. It was a huge operation, designed to serve hundreds of new draftees. Accordingly, there were about 20 of us KPs. The kitchen was pretty well automated even at that early date, having for example, automatic potato and carrot peelers. Actually, the machine buffed the outer skin off, rather than peeling them.

Planned for the meal that day were carrots and about four of us were put to work preparing them. First, we put them in the big buffer and they came out pink and pretty. The next job was to cut them into smaller lengths—two or three inches. This was where we were to get into trouble.

The four of us sat around a large GI can and began cutting the carrots with sharp butcher knives. The short pieces of the carrots dropped into the can and before long we had about a half can full—equivalent to about a bushel of carrots. We were chatting away about what towns and states we were from and what type of unit we hoped to get assigned to.

If we had left it right there, we would have been okay, but we had to get a little fancy and cute. We began to chop the carrots with the butcher knife and found we could go twice as fast. Maybe we thought if we got through earlier we would be excused. Fat chance of that!

As I chopped merrily along, one of the other guys suddenly yelled out and stood up. He grabbed his hand and as blood dripped into the can with the carrots, I saw the tip end of one of his fingers was gone! To my horror, I realized that I had chopped off the tip of his index finger!

We grabbed a towel and we wrapped his hand in it and squeezed above the cut to stop the bleeding. All the cooks came running and someone got him into a vehicle and took off for the post hospital. That was the last anyone ever saw of that guy and to this day I have no idea who he was or if he also ended up in the 17th Airborne.

We were all shook up and I especially felt bad. However, there was really nothing I could do. I began to wonder if I would be court martialed or receive some other horrible punishment. Nothing ever happened, and actually, the cooks seemed to get a big kick out of it. They laughed and laughed and said I was the quickest KP they had ever seen on the carrot detail!

After all the excitement died down, we were put back to work on the carrot job. This time, however, two of the guys were given another can so that we would not be so close together.

Another guy and I went back to the original can and resumed cutting the carrots. I did notice that the other guy sat way back from where I was and carefully cut his carrots out of the reach of my butcher knife.

We finally realized that when the guy had got cut, he had bled into that can. Also, I wondered where that little tip of his finger had gone. Surely it must have tumbled into the can as well. We needed to do something about this as we were preparing these carrots for lunch that day.

I told one of the sergeant cooks about this situation and he just laughed! "Hell, boy," he replied, "we're late already on those carrots and besides, ain't no one gonna see blood in orange-colored carrots and that tiny piece of finger will just add a little bit of protein to the meal!"

I thought surely he was kidding, but then he told me to shut up and get busy or my tail was going to be in a mess of trouble! What was I to do? At this point I thought discretion was the better point of valor and I went on cutting carrots.

I ate everything on the menu that day, except the carrots. Being on KP, I had no way to warn Pearce or Izzie about not eating them. I asked them later if they had both eaten carrots and they replied that they had. I asked if they were good, as I had prepared them with my own special recipe. They said they were fine, but when I told them what had happened, they nearly threw up!

During the time I was in the Army, I know I ate a lot of terrible-tasting food, but I feel sure I didn't eat any that had blood and fingers mixed in! I guess there's some guy out there today who's a cannibal and doesn't know it!

CHAPTER 3
DESTINATION: THE SANDHILLS!

O
ur stop at "Fort Ben" only lasted two or three days. The Selective Service System was in full swing and draftees (as well as volunteers) were arriving all day long and just as quickly, were being shipped out to various posts for training.

Everywhere you looked there were columns of twos marching somewhere. The marchers were usually out of step, a couple of them were trailing behind, and all were wearing ill-fitting uniforms. They were a sorry lot and I know we looked no better.

I'll always be thankful for the two quarters of ROTC that I had had in college. It gave me a sense of confidence. At least, I felt better than the general rabble I saw. I felt like a soldier, even if I might not have looked too great in my unaltered and unpressed uniform.

We knew that another good buddy of ours from Bowling Green, Tom Uhl, had entered service a few days before us, so we figured he was somewhere on the post. Somehow—I can't remember how—we did locate him and as usual, old Tom had everything scouted out and was loaded down with all the latest rumors as to where we were headed.

I can't recall just where his first rumor said we were slated to go. He brought us several new rumors during the next few days, but the actual designation remained a mystery. No one in his right mind could have dreamed up a place like the one that actually awaited us!

They had things for us to do every minute of the day during our short stay at Fort Ben. There was intelligence and aptitude testing, close-order drill, lectures, training films, shots and orientations on everything from guns to venereal disease.

In addition to learning how to make a bed the army way, we also learned how to salute officers and how to address them. I do recall that rather than hating to salute, we were all pretty eager to throw those highballs just to see how the officers reacted! I recall seeing a young second lieutenant stray down our street one day and before he could "escape" the recruits made him return nearly a hundred salutes! His arm was about to fall off before he managed to get away.

One day our buddy Uhl brought us the latest scuttlebutt. We were going to go to some east coast camp to get basic training and then we were all going to be assigned to the Air Corps. It turned out he was only half right—if you consider Camp Mackall, N.C. an east coast training center. The Air Corps part was purely a pipe dream never to come true!

Uhl shipped out a day or so before Pearce, Izzie and me. We never doubted that once we got to wherever we were going that we would find old Tom there with all the latest information and the latest hot rumors for us. In this we were right.

I guess I really realized I was in the Army when one day they told us to ship our civilian clothes home, we wouldn't need them any more. They also said we probably should just junk them because if we ever needed them again—and we probably wouldn't—after five or six years they wouldn't fit us anyhow!

I did ship my clothes home and true to what they had said, they never did fit me anymore. Unlike the present, in those days military personnel were not permitted to change to civilian clothes when off duty. We really didn't mind this as there was a lot of pride in wearing the uniform and no one seemed to mind.

One day they marched us to a large building. We were placed at individual desks that were separated by plywood partitions. There was no way a person could look at the test paper of another person. It was plain something big was up.

We were told that this was the most important series of tests that we would ever take because it would determine the branch of the Army to which we would be assigned. For example, they said, officers were badly needed in the army and to gain entrance to Officers' Candidate School, you had to make a score of at least 110 on this test.

First, we put on a set of ear phones and were given an aptitude test in Morse Code. After a quick review of what a dot and a dash sounded like, they sent a short message for us to copy. After the first few noises, I was lost, so I was pretty sure if they were planning to send us to the Air Corps, I was not going to be a radio operator or a navigator.

Most of the test was pretty simple stuff. Being a honor high school graduate with almost a year of college, I did well, scoring 117 overall on the test. I thought sure I was a cinch for OCS. If Tom was right about the Air Corps, I wondered what kind of job I'd get. I knew with my poor eyesight I was not a candidate for pilot or guner training and I had just eliminated myself from the jobs of radio operator and navigator. Maybe they were planning on training me as a bombardier!

Then each of us was taken to a private area where a non-com gave us a personal interview. My interviewer was a corporal, probably with less than six months in the service himself, but at the time I was impressed. I felt sure I was headed for OCS and he was going to ask my wishes as to where I wanted to go.

The only memory I have of that interview is this corporal asking me if I would object to service in the "air forces". Again I took that to mean the Air Corps. Immediately, I had visions of a nice cushy job as some sort of officer in charge of a crew of mechanics. I would be far from danger back at the airdrome and I would sleep in a nice, warm bed with white sheets and go to town every night.

I have never been lead farther from the truth. I guess by saying "air forces" he was really thinking "Airborne", but as I had never heard of "Airborne" either, I had no idea of the adventuresome life he was planning for me.

One other thing happened while we were at that building that I often thought about in the years to come. The NCO in charge of us announced that over in a certain corner of the building was a representative of The Parachute School. He said if any of us were so stupid that we wanted to learn how to jump out of an airplane, we could go over and talk to him.

I looked over where he had pointed and there was this sharp, young paratrooper with shiny boots, tailored uniform and his overseas cap cocked at a jaunty angle. He looked great, but I laughed with all the other guys in my group. I wasn't crazy! I wasn't going to jump out of a perfectly good airplane!

One day we were told to pack up our gear, we were leaving. In the Army everything starts early, so we got up about dawn, ate breakfast and fell out in front of the barracks with everything we now owned. Our barracks leader gave us "left face", and we marched off to the train station.

For the next two days that train was our home. It was a steam locomotive and it belched soot and cinders that poured in on us. There was no air conditioning and there were no sleeping berths—just hard, dirty bench seats and too many troops per car. We were forced to sleep on the hard seats or the filthy floor. Soon we were grimey, short-tempered and disgusted.

It was stop and go, criss-crossing across the United States. We would stop every four or five hours somewhere out in the country and get off and stretch our legs. MPs stood off in the distance and watched us. We had the feeling we were prisoners and they thought we were trying to escape. That idea wasn't too remote as the rumor started around that they were shipping us direct to a Port of Embarkation!

I have no idea where all we went. Back and forth. Some said it was normal troop train secretcy. It seemed more like poor planning to me. The only single place I could ever identify was Roanoke, Virginia. The train stopped as we went through Roanoke and our coach stopped right in the middle of a street. The windows were either sealed or stuck so we couldn't even yell at the girls.

On the train, we got pancakes for breakfast, a sack lunch and a luke-warm supper. There were no stops with Red Cross ladies offering hot coffee and doughnuts like we had seen in the newsreels. The food was pretty bad, but we were young and excited about our new adventure, so we managed. There were also no facilities for bathing or shaving so we were soon covered with soot and dirt thrown back by the coal-fired locomotive. We were a sorry looking lot when on April 18, 1943, we arrived at our destination.

I'll never forget looking out the window when we pulled into Hamlet, North Carolina. There were signs that said: "Welcome to the Sandhills!" We also saw some other signs that no one could understand. Signs like: "Home of the 17th Airborne Division" and "193rd Glider Infantry Regiment". What was an "Airborne Division" and what in the world, we wondered, was a "Glider Regiment"? Surely this whole train load of soldiers weren't going to to be taught how to fly gliders!

Then we fell out and formed in a column of twos, shouldered our two barracks bags and marched off to board a long line of waiting trucks. We were all saying to ourselves, "What have I done to deserve this?"

Finally, we found out where we were going. The trucks arrived at a gate marked "Camp Mackall". No one had ever heard of the place. But, there stood more MPs. They were still guarding us! We knew then for sure we were in big trouble. This place was not on any maps and the chicken-house barracks we could see sprawled everywhere looked like what you would expect to be provided to house prisoners.

As we drove down the streets inside the camp, we would stop at every block or two and drop off a few men. The NCO would read off a few names and some weary guys would pile out. Another NCO was waiting there and he would take over and start screaming commands. Finally they called my name so I grabbed my bags and got off. Bidding Pearce and Izzie good-bye, I shouldered my gear and with sweat dripping from every pore in my body, I struggled down the street trying to keep in step with the others. It was useless.

Finally, the group I was with arrived in front of what would be our new homes. Names were called out until all of us were assigned to one of the five barracks buildings that were located on our "company street". It was only then that I learned I was to be in the 1st platoon, Company D of the 193rd Glider Infantry Regiment. Whatever that was!

CHAPTER 4
WELCOME TO CAMP MACKALL

When we reached Camp Mackall I believe all of us were impressed—in a negative way—with the primitive facilities that were very much in evidence. It was almost like the builders had been called away and surely would be back later to finish the job. Not so. This barren, sand-covered acreage was to be our home and if we wanted it to be more comfortable, it was going to be up to us.

Camp Mackall was one of those wonders of wartime construction. With the war escalating, the United States needed more land to train its soldiers. And, for Airborne troops, the more rugged the better. Named for Pvt. John T. Mackall, a member of the 509th Parachute Infantry Regiment who in North Africa became the first paratrooper killed in World War II, the camp was ideal for training Airborne troops.

On November 7, 1942 when construction began, Camp Mackall was nothing more that 62,000 acres of rugged wilderness. By March 1943—only four months later—it had 65 miles of paved road, a 1,200 bed hospital, five movie theaters, six huge beer gardens, a complete all-weather airport with three 5,000-foot runways and 1,700 buildings. However, when we arrived in mid April, there was still a lot of building to be accomplished.

The barracks were all one-story, long like a chicken house and covered with tarpaper. Two potbellied stoves—one in each end—were to provide the heat. We soon found out that if your bunk was adjacent to a stove, (as mine was) most of the time you were uncomfortably hot, but if you were too far away, you almost froze at night!

The latrine was next door in a separate building. It was functional, but crude and hard to clean as we all got to learn. Outside it were wash tubs and racks where we could wash and scrub our web equipment and any clothes which were not sent to the GI laundry. Clothes sent there might never be seen again or if returned, were often torn and poorly pressed.

Outside our barracks was a large coal box. Stockade prisoners delivered coal to the boxes once a week. If you ran out before the next delivery, you either went without or stole coal out of another unit's box! I never remember us being cold because of lack of coal.

Sand was everywhere. There was no dirt to be seen anywhere. This was the "Sandhills" area of North Carolina and it couldn't have been named more appropriately. With the sand came the sand flies and mosquitoes. They said that the mosquitoes were so big, they would carry their victims away to eat them!

Amid this heaven on earth, there were only about 5,800 men in our division when it was first organized. Probably the same number, or maybe a few more, were in the llth Airborne Division which was located on the other side of Camp Mackall. There were also other special housekeeping units scattered here and there. They had all been there a few months longer than we had, but they were also still struggling with making their areas livable.

The truck carried us to within a few hundred yards of our destination and then we walked the rest of the way carrying all our belongings in two duffel bags. When we arrived we were immediately dropped and given 10 push-ups. That was our welcome to the Airborne. Few of us, even those in pretty good physical condition, were able to do 10 push-ups after the physical exertion of carrying those bags all that way in the hot April sunshine.

We found vacant metal cots in the chicken-house barracks, unrolled the mattresses on the flat springs and collapsed. Soon a number of troops arrived and came tearing into the barracks. They were dirty, covered with soot and smelled of sweat. They treated us new guys with contempt and disgust. It developed that they thought we had been lounging around the barracks all day while they had been out fighting, of all things, a forest fire!

This was only a warning of what lay in store for us. We got to join in this fun when we were ordered to fall out at 5:30 a.m. the next morning. We could see the 2 1/2-ton GI trucks waiting to take us to the fire area. As we were to be gone all day, we were given a sack lunch as we left the mess hall at breakfast. It consisted of a "jam" sandwich (a slice of cheese and two slices of bread "jammed" together) and an apple. We were used to better than this for an afternoon snack.

It seems that half of North Carolina was on fire. As we were in the heart of the pine tree country, the resin in the trees often would actually explode when ignited by the spreading fire. The fire could jump across a swamp burning the trees protruding above the water. It was no place for the unwary. It was dangerous work.

This is where I met the guy that was to be one of my best friends in the service. I had been fighting the fire one day and was worn out. I saw the opportunity to sneak off the line for a few moments and grab some rest in the shade of a little clump of woods. Undetected by the cadre that was directing our efforts, I hid under some trees and relaxed.

Off to my side I heard a muffled laugh and saw the brush stir. Fearing I had been found out, I peered through the bushes and saw another soldier also stretched out relaxing. Apparently, he had had the same idea as I had had and we both laughed at how much smarter we were than those poor hot and tired guys out there fighting the fire!

After only a few words, I realized that I had found another Southerner in this company of seemingly all Pennsylvania and New York natives. Boy, his slow southern drawl sure sounded good to my ears! He turned out to be Burl Ray Crabtree and he was from Fort Gay, West Virginia. I called him Ray as I couldn't seem to remember the name Burl. We immediately became good friends and remain so to this day.

We continued to fight the fire for about a week. I thought the whole camp was going to burn down. Thanks to a couple of days of rain, things finally got back to normal. The fire did burn through our training areas so when we finally began basic training on Monday, May 3, we had to contend with the ashes for the next 13 weeks. When we ran and stirred them up, they would fly up and around choking us and clogging our nostrils.

On or about April 23, we were marched over to the dispensary and everyone was given two shots. I don't recall what they were for, but I know I had already had them as my parents saw to it I had good medical care. However, the army doesn't bother to ask you if you've had a certain shot, they just give it to you and then they know you've had it!

Loaded up with the serum, they ran us a mile or so to a new barracks area on the far side of the camp. This was an area that was being made ready for some new troops slated to arrive in a few days. The area was even less developed that ours and the ground around the barracks was rough and pitted like it had been plowed.

Each man had been issued a small entrenching tool and we were put to work smoothing and leveling the area around these new barracks. The sun was out in full force that day and it was hot as the devil. It was hot, sweaty, backbreaking work and with the small entrenching tools, it was like attacking an elephant with fly swatters.

After an hour or two of this, I was sick as a dog. I could feel my forehead and it was very hot. I knew I was running a fever, but there was no relief. Then, one time when I straightened up, the world began to spin and I passed out cold as a cucumber.

When I woke up, I was being loaded in an ambulance to go to the camp hospital. Upon arrival, I was given cold liquids and some pills, an ice pack for my head and put to bed. I had come close to having a heatstroke.

I think I slept all the rest of that day and that night, but by morning I was okay, although very weak. By the end of the day I seemed to have recovered, but I decided to fake it and enjoy another day's rest before I went back to the rugged training I knew awaited me with my company.

The hospital was a large, sprawling facility that covered a large area. I roamed around to get my legs back and even got lost one day as I walked to the mess hall.

One day I ran into Paul Ankeny, a Business University student I had known back in Bowling Green. Paul was in the XVIII Airborne Corps and had broken his leg during judo training. It was good to see him and later, after we had both returned to our units, we got together several times to have a few beers and talk about our school days back in Bowling Green.

The hospital was badly understaffed and I went the next two days without seeing a doctor. I realized I was stuck here until someone okayed me and marked me for "return to duty." As I was feeling okay now, I wanted to get out of the hospital and back with my buddies. The next morning, when still no doctor came around to examine me, I decided I wasn't going to stay any longer.

I went down to the dismissal office to see how the process worked. The room was filled with 30-40 guys sitting around waiting for their names to be called. When called, an orderly checked their name off of a list and they filed out and got into a vehicle to be transported back to their unit.

I noticed that several times a name was called and that soldier would not be there. The orderly would call it again and if the person still didn't answer, he'd just go on with the list. I decided that that would be my ticket out of there!

I went back to my ward, gathered up my gear and after lunch returned to the dismissal office and took a seat in the waiting area. I waited while they called out the names of the guys who were scheduled to be discharged from the hospital that afternoon.

Soon some guy's name was called and he failed to answer. I got ready. On the second call when he didn't respond, I answered "Yo"! Then I got up, walked out and loaded on the truck. That's all there was to it. The truck driver asked each of us where we wanted to go and I was driven right to the corner near my barracks.

I have always wondered what happened to that guy whose identity I assumed. The hospital is no longer there, but could the ghost of that poor guy still be wandering around there trying to convince some ghostly orderly he is now well and wants to return to his unit?

CHAPTER 5
ARMY CHOW

W hen you leave home for the first time in your life and join the Army, there are a lot of adjustments a young man needs to make. He must forget his personal desires and learn quickly that everything he does must be for the good of the unit. Those who have been entrusted with making what could be life and death decisions have to forget personal feelings and do what is best for the accomplishment of the mission.

One of the first things that get "standardized" is the food. If you were picky about what you ate when you came in the service, you soon learned you had only one alternative: eat what was provided or go hungry! Although at first some tried to solve this problem by running to the Post Exchange for a quick burger, eventually, all were forced at some time to either eat the army chow or else.

I was fortunate in that I liked all foods. There was not a single fruit, meat or vegetable I disliked. Although I now dislike sweet potatoes, I can't remember if I disliked them back in 1943. In any event, I suspect we had them so seldom, it was no big problem.

Cooking, however, was something else. My mother was a wonderful cook. I never really knew how wonderful until I dug into some of that army half-cooked food. It had a personality of its own!

Considering the circumstances, the cooks (aided by a crew of unhappy recruits forced to serve as KPs) did a pretty good job. While we were at Camp Mackall, we had a battalion messhall, meaning they had to prepare for about 600 hungry men at each meal. It was small wonder that many times one found himself with a half-cooked or even an uncooked portion. Even worse, sometimes the food began to run out and the portions got smaller and smaller.

The companies alternated as to who ate first, second, etc. The ideal position was to be the first company to be fed. With the first troops the portions given out were larger as it could not be detected at this point if there was going to be a shortage. The food was also better cooked in this first serving as that was where the mess sergeant usually did his "tasting" to check on the quality of work of the cooks and their helpers.

As the companies filed through, the food was dumped on their trays. The mess sergeant and the first cook watched carefully and when it looked as if there might not be enough to go around, they ordered that the helpings be reduced. And, as we got nearer the bottom of the large GI cooking cans, the quality of the food tailed off noticeably. Woe be to the last company to eat. They were lucky to get a little of anything.

Complaining usually got one nowhere. In fact, if you weren't careful, it could end up getting you put on KP the next day. The officers made a bit of fuss about the level of food their men were receiving, but that also seemed to go nowhere. In any event, in the 10 months we were at Camp Mackall, the problem never seemed to get much better.

Potatoes were on the menu every day and in one form or another were served at almost every meal. Some other favorites seemed to be spaghetti or macaroni, beets, peas and beans. All kinds of beans. Franks, bologna, chicken and ground beef appeared occasionally as did some other dishes that no one seemed to be able to identify.

Tasteless white bread seemed to be in ample supply. For breakfast it was toasted. We often had eggs, but butter was unheard of. For lunch the bread often appeared in the form of sandwiches with bologna and what we called "rat cheese". That cheese was like plastic and it took strong teeth just to chew it.

Sometimes the day's left-over bread showed up again at supper time. It was usually toasted and resembled a hard shingle by this time. They then covered it with a thick, gravy-like mixture that included all the left-overs of the day. We called it "S.O.S." Some refer to this dish as "Something On a Shingle", but the troopers had a more descriptive term for that first word!

Fortunately, there seemed to be no shortage of salt and pepper and we soon learned that if you put enough salt and pepper on any food, you could eat it. That was a hard lesson for me to learn as I had never used salt and pepper beyond what my mother had used in her cooking. I did what I had to do at that time, but since then I have cut back on both.

I have saved the subject of liquid with the meals until last. This is where I probably had my biggest problem. In the morning we had coffee, period. If you didn't want coffee the only other thing to drink was water. The milk, always in short supply and seeming to be watered-down, was reserved for use on cereal and woe be to the soldier caught drinking it.

All my life I had enjoyed milk for breakfast, lunch and supper. It's all I ever thought about drinking, all I ever wanted to drink. After about a month of drinking water for breakfast I was about ready to kill for a glass of rich, creamy, cold milk.

For lunch and supper it was coffee or Kool-Aide. We called Kool-Aide, "bug juice". We were not far off. Sometimes, especially in the summer months, we had luke-cool tea. (You couldn't call it "iced tea"!) I drank a lot of tea and bug juice in those days and a lot of plain water. I only managed to quell my milk thirst by also eating a lot of cereal.

My buddies drank cup after cup of coffee and continually complained about how rotten it was. However, when we were in the field on problems, they were always looking for a cup of coffee and wanting the cooks to bring up some. They said it tasted bad, but it was hot and it lifted their spirits.

Finally, one dark, cold, rainy night I got to the place where I badly needed to have my spirits lifted. Enough so that I decided I had gotten to the place where I needed a cup of that dreaded "GI coffee". I just knew I wouldn't like it and I knew it would probably keep me awake all night. But, I was wet and cold and about to freeze and if that coffee was hot, I needed some of it!

I had been put on guard duty that particular evening. We had to memorize what they called "General Orders", stand a formal guard mount and pass inspection on our uniforms and weapons. The military treated it as deadly serious. Actually, it was all intended as a training vehicle as the posts we walked and guarded were meaningless as far as security was concerned.

I was sent for a two-hour shift to guard a lonely post that in reality needed no guarding. I did realize, however, that possibly I would be tested that night and if I didn't perform correctly, according to "the book", I would be chewed out royally and in all probability, find myself on KP or some other revolting detail.

It was a great night for this kind of foolishness. It was cold—at least in the 30s—and it was raining cats and dogs. My post was an area from a tree to a building some 50 yards away. When I reached the building, I would stand in a narrow doorway for a minute or two trying to wipe the rain from my face before I would start the walk back to the shelter of the tree.

I chuckled to myself knowing that if some officer or sergeant came to check me out, he would also have to come out in this bitter weather and be miserable too. The fact of the matter was, no one ever came to check me. They were smart enough to stay inside on a night like this.

The building on my post was some sort of headquarters and there was a CQ (Charge of Quarters) on duty there. I guess he heard me when I would stop for a couple of minutes in the doorway. On one of my stops, he opened the door and offered me a cup of hot coffee.

I was so miserable at the time, I would have drunk anything that was hot. As I cupped my hands around the steaming cup of coffee and inhaled the aroma of the steam curling up under my steel helmet, I knew right then what I had been missing! I gulped it down and I never had anything that lifted my spirits like that and made me forget how forgotten and miserable I was!

After that, I drank coffee as often as I could find it. It became more like food than drink and no matter how bad things got to be, it always seen to settle me down and bring things into perspective.

Later on, when we were in combat during the Bulge and the weather was almost as menacing as the Germans, it was a wonder what a cup of coffee could do for your spirits. As soon as we would stop for any length of time, the guys would break out their little packets of instant coffee, get a fire going and start brewing up a cup.

I've heard my buddies poke fun at the Brits and their knack of finding ways to brew their tea, but believe me, they are no more skillful in ways to do that than the Americans were in whipping up a cup of coffee. The true genius of a soldier can often be measured in terms of his ingenuity in finding ways to come up with his "comfort items".

That's how coffee came into my life. Even today, my wife gets the coffee going before I get out of bed. I suspect that she doesn't want to have anything to do with me until I have had that morning cup of coffee. After a good hot cup of coffee, I'm ready to deal with the world!

CHAPTER 6
POST RECREATION

For the first few weeks at Camp Mackall I feel sure most of us suffered from varying degrees of homesickness. After all, for most of us this was the first time we had been away from home for an extended length of time, and it took a bit of getting used to it before we were very civil to each other.

During this time, it was especially nice that Pearce, Uhl and Izzie were billeted nearby. Sometimes Ken Holloway joined us. Many evenings we would meet, talk and exchange news we had received from far-away Bowling Green. This really helped us fight homesickness and to pass the time.

Once we got through the grumpy stage and somewhat adjusted to the rugged training they were giving us, we began exploring around to see what entertainment and recreation was available to us. Believe me, it was pretty thin. It consisted of a movie theater, a PX (Post Exchange) with a soda bar, and a service club. For basic trainees, stuck on the post with no passes allowed, that was it.

At first, when we returned from the field, we were so tired that we fell on our bunks. Then it was chow time and then time to clean our weapons and be ready for an inspection by our Platoon Sergeant and/or Platoon Leader. Then we showered and shaved as there would be no time for that tomorrow morning.

Finally, if we were still able to move, we were allowed to leave our company area and enjoy an hour or two of our own choosing. These sojourns were brief because we were always bone-tired and the whole cycle began over again at 0530 the next morning.

There were the few that always went to bed just after chow. However, most of us wrote a couple of letters and several times a week we went to the PX. If I had the money, I loved to get a milk shake or some ice cream. (I still haven't broken that habit!)

After basic training was over and we were used to the physical grind, we found we could do more and still operate near 100% with only about half the sleep we normally required. This adjustment would stand us in good steed later on in combat.

On the post we soon discovered the beer gardens and the 3.2% beer the Army served. We became experts on filtering that slim 3.2% of alcohol out of a pitcher of beer. It took a healthy set of kidneys to do it, but we were young and able! The beer gardens were popular places, especially after pay day.

The post theater was the coolest place available to us. It had real air conditioning and even if you didn't want to see the movie, it was a nice, quiet and cool place to take a nap. The popcorn was good, but the bare wooden seats were uncomfortable as hell.

Getting in the theaters was a problem. There was usually a mob for the first showing and the second showing put you out too late for most of our bedtimes. The cost was only 15¢ for soldiers and 30¢ for any guests, so that admission schedule fit our budgets nicely.

A GI audience was a noisy one. The troopers often made out-loud comments in regard to the dialogue on the screen. They hated any patriotic over-doing by Hollywood and they would boo any reference to the regular Army or to other branches of the service. The paratroops would boo any mention of gliders and the glidertroops would boo any mention of paratroops. One soon got the idea that the audience didn't particularly like anything! Mostly they were just having fun and trying to keep cool.

The service club was sometimes a fun place. A few guys could always be found there writing letters, reading magazines or making phone calls home. The big nights, however, were the nights they had boxing or USO shows and dances. And, those nights were too few and far between.

The shows often consisted of orchestras or combos with singers and at times, some lousy comedians. When a show came without a band, our own post orchestra usually performed. They were good. The leader was a GI named Blue Baron—or at least, that was his stage name—and after the war he became the leader of one of the top "Big Bands" of the '40s.

Occasionally, we got a USO show. Some big names toured the country in those days and visited army camps. We always felt Camp Mackall was so barren and rugged and the accommodations so Spartan, that the really big stars probably shunned us. However, Bob Hope played there one night. I don't recall going. Our company was probably out in the boonies that night, as they often were!

The shows that really packed them in were ones in which the GIs themselves participated. I remember seeing some really dumb sketches in which GIs played the part of women with mops cut off and used for wigs and their muscular hairy legs showing. Somehow, I thought that hilarious at the time!

Then, there were the dances. The music was great and the USO brought in dozens of girls by bus from neighboring towns. Some of the guys really took advantage of this opportunity and met some girls that they later went to see when they got a pass. I never seemed to get into the flow on this. The girls I saw all seemed to be ugly or too fat—maybe both.

There was one more type of recreation or entertainment that abounded at good old Camp Mackall. Gambling. We often had either a card game or a crap game going in the barracks. At "lights out" it was usually moved to the latrine where the lights stayed on all night. I often took part in this activity and my skill as a crapshooter was a known fact in our company!

The beauty of this entertainment was that you didn't have to have elaborate facilities. Most any old place would do and the tools of the games could be carried anywhere, even into the field while we were on problems or maneuvers. I continued my devotion to these two sports and while overseas, I am sure I did not miss a month when I didn't send home the limit in money orders.

Laugh if you will, but when I returned home and married, my wife and I lived off these savings for six months while I attended the University of Georgia. It was that long before the VA got my papers in order and I began to receive payments under the GI Bill of Rights!

CHAPTER 7
VISITORS FROM HOME

By the beginning of June, we were only about four weeks into our 13-week basic training schedule. We had only been in the army about six weeks and although we had toughened up considerably, we were still trying to find our way. There was still a tinge of homesickness in all of us.

It really wasn't a good time to have visitors from home and the raw facilities at Camp Mackall were certainly not inviting. Nevertheless, when my mother and father wrote me they would like to come visit me, I sure wasn't going to discourage them!

In addition, I urged them to bring Georgeanna with them, because I was really missing her more than anyone at that time. Nell Jones was apparently really missing Ken Holloway too, and with that, the visiting party grew to four people.

Finally, all the details were worked out and they made their plans to come on June 3, 1943. I could hardly wait and I counted the days! I made reservations for them at the 11th Airborne guest house on the opposite side of camp—our own 17th Airborne guest house being full at the time. The little towns around the area had few if any motels.

The trip they made from Bowling Green to Camp Mackall must have been a real ordeal. With the gas rationing in place at that time, there was no question about being able to drive the family car. The long, hot trip had to be made by Greyhound Bus and I am sure it lasted for hours upon hours.

Even when they arrived in Hamlet, North Carolina, they had to catch the "cattle-car" bus the GIs rode out to the camp.

Worn out, they finally arrived. Dad made a phone call to my company orderly room and a message was delivered to me that they had arrived. Our C.O. at the time, Captain Rosario Sorbello, let me off training early and I showered and headed off across camp to meet them.

As it would be an hour or so before duty hours were over, the camp shuttle buses were not running as yet, so I had to walk over to the 11th Airborne guest house. I was so anxious to see them that I ran all the way—a distance of one or two miles—and when I arrived, I was wringing wet! Nevertheless, it was heaven to see them!

We sat and talked a lot. There was really nothing to do, but enjoy being together. I had to return to my barracks by last call, but as it was the weekend, we spent the entire next two days together. We got together with Uhl, Pearce and Izzie and took lots of photos.

Nell and Ken were mostly off to themselves during the time and I think they got married during this time. Georgeanna and I talked about marriage ourselves, but decided that we would just get engaged at this time. Wise decision.

I recall how Mother shuttered when she saw our barracks where her little boy now had to live! It was pretty bleak with the black tar-paper siding, rough wooden steps, unpainted eves, skinny stove pipes jutting from the shingled roof and the blue (for infantry!) butt can hanging outside the door. Only the small wooden sign "T6l03" distinguished it from hundreds of others just like it that lay in every direction you looked.

The time for them to leave came way too soon. It nearly broke my heart to tell them good-bye and soon we were all in tears. Camp Mackall was a miserable place, good only for training soldiers and I can understand how later, my parents told me how they hated to go home and leave me in that dump! As a parent now myself, I fully understand their anguish.

My mother and father weren't the only ones that made that rough, hot trip to see their son. We saw parents on the post all the time. In fact, Mr. and Mrs. Uhl came that same June to see Tom. The first day they arrived Tom's company was in the field, so they took Pearce and I out to eat.

I can remember one other interesting happening at Camp Mackall that June of 1943. We all got excited when we saw a movie crew on post making a movie about the Airborne. I believe this was the movie "Paratrooper" with Harry Carey. Naturally, they never mentioned anything about the poor, forgotten glidertroopers! As far as I was concerned, nothing could top having your mother and father, AND your girlfriend, visit you!

CHAPTER 8
BASIC TRAINING

W e officially began our 13 weeks of basic training on Monday, May 3, 1943. I say "officially" because it seemed as if it had begun that first day we arrived on post. We thought that very first day was a tough one, but it never got any easier during the whole 13 weeks of the basic training cycle. In fact, it got worse.

We started our day at 5:45 a.m. with "first call". There was no time to leisurely get up, rub your eyes and stroll over to the latrine to wash up. We slept in our underwear, so we put on our fatigue shirts and pants, pulled on our socks and GI shoes and began to lace up the uncomfortable leggings some nut designed back during World War I.

If you went about your dressing routine in an organized way, you had a fairly good chance of being ready 15 minutes later when the whistle blew to "fall out!" When that time came, there was always a wild scramble for the barracks front door. Woe be to the slow of foot when that scramble began. One day when our sergeant had us practicing getting out of the barracks in record time, we tore the screen door completely off the hinges. He was as pleased as punch!

Within a minute of the whistle we would form in four ranks in front of the barracks. Each squad then reported all present and the platoon sergeant then reported that fact to the first sergeant and he in turn reported to the officer in charge. Usually, all the company officers were present for reveille, but I feel sure sometimes there was some covering up done for this early morning formation!

Most of the time that was it. We were dismissed and returned to our barracks to get ready for chow. But, sometimes we got a surprise! We were ordered to open ranks, take off our shirts and helmet liners and stack them neatly in front of us. The company was then marched off in a column of twos and the dreaded command of "Double time, March!" echoed down the line. We were off on a morning run.

I recall one rainy morning when several of the fellows tried to get a few extra minutes of sleep and didn't leave themselves enough time to dress. They fell out for the formation after jumping into their shoes, grabbing their helmet liner and pulling on their raincoat over their underwear. You know what happened. It was a run morning and they were forced to make it clopping along in their untied shoes and underwear!

Usually we were a bit slow to get into the spirit of things, but once we were good and awake, we rather enjoyed the run. We would count cadence in different ways, but always ending with a loud "Airborne!" When we passed a column of paratroops also running, we would straighten up and pick up the pace to let them know we were just as tough and physical as they were! The espirit de corps was growing in us, we just didn't know it!

If you were not fully awake by the time we got into the run, you were in deep trouble. We probably did five miles before we returned to our company area to recover our clothing and retire to the barracks. If you have never tried that when you were half asleep, needed to go the toilet, and were hungry, let me tell you it will get your attention!

Around 6:45 a.m. we were back from the run and were dismissed. We made up our bunks and were in line at the mess hall by 7:00 a.m. ready to eat. By 7:30 a.m. we were back from chow, did a quick clean-up of the barracks and were ready to fall out by 7:45 a.m. and start the day's training. We never had an idle moment from the time reveille sounded. And, it would be that way for 13 long weeks.

We had several training areas that were assigned to our company and all were at least a mile away. We ran and marched to the areas and spent the morning there learning judo, bayonet fighting, map reading, military courtesy, sanitation, weapons training, individual and unit formations and a lot of other subjects that eventually made us into soldiers.

At about 11:30 a.m. we did our march/run back to our company area. Upon arrival, we washed up, had mail call and went to chow. By 12:45 p.m., we were ready to return to the field for more training. We usually returned to the barracks about 5:00 p.m., had another mail call and were ready for our evening meal at about 6:00 p.m. Some nights we had extra training, but after the first few weeks we were permitted to leave the company area for the nearby movie and Post Exchange. During basic none of us could receive a pass to leave the post. But, it really didn't matter as we were too tired to go anywhere.

By 10:30 p.m., most of the barracks had quieted down and a lot of the guys were already asleep. At 11:00 p.m. we had "lights out" and if you listened hard, you could hear "taps" being sounded over at Division Headquarters. The only lights in the company area came from the company orderly room and the latrine. On some nights we had "bed check" and on those nights the non-commissioned officer serving as the Charge of Quarters actually checked to see if everyone was in bed!

Mixed in our training were several overnight training problems. They weren't really tough problems. At least, not as tough as they would be later on or when we were on Tennessee maneuvers. But, they were plenty tough for many of our guys. We had several who had been farmers or outdoorsmen, but I was surprised at how many "big city" boys we had that had never "camped out" or even slept on the ground! For those of us who had been Boy Scouts or hunters and fishermen, it was really no problem. In fact, it was a welcome break from the monotony of garrison life.

One thing that happened during basic was our assignment to the squads that we would soldier in all the time we were with the company. I was assigned to the seven-man mortar squad in the first rifle platoon on or about May 9th. Henry Clay Browning from Sikeston, Missouri, was our squad leader, Orville Frederick Linrooth from Mason City, Iowa, was the first gunner and I was the second gunner. Alfred Lee Barclay from Los Angles, California, Roger E. Gardner from Waterlou, Iowa, Robert L. Desin and Robert J. Ryan who were from areas I can't remember, were the ammo bearers. They were all a good bunch of guys. They did their jobs, pulled their weight and we all got along together very well.

There was some shifting around among the fellows chosen to lead the other squads but most of those initially selected, remained in the job until combat took it's toll. During basic training, the squad leaders and their assistants were given black arm bands with the stripes of their position sewed on them. We called anyone wearing these badges of temporary rank, "Lance Corporals" and "Lance Sergeants". The title was not intended as a compliment, but later when they had proven that they could handle the job and they were awarded the rank on official orders, all the teasing stopped and from then on we treated them with the respect the rank deserved.

At least twice a day, we had rifle inspection. We carried our individual weapons with us everywhere we went during the work day and dirt and sand seemed to be attracted to them. We were given ample time to clean them and if you failed any of the daily inspections, you usually lived to regret it with extra time served on after-hours details or restriction to the company area.

Some of the weapons issued to us were old and ill-cared for by their previous owners. Others were brand new, just out of the shipping cases and they oozed cosmoline for months. It was not an easy job to keep any of them in satisfactory condition to pass the daily inspections. Add to that the fact many of the guys were slow getting with the program and did not care for them properly. We had plenty of candidates for the details.

We were taught to play some old "army games" too. We would disassemble our weapons and put them back together again while blind-folded and we raced each other to assemble them. Of course, all this was designed to teach us the importance of keeping the pieces clean so they would not jam in combat and that it does not take long to break down a piece and clean it, even in a combat environment. Reluctantly, we learned these vital lessons.

We trained in all kinds of weather. Rain, snow, heat, it made no difference. Occasionally, we would have a bivouac problem canceled due to inclement weather and we would be delighted! Usually, the training substituted would be indoor classes or training films at the theater. We relished the idea of sitting down and resting instead of pounding through the boonies. We frequently would nod off to sleep in the warmth of the building and it kept the officers and the sergeants busy just keeping the company awake.

With the intense training schedule we followed, frequently we would have instances where nerves and patience clashed and an old-fashioned fight would break out. The officers and non coms would break it up after only a few blows were struck, but it helped to break the tension. Often the parties would be given boxing gloves during their off-duty hours and afforded the opportunity to "work out their frustrations". I got a taste of this activity and it is reported elsewhere in this book!

Guard mount was another "privilege" of basic training. This was not just the posting of a sentry while on a field problem, but formal, 24-hour guard duty at the division stockade and other on-post locations. It was a time for "spit and polish" inspection of the guards and it was serious business. Every individual guard post was treated as if it was important even if it was not. The guards had better know their duties and their general orders or they could find themselves in a lot of trouble.

One time during basic training our company was assigned post guard duty and I found myself "selected" for the 50 or so men that were to serve. They went to great ends to convince us that this was a privilege and not a detail! With the events that occurred, I would have gladly surrendered that privilege.

Sometime during the night while I was patrolling a barracks area on a bicycle, there was a breakout at the post stockade. To my knowledge, this was the only time such an incident occurred while we were at Camp Mackall. Four prisoners escaped and actually made it off the post before they were rounded up. I think they only did it for the thrill of it as the area was so remote, they couldn't have had much chance of carrying out their escape completely.

The MP officers grilled every one of us guards. That included me although I was far from the area of the stockade on my bicycle! It was scary at the time, but now I perceive it as just another training vehicle—especially for the MPs! After all, with unloaded weapons, we couldn't have stopped any escape or crime if we had seen it in progress.

Near the end of our 13-week basic training cycle, we got some news that really lowered morale. Basic was being extended for one more week! It seems we had missed too many days in the field during the 13-week cycle, so we were going to make them up during the extra week. It really didn't make that much difference to me, but to some of our married guys who had their wives living in the nearby towns, the idea of another week restricted to the post was a real blow.

There were several other "memorable" training events that spiced up those dreary weeks. The Airborne Command (ABC) required that every unit should be able to march (or run) five miles in one hour with full equipment and carrying all their crew-served weapons. That event ended up with one half of us carrying or dragging the other half, but we made it. And, there was the 25 mile march to the Fort Bragg reservation, running problems for two days and the march back. We reluctantly grew hard as nails.

Around the first of August, we were at last through with this phase of our military life. We could at last, call ourselves soldiers! Our full attention then turned to the furloughs that had been promised to us back in April. They were to start on August 9, and would be given on a rotating basis as training was scheduled to continue. Of course, the army does these things by rank, so even though I made Private First Class on July 30, I had a long time to wait for my turn.

Finally, about the first week of September, I received my 10-day furlough and I boarded a train and headed for home. I was really glad to see many old friends and the town never looked better. Being with Georgeanna when she was out of school was especially great. But, after a while I grew restless and after eight or nine days, I'm afraid I was ready to go back. Bowling Green was different during those days. Most of my close friends were also in the service and not home, so it just wasn't the same. And, it never would be again.

CHAPTER 9
THE "DEAR JOHN" LETTER

O ne of the interesting phrases or words that grew out of military service during World War II was the "Dear John" letter. This term was coined by some wag to describe that letter a serviceman might receive from his girlfriend back home telling him that she had fallen for someone else and that he was no longer her special love!

There were a number of "Dear John" letters that came to members of my company during our time together. Actually, more were probably received than were acknowledged. To receive one was to admit you were something less than the stud we all imagined ourselves to be, so usually their receipt was kept secret!

I got one of these lovely letters sometime during the fall of 1943. I never had a chance to keep it a secret, however, thanks to my old buddy, Bob Pearce! In fact, he knew about it before I did and made sure all my buddies knew it as well.

Pearce's barracks were only a short distance from my barracks. He was in 1st Battalion Headquarters Company and I was in D Company of the 2nd Battalion. And, as his company always seemed to get in from training in the field before ours, he would come over to my barracks and examine any mail I had received that day and had been delivered onto my bunk.

As we were all hungry for news from home, we would read each other anything in a letter that we had received that was of mutual interest. This, in Pearce's reasoning, meant if I was late getting in from the field, it was okay for him to open any letter he could see was plainly from home!

I guess I should have gotten mad when this happened a few times before, but I didn't, so on the day my "Dear John" letter arrived, I had no one to blame but myself. Naturally, Pearce, in his own special way, made a joke of it instead of being sympathetic to the shock I received.

"Hey, Hagerman," he said at the top of his voice when I came in the barracks surrounded by all my buddies, "wait until you read this "Dear John" letter you got from Georgeanna! She really has dumped you this time!"

Unfortunately, he was close to being correct. Georgeanna and I had been sweethearts since 1938, and although during those five years we had times when we "broke up", we always seemed to "make up". This time it was serious, however, as she had returned to my mother, an engagement ring I had given her while I was home on leave that past August.

Although I tried not to succumb to Pearce's taunts in front of my buddies, I was crushed and Pearce knew it. He began to lighten up on me then, but the damage was done and I had to take a lot of ribbing from the guys in my barracks.

Pearce said he had duty that night as Charge of Quarters (CQ) and for me to come on over to his orderly room that night and we would talk. So, later that night, I went over to spend some time with him hoping to shake the depression I felt.

We talked for a couple of hours with Pearce trying to convince me the break-up was a good move for both of us. He said she was back there at Western dating all those cute aviation cadets that were now stationed at the college, and I was better off being free to go after any good looking girl I might see.

I tried hard to believe this reasoning as I knew it had some truth to it, but I guess I just loved her too much to swallow the idea. I was hurt that she had done this to me and especially that she had returned the ring to my mother! I felt like a little kid that had had his hand slapped.

Then Pearce pulled a stunt that was true Pearce vintage! He went into the captain's office, opened a drawer of the captain's desk and emerged with a fifth of whiskey. He got two glasses, poured us each a drink and offered a toast to my future as "free and being on the prowl" for any stray females in the eastern United States!

After we had laughed over this, I called Bob's attention to the fact that the level in the captain's bottle had dropped considerably. I said surely he would notice it, but he said that was easy to fix. With that, he poured some water into the bottle to bring the level back up to where it had been and returned it to the captain's desk. Apparently, the captain never caught on to Bob's little deception although it is hard to imagine he didn't notice the change of taste in his watered-down booze!

One message I know Bob did get, was that in the future I told him he was not to open and read my mail. The newspapers from home he could open, but not the personal mail. We never had that trouble any more. The fellows in my barracks soon forgot about the "Dear John" letter—or so I thought.

Forty-nine years later, in March of 1992, I attended an "Operation Varsity" party in DeLand, Florida. While I was there I was delighted to be able to visit with Ray Crabtree, one of my best buddies from the old company. He inquired about my family and then admitted he still hadn't forgiven Georgeanna for sending me that "Dear John" letter!

I'm pleased to say I forgave her long ago. In fact, now that we have been happily married for over 50 years, I am sure she did me a big favor. An 18 year-old soldier in the Army Airborne has no business whatsoever getting married during the height of a war. Your chances are not very good for having a long life together!

CHAPTER 10
AIRBORNE ALL THE WAY!

O ne of the first things I learned about the Airborne, was that if you were unhappy, there were only three different ways you could get out. You could die. Getting slightly crippled wasn't good enough. You could obtain an appointment to one of the service academies and five or six guys from the whole division managed this. Or, if you had 20/20 vision, you could be accepted for aviation cadet training—if you could get permission to take the examination.

In the parachute units, if you refused to jump, they either transferred you to one of the glider regiments (which was a fate worse than death to the parachutists) or, they would ship you out to a line infantry unit. That also usually meant death, sooner or later.

During the physical and mental pounding they gave us during the special Airborne basic training cycle, most of the idle time talk centered around how to get out of this crazy Airborne. We had not yet cast off the memory of easy, cushy civilian life. We had a lot more toughening up to do before we would adjust.

I was no different at that time. I had visions of coming home in my uniform and strutting around and wowing the girls, but I really hadn't adjusted to the idea of paying the price to do it. I had no political connection, my eyes were far from 20/20 (or I would have been in the Navy) and I damn sure wasn't ready to die! I was stuck where I was.

Silly me, I thought that nearly one year of college plus the ROTC that I had had would earn me at least the chance to be considered for a non-com position. That wasn't to be. When the platoon was first formed, they put all the tall guys up front so we'd look better when we marched. All the short guys were relegated to the rear. Unless they screwed up real bad, the tall guys, marching up front, got the stripes.

Then, I reasoned, maybe because of the score I made on the test at the Reception Center, I would be selected for Officer's Candidate School. They had told us there it took a score of 110 to qualify. I had made 117, so I thought it was just a matter of time until they discovered this child prodigy they had buried in the ranks. That was before I learned that OCS was frozen for everyone in the 17th Airborne.

One day I sucked up the courage to ask the First Sergeant, Bob Kepler, about the possibility of going to OCS. I got no answer but only an icy stare of disbelieve from the "Top". However, I learned real quick what the answer was when my name appeared on the KP roster for the next day.

My friend from home, Bob Pearce, who was a mortar squad leader in 1st Battalion Headquarters Company of the 193rd, managed to get an alternate appointment to Annapolis. He worked through his brother-in-law, Kelly Thompson, who was a naval officer in Washington. Kelly pulled some political strings and got Bob the appointment.

Bob was discharged from the Army and was put on orders to report to the preparatory school at Bainbridge, Maryland. There he would undergo a refresher course and if any of the direct appointment recipients failed either their mental or physical exams, their replacements would be drawn from the preparatory school.

I remember vividly the day Bob left Camp Mackall. He and I waited at the corner of our company street for the bus that would carry him off post and to the Greyhound Bus Station in town. Flaunting his new status as a "naval-officer-to-be", he climbed aboard and in good humor, "ordered" me to put his barracks bag on board the bus! I laughed as I did, but inside I was sad as I bid him and the connection he represented with home, goodbye.

Later, I discovered there were two other ways to get out of the Airborne. One way was to become a "bed-wetter" and get a "Section 8" discharge. Naturally, to fake this was not an acceptable method for anyone with any self-respect.

We did have one guy in our platoon, Robert Weitknecht, who tried it and everyone made life miserable for him. He got all the bad details, digging kitchen sumps when we were on bivouac, working on the garbage trucks, latrine orderly and coal detail. He led a very bad life.

"Whitey" would sleep soundly until just before reveille when he'd roll over on the side of his bunk and wet the edge of the mattress. Then he'd make sure everyone knew it. Finally, they actually pitched a pup tent outside on the sandy ground and made him sleep outside. Still he wet his blankets.

Weitknecht soon was the laughing stock of the company and we who were in the same platoon with him were ashamed he was one of us. I guess he got the last laugh, however, because one day when we came in from the field, Whitey and all of his gear were gone. We never got the official word on it, but we understood that he had been given an "unsuitable" discharge.

One day another way to get out of the Airborne came to light. By this time we had gotten over our homesickness, we were well into basic training and already were as tough as nails. We had built a esprit de corp second to none and were becoming proud to be in an Airborne outfit. I had forgotten about wanting a transfer and was relishing the responsibility-free life a buck private enjoyed.

On May 4, when we fell out in company formation ready for more training in the hot North Carolina sun, the First Sergeant read out a list of about 10 men who were to report to the orderly room. My name was among them and naturally, I figured some raunchy detail was in the offing.

To my surprise, we were trucked down to Division Headquarters and led into one of the smaller buildings nearby. Here we were told that we had been picked to take an examination for the Army Specialized Training Program or ASTP, as it was called.

If our grades on the exam measured up, we would be offered the opportunity to transfer into the program. It would mean getting out of the Airborne, leaving Camp Mackall and going back to college to learn some specialized skill. Most of the guys around me were eager for such an opportunity.

At last, faced with a possible way to transfer out of the Airborne, I was surprised to realize that I no longer wanted to leave. I had gotten over my homesickness, I had made some good friends in my company and I was a bit cocky and macho about being in the Airborne. Besides, we were rumored to be ready to start glider training soon and I was eager to start flying. Even in a glider.

Then, like any normal private, I realized that taking the test in a nice cool building was better that training with my company that day in the hot sun. So, I decided to take the test and do the best I could. Who knows, maybe this could lead to a promotion in the company, I kidded myself.

The test wasn't hard even though it had quite a bit of math in it and that was never my long suite. We got through in a few hours and were transported back to our company. We spent the rest of the day piled up on our bunks and were all showered and cleaned up when the company, all hot and grimey, came in from the field. All in all, it had been a very profitable day!

We heard nothing else about the program until May 29, when several of us were ordered to fall out and be trucked down to Division Headquarters again. I was glad once again to be able to miss a hot day's training. I was not prepared for what came next.

One by one we were called into a room where a couple of officers sat behind a big table. When it came my time, I reported in and one of them gave me "at ease". Quickly, they told me I had made a good showing on the exam and had been selected for ASTP, if I so elected.

Briefly they explained the program. I would be sent to some college campus where I would live in a dormitory and undergo a program of highly intensified instruction, mainly in mathematical subjects. The plan was to train soldiers to work in fire control centers where they would plot artillery fire.

I asked where I would be sent, but they said that would be determined later and that they didn't know at this time. It would be a concentrated course normally a year long, but compacted into about four months. They made it plain that it would be a lot of work, but there would be rewards for those who finished the course successfully.

Faintly, I saw those stripes at the end of the trail, but suddenly they didn't look so attractive as they did in my own unit. I knew there would be lots of girls on any college campus these days and I knew there would be weekends and parties and good times. It wouldn't be all studying.

That was the plus side. There were some minuses, too. I hated math and figured I'd go mad if I had to study it 24 hours a day. I had begun to like the spirit of the Airborne and I hated to think of myself again as a just another non-descript soldier far from the action. And, I had gotten well-acquainted with the guys in my company and made a lot of good friends in my platoon. I hated to leave them and start all over again.

So, forced as I was to make a fast, on-the-spot decision, I sucked it up and respectfully declined the selection. I was hustled out the door and that was that. I think all of the other guys with me agreed to accept and in a few days they were gone, never to be seen again!

I returned to the company and no one in a command position ever mentioned it or complimented me on my loyalty in staying. Maybe no one ever knew what happened. Maybe they didn't care. The buddies that I told, thought I was crazy. Maybe I was. I didn't expect any orchids or hurrahs, but it sure didn't work out that my refusal to transfer out brought me any new opportunities.

Later, we heard the guys who went into the program had been sent to Georgetown University in Washington. The story went around that in wartime Washington there were 100 girls to every man. Some of the people in ASTP there were pushed to their endurance level trying to "service" all the availables.

I'm sure many of the people who took ASTP completed the course of study and directed many a successful artillery barrage. Many, however, were never allowed to complete the course as the whole ASTP program was closed down about six months later.

Tom Uhl, my buddy from Bowling Green who had been in the 194th before he went to ASTP at Georgetown, was sent to the 13th Airborne. There he completed jump school, made sergeant and went overseas with them. The 13th Airborne was the only airborne division never committed to combat during WWII.

Another old friend of ours at Western, Ken Holloway, also left the 17th and went into the ASTP program. From there, Ken transferred into another unit and never returned to the Airborne. He eventually got into OCS, got his commission and remained in the regular army after the war and retired as a major.

As our division Table of Organization and Equipment (TO & E) changed over the next few months, we received many of the men who had been forced out of the program. Most of them joined us while we were on Tennessee Maneuvers. They knew nothing about Airborne and we had to train them.

I don't mean to sell these guys short, however, as they were all smart and caught on rapidly. Many filled much-needed administrative and clerical slots. Two good examples are Ed Siergiej and Joe Quade. Ed became the company clerk in Company C of the 194th and ultimately, the Secretary-Treasurer of the 17th Airborne Division Association. Joe went to the Parachute Maintenance Company and after the war became the Association's newsletter editor.

It's easy to reflect back now on decisions you made some time ago and wonder if you should have done differently. I really don't want to let myself wonder about that decision I made back in 1943 to turn down ASTP. Maybe I would have been able to finish the course, made sergeant and had a cushy job in some headquarters. Then again, maybe I would have fallen out of the Washington Monument and been killed! I'm glad I stayed "Airborne all the way!"

Chapter 11
ABERDEEN: MY OASIS!

The North Carolina area where we were stationed is now a fancy resort area. Pinehurst is the site of PGA golf tournaments and million dollar homes in the area are quite common. Back in 1944, when we were packed into Camp Mackall and Fort Bragg was only some 45 miles away, it was country fit only for training soldiers on how to live in the boonies.

Near Mackall was the small town of Rockingham, now famous for auto racing. It was always packed with soldiers and sported businesses that made it by catering to military needs. There were beer joints, tattoo parlors, tailor shops, clothing stores and the usual junky stores selling pillow covers, posters and military insignia. After dark, you would be hard pressed to see a young girl out anywhere.

When I went on pass, I wanted to get away from all that. I did not even want to see another soldier, although that was probably asking too much. Mostly, I wanted to be treated like a human being—like I had been treated back home before I was in the Army. That too, was probably asking too much, but still I hoped there might be such a place.

One place I found seemed to be closer to that Utopia than any other place in the area. That was Aberdeen, a small town of maybe about 500 people only 10 miles off of the Camp Mackall reservation. It was not "on the way" to anywhere, so very few soldiers went there. There was also nothing to do in Aberdeen. A movie, a few stores, no big dances, but a small USO where you could get a milkshake and a bed to stay overnight.

Some Saturdays I would go to Aberdeen with a buddy—usually Ray Crabtree or Ernie Stull—and we would relax, take in a movie, write some letters and go to bed at the USO. Then, we'd sleep late, loaf around until that afternoon and go back to camp. Not a very lively weekend, but a relaxing one and away from the army routine.

Sometime after I received the "Dear John" letter from Georgeanna and was feeling real sorry for myself, I went in to Aberdeen for such a low-key weekend. I remember listening to the radio at the USO. The Ink Spots were singing their hit song of the day, "Paper Doll". The lyric fit me exactly and my eyes teared up. I left the USO and went for a walk and to prowl through a few of the stores. Anything to get my mind off my troubles.

I found myself walking through Woolworth's five and dime store. I didn't need anything, but I was just looking at the merchandise to pass the time. I suddenly was asked by one of the clerks if she could help me. I took one look and I knew instantly that this attractive redhead could definitely help me! I told her my name and she said her name was Lucille Davis. I stuttered and stammered around for awhile, but eventually we began to talk. Then she said she was going to have to move away or her boss would notice she had been spending too much time talking to me. I asked when she got off and could we meet at the corner drug store or somewhere as I would like to talk some more. That's the way it began.

Lucille was about a year older than me, she had two younger teenage sisters and a older brother who was in the Marines. The family lived on a farm just out of town. Meeting this family was about the best thing that ever happened to me while I was in North Carolina. They were good people and they made me feel at home.

The two younger sisters were soon introduced to Ernie and Ray, respectively, and the six of us spent many evenings together. We went on picnics, to the movies and drove around in Ernie's or Lucille's car, buying gasoline on farm machinery ration coupons!

When the time came for us to leave Camp Mackall and go on Tennessee Maneuvers, I'm afraid Lucille and I had gotten a bit more serious than I had hoped. I guess that was my fault although I never meant for it to happen. She seemed to want a long-term commitment from me that when the war was over I would come back to Aberdeen. She may even have had marriage in mind. On the other hand, I knew that when I left Camp Mackall it was over.

Feeling it was best to be truthful and part friends, I told her how I felt and that if I survived the war, I would probably go back to Bowing Green and hopefully, would marry Georgeanna. Naturally, this ended a beautiful friendship fast! She told me to "go to hell" and that she never wanted to hear from me again!

I was sorry it ended on such a sour note, but I let it go at that. I never answered her letter. I had more important things to worry about, including surviving the war.

In 1970 or thereabouts, when we were living in Ashland, Kentucky, a young family bought the house next to us and moved in. I was surprised to learn that my new neighbor, Joel Chrisman, had grown up in Aberdeen. One day I asked him if he had ever known Lucille Davis. He said he had heard the family name and thought she might be a friend of his mother. He said he would ask her the next time he called home.

I had almost forgotten about it until one day Joel came over to my house and said he had asked his mother about Lucille Davis and she did know her. His mother had just called and told him she had run into Lucille in town recently. She had mentioned the fact that her son now lived in Ashland and his next-door-neighbor was Bart Hagerman who said he knew her. She said the next words Lucille said was, "Did he marry Georgeanna?"

I don't know what this says about anything, but I think it may indicate that I did the right thing when I told her the truth because in the long run, the truth never hurts. I liked her, but I didn't love her and I don't think I ever told her that I did.

There are a lot of nice people in this world and they are everywhere you look. I have no regrets for having met and known Lucille Davis and her family, and I have no regrets about our parting. I will always feel indebted to her and her family for making my days in dismal Camp Mackall much brighter.

Chapter 12
WEEKENDS IN CHARLOTTE

For us, the weekend always started at Saturday noon. It seems like every other outfit except the Airborne got off on Friday after duty hours, but we had to huff and puff until Saturday noon before we were free to go on pass.

When noon did come we would eat, shower and dress and hit the bus stops. Then the fun really began. Hundreds of GIs trying to push their way onto the dinky little buses that made the rounds of Camp Mackall and transported the soldiers into Rockingham or one of the other small towns near the camp.

You could either fight your way through this mob or wait until later after the rush was over. We did it both ways and it was still an ordeal. The alternative-staying on post-was not good either, so we usually managed to go somewhere. The goal on the weekends was to go as far away from camp as possible and to try to get away from the sight of other soldiers!

Bob Pearce and I frequently went on weekend pass together. We went to Chapel Hill one week and saw North Carolina Pre-Flight play another service team in football. About the only collegiate level football being played in those days was between service teams and schools that hosted specialized military training.

One week we decided that we would go to Charlotte, North Carolina, a distance of about 75 miles from camp. We had both known a girl named Edith Lester, who lived in Charlotte and had visited in Bowling Green during some past summer vacations. So I contacted her and set up a date. She was going to get Pearce a date with a friend of her's. We would meet them on Saturday night and maybe again on Sunday before we left to return to camp that evening.

I had no romatic interest whatsoever in Edith, but she was a nice person and I looked forward to seeing her again. It would also be nice to be in a home again after all our days in dull army barracks. Pearce, however, conjured up visions of his date being a glamorous knockout that would fall head over heels in love with him at first sight!

As it turned out, Pearce's date was a nice, attractive girl, but hardly the knockout he had envisioned. My date, Edith, was probably more attractive and personable, so Pearce began urging me to trade dates with him. I was totally opposed to this and didn't want to offend either of the girls with such a show of poor manners.

That night after we had left the girls and gone to a overnight shelter for servicemen, Pearce continued to hassle me to trade dates. I continued to resist telling him to behave for once and enjoy being with some nice girls like it was when we were home and were civilians.

We met the girls again Sunday and eventually ended up that evening at Edith's home.

It was just beginning to get dark and began to pour down rain. Soon it was time for us to leave to catch the bus back to camp. We already had our tickets and had planned to catch the bus at a nearby corner, so we left under umbrellas to walk about two blocks to the bus stop.

Someway, in the confusion of leaving, I found myself paired off and huddled under the umbrella with Pearce's date and Pearce was at last alone with Edith. This wasn't the way things were supposed to be. I wanted no complications and if we hoped to come back to Charlotte, I was afraid a situation like this was likely to cause trouble.

Believe me, I was totally taken back when the girl told me she had been waiting all weekend to be alone with me and to get away from Pearce! It really wasn't that important to me, but there was little I could do about it.

When we reached the bus stop we were early so to get out of the rain, we went up on the porch of a house on the corner. No one appeared to be at home, so we took the liberty of waiting there, out of the rain, for the bus. Pearce and Edith went around on one side of the horseshoe-shapped porch and the other girl and I were left on the other side. Then, to my surprise, the girl I was with was suddenly all over me. She began kissing me and carrying on like I couldn't believe! She was wild!

Now, there aren't many soldiers in any country's army that could resist this sort of attack, so I finally gave in and decided that maybe Pearce had had a good idea after all! Besides, wasn't he around the corner with Edith and probably doing the same thing? He had been talking about doing just that all weekend!

Apparently, however, he wasn't faring so well because in a little while he appeared at the corner of the porch and began cussing me in his usual, friendly manner. It seems that either the bus never passed that way or we were so involved that we let it pass without hailing it to stop. In any event, we were now stuck in Charlotte, the last bus had gone and no doubt we would be AWOL when we got back.

The rain had let up a bit now, so the girls returned to their homes and we moved down to stand on the street corner. We began to hitch-hike as we realized this was our only hope of getting back to camp without being AWOL. We were soaking wet and I guess we must have looked pretty pitiful as a car soon stopped and motioned us to get in.

The car was driven by a lieutenant who with his wife was returning from a weekend trip to Charlotte. They had purchased several dozen bed pillows for some of his fellow officers and they had the back seat piled to the roof with the pillows. They told us to just root our way in and the pillows should mash down enough to give us room.

This is exactly what we did. The pillows were warm and soft and we were asleep almost immediately! The lieutenant woke us up when we got on post and then he dropped us off near our barracks. I'll never forget that ride—and for that matter, the entire trip to Charlotte. You can rest assured I never let Pearce forget how his devious plan backfired on him!

I only went back to see that girl one more time and that proved to be a mistake. On Saturday night, July 26, we had a date, but the magic of that earlier evening could not be recaptured. It was a long way to travel and as I really didn't care for her, I resolved that I wouldn't go back to Charlotte again.

One thing that helped spoil that second trip might have been the fact that it was near the end of the month, and I was about broke. I had made the date earlier so I kept it although I was really strapped for money.

When I left camp I had purchased a round trip bus ticket, so I was assured of getting back to camp, but I guess I spent too much on our Saturday night date. After I took her home that night, I had 10 cents left! Needless to say, I told her I had to go back to camp the next day and not to expect me to come back to her house on Sunday.

I was unable to get a room in the servicemen's center, and being broke, I headed for the bus station to sleep on one of the benches. When I arrived I found that they were all taken, so I went across the street and stretched out on the post office lawn.

After sleeping for awhile, I awakened with a start when an MP slapped me across the soles of my shoes with his billy club. Seems I was sleeping right by a sign saying "keep off the grass!" My pass was in order, however, so he didn't lock me up. I spent the rest of the night hours sleeping on a bench in the bus station.

When daylight finally came, I washed up and went for a walk while I waited for the next bus. I was hungry, so I went in a little "hole-in-the-wall" type of restaurant and bought a candy bar with that last dime. The counterman also gave me a glass of water. As I sat there and wondered what to do next, I got a weird idea.

I poured some tomato ketchup into the glass of water, added some oyster crackers—both free and obviously on the counter for customer use—and presto! I had me a free bowl of tomato soup! The counterman looked at me a bit perplexed, but said nothing. Maybe it was because I was a serviceman or maybe it was because he had not delt with a situation like that before.

Finishing my bowl of soup breakfast, I walked out on the sidewalk and headed back toward the bus station. It was only by accident that I happened to look across the street and notice an attractive WAC officer walking by. Suddenly, I realized that the WAC officer was my own Aunt Elsye!

She was my mother's younger sister and she had joined the WACs after her husband and my uncle, Dr. V. A. "Jack" Jackson, was called up for service. He was presently a major in the Medical Corp serving in the Pacific Theater.

As the lieutenant in charge, my aunt had come to Charlotte with about six enlisted WACs to seek recruits for the Women's Army Corp. I had no knowledge that she was even there and it was just by accident that I happened to see her. She was just as surprised to run into me!

After we hugged each other, she took me to the hotel where she was staying and I met her detachment of WACs. I remember one great looking girl who had been "Miss Chicago" and it was not hard to understand why they had put her on recruiting duty!

I admitted to being broke and still a bit hungry. Aunt Elsie made me take a $5 loan so that I could buy something to eat. Although I was invited to spend the afternoon with my aunt and her girls, I really thought it best that I get on back. I left after a short visit and caught the next bus back to camp.

That wasn't the end of my adventures that weekend. The bus that I took back to camp was one of those cab and trailer types. It wasn't very comfortable and was even more unstable. On the way back, the driver swerved suddenly to miss a dog and the bus jackknived and went over on its side in the ditch.

Everyone was thrown about and most of us landed in a pile of bodies in the front end. I think one soldier suffered a broken leg, but most of us were just bruised and shook up a bit. We were really lucky. A new bus was called for and we finally made it back to Mackall.

By the way, I later repaid the $5 loan to my Aunt Elsye. That was a lot of money in those days! She and her team of recruiters soon moved on to other locations and I never saw her again while we were both in service. I never went back to Charlotte and the girl I had known there soon faded from my memory. We left for Tennessee maneuvers soon after that and life in the military went on.

Chapter 13
THE INSPECTIONS

D
epending on the type unit to which a soldier is assigned, he might find his entire allotment of free time is tied directly to his ability to pass inspections. It's simple: fail inspection and you get no pass. Many seem to skim through on their wits, but nothing ever beats preparation and a bit of hard work. Trying to beat the system is hardly worth the effort.

There were no passes for any of us during those first 13 weeks of basic training, so the threat that hung over us then was extra detail. Nothing could interfere with the training schedule, so extra detail was done after duty hours or on Sunday. These were necessary details and someone had to do them, so we were intent on being sure it was "someone else".

Try as we did, the "privilege" of pulling some kind of detail was usually passed around so that no one completely escaped. For the men who had been tapped as potential NCO's, they were made to serve as Charge-of-Quarters (CQ) and fire guards. For the rest of us, we served as latrine orderlies, swept and mopped the barracks floor, policed the company area and served extra turns as kitchen police (KP). About the only duty we avoided was the garbage truck. That was still reserved for military prisoners and AWOLs.

At first, being picked for latrine orderly duty was regarded as demeaning. Later we learned to appreciate this duty. It meant a few hours of hard work getting the latrine cleaned up for the morning inspection, but after that, with a bit of touch-up after the lunch break, the latrine orderly could take it easy the rest of the day. It sure beat going to the field.

The one thing I could never understand about latrine duty mentality was the fact five of the commodes had a sign reading "Reserved For NCOs." Was that to protect the private soldiers or the non-commissioned officers? And, from what?

The way to avoid extra duty of any type was to make sure you passed all inspections. This not only applied to the big Saturday "show-down" inspection, but to the everyday formation inspections that could come completely unannounced. Your uniform and web equipment had to be clean, all buttons buttoned, insignia properly sewed on and your weapon spotless. You yourself also had to be clean, have a neat haircut and a fresh shave.

The Saturday inspections were the worse. During basic training we would train most of the day and then be given time to prepare for a "show-down" inspection to finish off the day.

All uniforms and gear had to be properly displayed according to a pre-determined system, foot lockers had to be arranged just so, beds neatly made and the area swept clean. Our weapons had to be spotless and coated with just the right amount of oil. Woe be to the man whose rifle had a pitted barrel!

Another cute trick added during this period was the memorizing of the General

Orders. This was a set of twelve directives all soldiers who pulled guard duty were supposed to know. If you adhered to these directives and let yourself be guided by same, you hopefully would do the right thing in all emergencies. Mostly, it became an exercise in improving our memories and just another way to get us all "thinking the army way".

This memory test was usually thrust upon us when we least expected it. It came sometimes while we stood in formation, during an inspection and always when we reported to the Orderly Room to pick up a pass. You would be asked what is the third General Order or any other number at random and you had to come right back with it or there would be no pass for you.

One thing that always amazed me was the inspection of our extra clothes that hung on the racks beside our beds. All hang-up clothes had to be on black wire hangers, all buttons buttoned and all hangers hanging in the same direction. It seemed that no one could manage to button all their buttons. If an inspecting officer looked hard enough, he could usually find an infraction.

It was no secret that if you had a beef against someone, it was easy enough to unbutton a couple of his buttons when he wasn't looking and see to it that he received no pass that weekend. I didn't have a lot of trouble with this. I would check my buttons just before the inspection began and then keep my eye on them until the inspection was over. And, I was blessed by being billeted around some pretty good fellows and we sort of looked out for each other.

The other trouble spot was the foot locker. Everything had to be folded a certain way and be in the proper location. There was no excuse for any breach of uniformity. Some guys just couldn't fold a pair of socks. The top tray had to be perfect and the bottom area, where you were allowed to have a handful of personal items, had to be neat and "military-looking", whatever that meant.

Rust on a mess kit, eating utensil or canteen cup would also do you in. I could understand this as neglect here could cause food poisoning. Web equipment had to be scrubbed weekly and this left little time for drying. So we wore it wet. We even scrubbed tent pegs. There was no place for dirt or rust.

The beds, made of flat wire springs and cotton mattresses, were a big problem. It was May 10 before we got pillows and still we had no pillow cases or sheets. The beds always seemed to sag making it almost impossible to tighten the blankets to the tolerance that was demanded. The test of bouncing a coin on them was finally abandoned, but those blankets still had to be taunt and without a wrinkle. And, the "US" on the blankets had to be positioned at just the right location.

Finally, if everything else seemed to be correct, the inspecting officer could always get you when he checked your weapon. There were just so many things that could be wrong. Sometimes it was a speck of rust that the poor GI couldn't even see or too much oil or too little oil. And, once a rifle bore was allowed to pit, the owner was gigged from then on. There was no escape for him. He had to live with this burden until he could transfer out of the unit or loose the piece in combat.

A few times we managed to beat the system. To the GI this was a wonderful feeling. He began to think he had some control over his own destiny. It didn't happen often, but when it did it made a lasting impression. I can remember only one such case, but it was a good one!

Late one night Ernie Stull, Ray Crabtree and I were returning to camp from one of our visits to nearby Aberdeen. We were in Ray's car and he was driving. As we rode down the two-lane road toward camp we suddenly passed through an area where we saw a number of parachutes scattered over the fences and the open field adjoining the road. Apparently there had been a tactical jump that night and as yet, no one had policed up the chutes.

For some reason, we decided to help ourselves to one of the parachutes. We were still only glider troops at the time and it would make a nice trophy to take back to our barracks. Also, nylon was impossible to buy during those days and all women were anxious to get an old parachute canopy to make dresses. One popular use was to make a wedding gown.

Whatever the reason, we bundled the chute up, put it in the trunk and returned to camp. The next day we proudly showed our trophy to our buddies. Next, we began to wonder what we were going to do with it. It was too big to hide and it couldn't stay in the car. The answer was to store it in the attic of our barracks until Ray got a three-day pass and could take it home.

The chute was stored away in the attic just in time before one of our Saturday inspections. If it was discovered, it meant not only restriction for the entire barracks, but someone would have to answer for theft of government property. It was a very tense moment when Captain Stuhrman came down the line that day inspecting each of us and our layouts.

I watched out of the corner of my eye as the captain stood face to face with Ray and looked him over from head to toe. Then in horror, I saw Ray's eyes lift up and glance at the ceiling. Captain Stuhrman glanced up, but seeing nothing and not guessing that the attic held some secrets, he went on with his inspection. Soon he passed on down the line and we all breathed a sign of relief.

Ray got his pass and took the chute to his home in West Virginia. We were all glad to see it go. Some time later we learned that on that night of the jump, two troopers had been killed. During wartime, these sort of mishaps were hushed up. The story was that because the rain had made the blacktop road shiny, the troopers had mistaken it for the river and according to set procedure, cut out of their chutes before landing. I imagine this was not the only case where paratrooper deaths were hushed up.

Inspections continued to be a big part of our lives throughout our entire time in the military. Even after combat when accountability was thrown out the window, the Army managed to come back with toughness on inspections to whip us back into shape. It wasn't so much an effort to conserve equipment as there seemed to be an abundance of that, but it was more for discipline reasons. All armies really liked this sort of thing!

CHAPTER 14
GLIDER TROOPS VS PARATROOPS

E arly in our training as glider troops we took a lot of harassment from the paratroop units. Most of this, however, came while we were stationed at Camp Mackall. Living on the same post with paratroops from two Airborne divisions—the llth and our own 17th—provided plenty of opportunities for disagreements. We were just packed in too closely. Fights were quite commonplace and accordingly, I don't know how many times the beer gardens were closed down due to unrest among the troops!

One evening I was with five or six of my buddies from Company D and we were enjoying a few 3.2% beers at the stockade-type beer garden located near our billets. We sat at a table near the wall in back and were quietly minding our own business. Suddenly, a fight broke out across the way and as we watched, it spread rapidly toward our location.

We had no desire to join in what was sure to become a giant free-for-all, and at this point only wished to save our necks. As usual, we could see that it was becoming a glider-paratrooper affair. Someone got the idea to turn our table over as a buffer against the spreading fight. This we did and we were able to almost disappear behind the table and its attached bench seats.

Maybe that was cowardly of us. Maybe we should have joined in and helped our fellow glidertroopers fight the paratroops. Maybe we should have gotten our faces pounded in for no good reason. At the time, however, self preservation seemed to be the best choice and we laughed at how we avoided the senseless fight.

In a few minutes, some MPs arrived on the scene and one of them fired his .45 in the air. The whole place became as quiet as church. The MPs quickly sorted out two or three of the combatants who seemed to be the most heavily involved and hustled them out of the beer garden to heaven knows where. The place was immediately shut down and the rest of us filed sheepishly out and returned to our barracks.

There was another incident we heard about. Somewhere out in one of the dusty training areas, a parachute company marching in column passed a glider company also marching in column. The two columns of men began to shout insults and curses at each other as they passed and finally it erupted in a free-for-all fight there in the woods. I can just imagine the chaos that resulted and the officers from both companies trying to separate the troops!

Finally, the day came when all this animosity was put aside. Strangely enough, it came about through a simple matter of augmenting the training schedules. The paratroopers were given an orientation flight in a glider and we began our training flights in the gliders. We were given something to be proud of and the paratroopers quickly learned to respect the men who would dare to go up in the flimsy crafts.

The fellowship between the two type units became even more secure when in the summer of 1944, at Camp Forrest, over 2,500 glidertroopers volunteered for a division jump school and about 2,200 qualified as jumpers. After that, maybe it wasn't exactly one big happy family, but you never heard of fights between the units. When there was trouble in town, the men hung together as a division and not separately as glidertroopers and paratroopers.

The brass was not unaware of this competition between the two branches of the Airborne. In some cases I think they actually promoted it in an effort to "toughen" the men for the combat ahead. However, as that time drew near, there was a general backing-off in favor of division harmony. Several things helped bring this about.

Undoubtedly, the prime event to encourage intra-unit harmony was the division jump school. There was probably no real tactical advantage in having the glider troops qualified both ways, but it was a big morale builder. They became more confident of their own abilities. Justifiably, they could reason to themselves that they could do anything their cross-camp rivals could do.

Maybe the main motivator was the fact that the newly-qualified paratroopers now received an additional $50 a month in jump pay. That put them in the position of no longer being the poor step-children in the division. It was several more months before congress authorized hazardous duty pay for the glider troops.

The new paratroopers also received two other premium advantages. They now could proudly wear the silver jump wings and the shiny paratroop boots with their pants legs bloused! This might not sound like much, but at that time, and even today to some extent, that is a much-cherished privilege. There are few awards that can measure up to the Combat Infantryman's Badge and the Parachute Wings.

Finally, all qualified glider troops were awarded the newly-designed glider wings and both units adopted a combination glider-parachute hat patch. This seemed to complete the marriage. When the units went in combat, the camaraderie became even more apparent and with the respect each gained for the other, all forms of the old hate relationship disappeared once and forever.

CHAPTER 15
A LOSS OF SACK-TIME

O ne thing I had to give up when I went in the army was plenty of sleep, or "sack-time" as we called it! In civilian life I often slept eight or nine hours each night and on weekends I frequently slept-in for even more. Not so in the army. It seems we were always getting up early and working late. We quickly learned to grab our sleep when we could.

While we were in training back in the States, we had lights out at 10 o'clock and reveille was at an early 5:30 in the morning. With seven and a half hours sleep each night you could manage quite well, but if you went to town or happened to catch some late duty, it cut into your "sack-time". We seldom averaged over six hours a night while in garrison and way less than that when we were in the field.

Faced with this situation, we were always ready for a nap whenever the training permitted. If we went to the theater for a training film, in 10 minutes nearly everyone was asleep. If we were in the field and away from the officers or sergeants, we usually found a cool spot and dozed off.

Monday mornings were the worse. After a big weekend on pass we were always beat. Generally, we could grab nine minutes sleep during each 10-minute break. If we stopped while on the march, it often was an ordeal to get everyone awake and back on their feet when the break was over!

One week while we were at Camp Mackall, we had a three-day problem on the Fort Bragg reservation. Bragg was only about 40 miles away, so naturally, we just walked over. No need for transportation. We hoofed it. We started out after the sun had gone down and walked all night. Then we ran problems all the next day.

After the evening meal that day, everyone was asleep in 10 minutes. Amazingly enough, after a decent night's sleep, everyone was ready to go the next day. We ran problems all that day and the next. We may have gotten a few little cat naps in, but not many. That night, when the duty day was over, there was no horsing around. Everyone hit the sack once it was dark.

The next day we had a shorter problem that finished earlier. We packed our gear, had chow, and after the sun had gone down, we started our march back to our barracks at Camp Mackall. Once again we marched all night to get there. It was on this return trip that Phil Recupero and I made an interesting discovery. We could sleep while we were marching. Sounds impossible, but I swear that it is the truth.

Phil was a scout in the third squad and when we marched in a column of two's, Phil and I marched side-by-side. We always talked a lot as we walked and that night we decided that we might be able to sleep and walk. We decided to try it during that night's long march back to camp.

We would take turns. The one who was going to stay awake would carry the rifle of the one who would sleep. He would take the sleeper by the arm and thereby keep him from wandering off into the ditch. Then he would count 1000 paces which usually took about 30 minutes and was close to a mile. Then he would awaken the sleeper and they would change roles.

We did this all the way back to camp, interrupted only by the breaks which came approximately after each of us had had one turn at "walk-sleeping". It was not as restful as sleeping in a bed or even on the ground, but it was better than no sleep at all! We figured if sleep-walkers could do it, we could too. And, we did!

When I went home on furlough I usually slept-in late on that first morning, but time was too precious to waste it sleeping! The same applied to those weekends I got to come home while at Camp Forrest. There were people to see and things to do! However, when I got back to camp I quickly reverted to the old ways, trying to find any "sack-time" I could.

You really have to need sleep to doze off while riding in a GI truck. The shocks are not designed to provide a soft ride. However, we soon learned to handle the rough pitching and banging around on the wooden seats and would nod off on a ride of any real distance.

The same great need for sleep persisted when we reached England. On the weekends when we went to London, we would return only about an hour before we were to fall out for revielle. We would change from our Class A uniforms into our fatigues and be ready to fall out when the whistle blew. Then we'd lie down on top of our bunks and grab a last hour or so of sleep.

When we boarded the C-47s in England that were to take us to France and the Battle of the Bulge, instead of being all keyed up, most of us were asleep before the planes reached the English Channel. Even after landing and going into the woods, we curled up in the cold and grabbed a few winks. Whether it was nervousness or a genuine need for sleep, we seemed to be obsessed to sleep whenever we could.

The first time I remember sleep not being our number one priority was when we entered combat in Belgium. We knew this was the real thing, but green as we were, we thought there was a German behind every tree. At last no one had to tell us to stay awake. We occupied two-man holes and one man was supposed to stay awake at all times. They didn't have to tell us twice.

There were a few cases of patrols probing our lines, but in those first few days, nothing much really happened at night. Nevertheless, we observed the "one awake" rule pretty well. I remember I did not sleep at all the first night. The next day was quiet so I may have dozed off several times for a few minutes, but all told, I went about 48 hours with maybe one hour's sleep. That was a record for me!

The dumbest time I found to take a nap while we were in combat came one night in Luxembourg. It was January 26, and our company was in reserve as the battalion was mopping up resistance in the little village of Hautbellian. The plan was to maneuver into positions where we could attack Hosingen on the Our River. It was a bitter cold night, dark as pitch, about two o'clock in the morning, and as we were moving through a cluster of farm buildings, a halt was called. Several of us ducked into a nearby barn seeking both cover and warmth during the halt.

The roof at the far corner of the building was slowly burning, apparently set on fire by artillery. The fire didn't bother us as we thought we would only be halted there for a few minutes. Just inside the door lay a dead horse. It had been dead for some while as it was swollen up and its legs pointed up into the air.

By this time a dead horse was nothing. For that matter, neither was a dead person. As the barn door was gone, another trooper and I huddled down in the hay behind the swollen horse using it as a shield against the cold wind. In no time we were sound asleep. We lay there a good 20 minutes before the word came to move on up.

As we walked, I became aware of some itching or something biting me around my neck. My friend reported he was having the same problem. To make a long story short, we had picked up some lice during the nap in the hay behind the dead horse. For the next three days, I scratched and itched as a few of the lice seemed content to follow me the rest of the war.

I only had to put up with them for about three days because I was then wounded and sent back to the hospital. Some nice orderly had to clean me up and delouse me before they could put me in a bed. Would I be so careless again? Would I lie down by a dead horse and sleep? Sure! A soldier has to get his "sack time" whenever and wherever he can!

CHAPTER 16
LOST IN THE BOONIES

A lot of dumb things can happen to a person, but if they're smart, a lesson is usually there to be learned. I learned a good lesson one day while we were running company problems in the pine forests of Camp Mackall.

Our company was set up in a defensive position late one afternoon and we were preparing our Main Line of Resistance (MLR). For our mortar squad, that meant mass clearance for the tube and preparing a range card that would plot every possible target in front of our sector. By having the range already plotted, a mortar squad has a better chance of getting on a possible target quickly or of firing accurately during the hours of darkness.

This time our squad sergeant, Henry Clay Browning of Sikeston, MO., asked me to perform this duty. I was eager to do a good job so I went out in front of the gun and began looking for a good vantage point from which to plot the targets.

We were really out in the boondocks. We were surrounded by the dark, thick pine forest and there was no hill from which the surrounding countryside could be viewed. I realized that the only way to accomplish my task would be to climb one of the tall trees.

I went out some 100 yards ahead of our position to scout the ground. I picked out a big, tall pine and up I went, higher and higher. From this perch I could see all the draws, rock outcroppings, and road intersections in the area. I soon had everything plotted, so I started down to return to the gun site. Then it happened.

Maybe I slipped, maybe a limb broke. Whatever happened, I lost my balance and started falling. I grabbed for anything to break my fall, but had little luck as I came down fast. I think I hit every limb on the way down as my body was covered with black and blue bruises the next day.

When I hit the ground it knocked my breath out and a lick on the head rendered me unconscious. When I came to, I was not only stunned, but quite embarrassed and looked around to see if anyone had seen my dumb stunt. Apparently no one had as it was quiet as could be in the area.

I never thought to use the compass that I had, but started out immediately to go back to the gun position. I guess I must have started off in the wrong direction as the farther I walked the more deserted the area became. Still unwilling to admit that I might be lost, I walked on trying to find the company area, but to no avail.

After about an hour of aimless wandering, I realized I was hopelessly lost in the boondocks of this large training area. I tried to remember all my Boy Scout training about moss growing on the north side of trees and the sun setting in the west, etc. I couldn't find any moss and it was so overcast I could not locate the setting sun. Nothing seemed to work for me.

I knew the general direction of the training area from camp, so I sat down and waited for it to get dark. Then, to add to the misery, it began to rain and rain hard. Finally, I was able to see the glow in the sky of the main post area. I started walking in that direction and must have gone two or three miles before I hit a spot that was familiar. Then I headed for the training area, another good two miles.

After walking about a mile, I met some trucks heading back toward camp. I stepped to the side of the road in the shadows so I wouldn't be seen and then watched as I realized it was my own company roaring by, heading back to camp. Later, I found out that the problem had been called off due to the inclement weather and everyone had been trucked back to the barracks. Everyone that is, except me and I had been left way out in the boonies!

I turned around and started hoofing it back. It was a good two miles so I had ended up walking over six miles and my body felt like I had been hit by a tank. As I walked, I slowly came to realize that they had to know I was missing and yet, had left without finding me! They apparently were going to leave me out there for the night!

Well, I finally got back after every one had cleaned his equipment and was ready to bed down for the night. "Why," I asked, "didn't someone come find me and why did you come on in to camp and leave me out there?"

The answer was simple. They did look for me. A little. Then when the weather turned so sour they reasoned I had found shelter—maybe even returned to camp on my own. They added that if I wasn't back by morning they were going to come back and find me.

Well, that was hard to argue against. If it hadn't been for the fall out of the tree and the resulting disorientation, it wouldn't have happened anyhow. Brownie gave me another good answer too. He said I ought to be glad the old man didn't rip me good for goofing off and going for a walk in the boonies!

Yea, I learned a good lesson that night, but somehow, with my body aching all over it was a tough one to learn. Needless to say, I never climbed another pine tree while we were in the boonies of North Carolina.

CHAPTER 17
NEVER VOLUNTEER FOR ANYTHING!

They have a saying in the service: "Don't ever volunteer for anything!" And, I might add the fact that the greener the recruit, the more likely he was to get suckered in. I guess I took the bait once, but after that I was a much smarter soldier!

One day, just a week or so after we had completed basic training, I made the mistake of volunteering. We had just returned to the company area and were standing "at ease" in company formation in front of our barracks. It was the time just before we were dismissed when announcements were usually made to us by our First Sergeant and/or the Company Commander.

Captain Jerry Stuhrman turned the company over to First Sergeant Bob Kepler and we were all anxious to be done with the day's work and to be dismissed. "Kep", in his slow, western drawl, had only one announcement that day. I nearly dropped my weapon when I heard him say, "Private Hagerman report to me at the orderly room following this formation."

What had I done now, I wondered! I was sure I hadn't screwed up in anyway. Surely this couldn't be something good. Good things just didn't happen in this man's army! I readied myself for the worse and reported to the orderly room as told. I was ready to face the music—whatever it was!

"I see from your 201 file, that you attended Western Kentucky Teachers College," Kepler began.

"Yes, Sergeant," I replied. "I went there for two quarters before I came in the Army."

"Well," Kep drawled, "we've got some men in the battalion that have had a limited education and we need someone to give them a little instruction in the "three R's": reading, 'riting and 'rithmetic! You would meet with them three evenings a week just after chow for about an hour or so."

My brain was racing way ahead of him by this time. What was in it for me, I was wondering! Give up three evenings a week? Those one-hour sessions would last longer, I knew. I hung on every word the sergeant said.

I knew I wasn't going to make non-com in the platoon, those positions had already been decided and sewed-up during basic. Was this a chance to get a couple of stripes and earn more money? Would it be worth it to me in the long run?

I began to realize that Kep wasn't telling me I had to do this. He was painting a pretty picture and was hoping I would be so carried away that I would volunteer. Gosh, how long it had been since I had had a choice about anything! Finally, he got to the tough spot for him.

"Well, how about it," he asked, "want to take a shot at it?"

"Gee, I don't know, Top, I'd like to help those guys, but I hate to give up three of my evenings each week," I replied. "Does the job carry any stripes?" I ventured.

That's where I gave him an opening to sucker me in. I guess I'll never know if he meant to mislead me or whether he just didn't know for sure, but he cocked his head, looked down at the floor and replied: "Well, could be. I'm not for sure, but if we can work it out, I'll do what I can."

Now, Kep was a good guy. He was stern and all business, but everyone liked him because he was fair. He always kept his word and I took what he said to be the gospel. So, I said I'd give it a try. That was where I made my big mistake.

That first evening when I reported over to the building where we were to have school, I found about 12 or 15 guys waiting. Some were of foreign decent—Italian, Cuban or Mexican—and I could hardly understand them. Others were grade school dropouts and some were of limited intelligence. I wondered what the devil I was going to do with this mixed bag!

The military had been authorized to draft a limited number of men who had a limited education, but I doubt if much thought was given to what type of assignment they should have. Someone apparently decided that a good place for them would be in a hazardous duty unit. So, the Airborne got their percentage.

The study guide I was given was not really aimed at educating these people, but just getting them to the point where they could read or write a simple army message form, follow written orders and hopefully, not jeopardize their entire unit.

I was right about another thing too. The classes lasted longer than an hour. It was 6:30 until 8:00 each of those three nights. Soon some of the guys began cutting class and apparently memos sent to their companies were ignored. After about three or four weeks we were down to about eight or ten students.

To make it worse, by this time I had begun to feel sorry for them and I got to where I wanted to help them learn.

One of my students was Pvt. Joseph J. Czubak—"Chulsby" we called him—and he was in my own platoon. He could not write his own name. He even signed an "X" on the payroll! I got to thinking about this. I could be in a situation where I was depending on this guy and I figured my chances would be nil. It really behooved me to teach him something.

We went on for weeks like this. Not one single time did any officer or NCO from any of the battalion's companies come by to see how it was going or to check on us or to see whether we were even meeting. No one, including Kepler, ever asked about the school, or cut me any slack so that I could prepare for the classes.

Naturally, I realized by this time that I had been suckered into a deal. Someone up above must have said it would be smart to set up such a school and the order was cut and sent down. Nothing else was ever said and everyone just forgot about it. I was wanting to call it all off, but I had a real problem and I couldn't figure out how to get out of it.

I got my opportunity when they announced we would have a week-long field problem. When I mentioned the school to Kepler, he said I should call it off until further notice. I then told the students they would be advised when to report back. With that, we all went happily to the field for the problem.

That proved to be the last of the school. I decided I would just keep quiet and wait until I was advised to resume classes. Apparently the students didn't ask either as I'm sure they were tiring of the routine. The whole thing just died right there. It was one of the very few things that I ever saw in the military that just seemed to go away!

Of course, I didn't get another stripe out of all that effort. But, after what I had voluntarily given up, it was enough just be relieved from teaching those three evenings a week and to get back that time for myself. I guess I had to learn it the hard way: "Don't ever volunteer for anything!"

CHAPTER 18
THE LONG-LEGGED SWEDE

I f there was any blessing that was bestowed on Company D, it was in getting Captain Jerry Stuhrman for our company commander. You could just look at him and feel strength and know he was a cut above the rest. I feel sure there was no one in the company who didn't like and respect him.

During the early weeks of our training, Stuhrman was our executive officer, the XO. The company at first was commanded by a captain named Rosario Sorbello. However, it wasn't long before Sorbello was promoted to major and transferred. We never saw him again. Stuhrman, then a first lieutenant, made captain and took over.

Probably the first thing that changed in the company was the pace at which we marched. Sorbello was a squat, athletic built man of short statue and the pace at which he led the company, although brisk, was no real strain on the men in the rear ranks.

Stuhrman, on the other hand, was a long-legged, blond-headed outdoorsman who loved to stride out and travel at a really brisk pace. This often meant the men in the rear of the column (and these were often the shorter men) practically had to run to keep up with the company and the long-legged Swede who now commanded it!

I really don't know where the idea of him being a "Swede" came from. The name is of German orgin, but as Germans were not held in high esteem at that time, and Stuhrman was a decided blond, someone started it around that he was Swedish. At that age and time we would believe anything and we bought it without question.

Stuhrman was from Missouri and had grown up on a farm. Although at the time he entered service he had been working as a rural mail carrier, he continued to live on the farm and maintained his love of the land and farm animals. That included ducks. Ducks seemed to be his favorite tie back to his rural, civilian beginnings.

Maybe that was why a scrawny, white duck suddenly appeared in our company area one day while we were stationed at Camp Forrest. I couldn't believe my eyes when I first saw it, but when I saw Captain Stuhrman throwing some feed to it, I knew it was no accident that it had chanced to be there, and, that it was there to stay.

In no time that duck staked out the company area as his territory and took over the free run of it. Nobody dared to challenge him as the word spread fast that this was the captain's duck. Some griped about it—especially those who were assigned the detail to police up the area—but most became fond of the bird and we delighted in having something the other companies didn't have: a mascot!

This was about the time the division was starting a jump school for all the glider troops who wanted to volunteer to qualify as parachutists. It was only natural that the men not only named the duck "Airborne", but started the rumor that the "old man" (an army term of affection for a commanding officer) was going to jump with the duck and "qualify" it.

Although that was not to be, the story went around about Company D having the jumping duck. We took great pleasure in enlarging on various stories of the duck's exploits to the wonderment of our comrades in the other companies.

I remember the one where we bragged that Captain Stuhrman had jumped with the duck and then released him just before he came in for his landing. The duck was said to have done the last 50 feet as a free fall, not knowing that it was supposed to spread its wings and that it should be able to fly!

Stuhrman, of course, made no jumps with the duck. Whether he was more interested in his own safety or the duck's is a matter to be debated, but the stories grew as did the enlisted men's love for "Airborne". That's what made the end a bitter pill to swallow.

The time finally came for the division to prepare for our move to the Port of Embarkation (POE). This meant getting rid of all personal items and excess baggage we had acquired during our days of service to date. Men were given 3-day passes to take cars home, or get wives settled in their hometowns or to wind up any other personal affairs.

Naturally, that also meant something had to be done with "Airborne", the duck. Word got out that Lt. Van Sycle had taken the duck to a farm residence he had leased near Camp Forrest and that his wife planned to stay there and would look after the duck. This made sense and everyone was pretty happy with the arrangement. Then the bad news got out and the men turned violently mad.

It seems that Van Sycle invited all the company officers to a farewell dinner at his house and the rumor went around that the main course was duck! Everyone was said to have really enjoyed the meal and that there was no remorse in their eating what had been our proud mascot. There was, of course, no truth to the story, but we didn't find that out until some 35 years later!

Stuhrman told an interesting story on himself years later to the amusement of former company members. It seems one day while we were at Camp Forrest, he was in his office in the orderly room and was fooling around with a defective—or so he thought—parachute flare. For some unknown reason he was trying to remove the small parachute when the device went off.

Up went the flare, through the roof of the orderly room and high in the air. Totally shocked by the ignition of the device, Stuhrman was nevertheless, miraculously uninjured. As First Sergeant Bob Kepler and Supply Sergeant Wilbert Springstubb rushed in to investigate, Stuhrman put them to work covering the hole in the ceiling and swore them to secrecy. By some wild twist of luck, the incident went undetected.

Even in combat, Stuhrman's luck held. At one of our reunions long after the war was past history, he told another one on himself. It seems he was at the head of the company as they filed along in column on a dark, snowy January night winding their way through the dense Ardennes forest. Movement was by map and compass and it was tough going all the way.

The scouts up front halted the column and came back to report to Stuhrman that there seemed to be a German bivouac area in the woods just ahead. They had spotted the enemy troops but had not been seen themselves. Stuhrman calmly led the column in a 180 degree turn, reversing the direction to lead the column back the way it had come. No one—neither friend nor foe—ever knew what had happened and how close we had come to a disaster!

My own personal Stuhrman story comes from an incident that took place while we were in England. It was early in December of 1944, and we had gone down to Southhampton for some training in house-to-house fighting. There were several city blocks there that had suffered a terrible pounding by German bombers and the ruins had been set aside and reserved for training troops in the art of house-to-house fighting.

The training was quite good and we learned a lot. Before leaving the site for our trip back to our billets, the company was gathered together and several weapons were demonstrated for our general knowledge. We were shown how the concussion made by the English Gammon Grenades could knock down a wall and how you could "spray" a room with the new M-3 "Grease Gun".

Then, Captain Stuhrman decided to demonstrate the firepower packed by one of our white phosphorus grenades. No one had ever seen one go off so we were very attentive. Stuhrman pulled the pin on one and tossed it over against the wall of one of the bombed-out buildings.

Unfortunately, the demonstration backfired. The wall of the building acted as a reflector and the minute pieces of burning phosphorus ricocheted back into the troops seated on the ground and wreckage of the buildings. There was a near stampede as men scrambled to take cover and to beat out the fires starting in their clothing.

One piece hit me just to the left of my left eye and I felt the pain as it began to cook the flesh. The one thing that saved me that day was the fact there was snow upon the ground. Water neutralizes the phosphorus and will wash it away. You should see the guys scooping up snow and rolling around in it!

I grabbed a handful of snow and slapped it to my face and the problem was quickly solved for me. I did get a good burn, but an English Red Cross lady put some salve and a bandage on it and I never had any more trouble. I was just glad the phosphorus had missed my eye. The burn was bad enough, however, that I still have a small scar there today.

To his credit, Captain Stuhrman apologized to the company for the incident and later came by my tent to see how my burn was healing. Years later, I teased him about the parachute flare, the goof with the grenade and pointed out to him the scar I have. He responded that the training must have been good because I sure learned to respect those grenades that day and that I should be glad he hadn't decided to demonstrate a fragmentation grenade! I'll agree to that!

Stuhrman got out of the military after the war. He had received the Purple Heart, Bronze Star, Silver Star and three battle stars. He went back in the 82nd Airborne during Korea and finally retired from the service as a lieutenant colonel.

He was and is, one of the most respected and best-loved individuals I have ever known. He was a very positive role model for me. Although a number of our company were killed during the war, I know that because of him alone, many more of us made it home safely. I don't know how you can pay a higher compliment to a man.

CHAPTER 19
THE BEST SOLDIER I EVER KNEW

I don't have any problem in identifying the best soldier I ever knew. Far and away it was T/Sgt Charles R. Pierre, our platoon sergeant. That isn't just my opinion. Every one who knew him would readily agree on that. Pierre was the best.

It wasn't because of his combat record that I say that. Unfortunately, Pierre was killed in action during our first combat assault. Had he lived longer, I feel certain that he would have been able to bring more of our guys home and I also suspect the Germans would have paid a dearer price when we clashed with them.

Pierre was from a small town in southern Ohio. He was married, but as far as anyone ever knew, the couple had no children. No one ever knew much about Pierre. His private life was basically a mystery to the men in his platoon and even to most of his close sergeant friends. That was the way he wanted it.

Maintaining a distinctive line between both officers and private soldiers, one often got the idea he did not like either. But, that was not true. He cared deeply for us private soldiers and woe be to anyone in another platoon or company who tried to harm any of his men. And, although most of us were always griping about the officers, he would have none of that and stood up for them regardless of the situation.

He was really tough on us and would not accept a mediocre performance. We were the First Platoon! First and finest! He saw to it we toed the line and he wanted us to take the toughest assignment and do the best job. He usually had his way and we took pride in being the best.

Pierre hated paratroopers. He was a glider soldier through and through and could not stand the "Superman" attitude some jumpers had. Several times we noticed that Pierre had a black eye or a cut on his face and we knew he had challenged some loud mouth while off post. We didn't dare to comment on it, but we knew!

He was a stickler for wearing the uniform correctly. All of our brass had to be shining and placed just right. Woe be to anyone who was detected wearing some item that was not authorized. He was especially angered by the fact paratroopers had the silver jump wings and in the beginning, the glider soldiers had no similar award.

I have a photograph that was given to me after the war that was taken of Pierre while he was on leave back in Ohio. Naturally, he never expected that photo to be seen by anyone in his company. In it he is wearing an old Sam Browne belt which I suppose he wore in the pre-war army, and to my surprise, a set of miniature glider pilot wings on his cap! I couldn't believe my eyes!

I remember clearly the day we glider troops were given the opportunity to volunteer for parachute school. I think the main reason this was done was to give us the opportunity to earn extra pay. I never believed the story that it was to train us to go into combat either way as the terrain might dictate.

At that time, glider soldiers, who were not volunteers, had no say-so about how they went into combat. They took their chances in the gliders and unlike the paratroopers, received no hazardous duty pay. We had been conditioned to regard this as the way we showed the paratroopers we were as gutsy as they were! Very few of them wanted to go up in the gliders.

Then, one day after we had completed a tough day in the field, we were standing in company formation alongside our barracks waiting to be dismissed. Although the rumor had been going around, Captain Stuhrman surprised us all when he announced that glidertroops were now going to be allowed to volunteer for jump school.

We had thought this might happen, but so many rumors were going around that no one ever believed anything. He explained the program, when it would start, when it would end and the commitment it would require. Then he turned the platoons over to the platoon sergeants to obtain a list of the men in each platoon who wished to volunteer.

Pierre called the platoon to attention, commanded us to open ranks and then to stand at ease. With no further comment, he ordered everyone who desired to volunteer to take one step forward. The vast majority of the platoon—about 30 of the 45 men—stepped forward. I did not hesitate for a second, but I noticed I was the only one in my seven-man mortar squad that volunteered.

Pierre cursed those of us who had volunteered and then he went down the line personally chewing out each of us. Next he gave all the volunteers 25 pushups. We were really pumped up by this time and we ripped them off with ease. Then, to our astonishment, he cursed himself and then he dropped and he did 25 pushups. His only comment was there was not going to be anyone in the first platoon that could do anything he couldn't do!

Pierre tore through jump school with no trouble whatsoever and afterwards was the most "gung-ho" paratrooper the Army ever had. Where before he had made fun of the prized jump boots the troopers wore, he now spent hours shining his to a dazzling brilliance! And, he also seemed to delight in giving the nasty details to the non-jumpers in the platoon.

The paratroopers at that time wore a small, round patch on their caps with a parachute on it. We wore the same round patch, but it had a glider on it. Naturally, now that we were jumpers, we wanted to wear the parachute patch, but that was prohibited. Pierre enforced this regulation vigorously. It was as if he was still trying to maintain the connection we had when we were solely glider troops.

One time he was showing some of us some photos he had made while off post and there he was wearing a cap with the parachute patch! When we called it to his attention, he got red in the face and replied that what he did on his own time was no one's business. But, he added, what he told us to do was also his business and we had damn sure better not forget it! I think we had no problem in understanding that logic.

One of the few times we ever challenged Pierre was just before we left Camp Forrest for overseas. The whole thing began with me. The idea grew out of the fact that we were restricted to the post and could not even get a pass to town. To me that was a real blow as I could be in Bowling Green in about six hours and I had been able to get home nearly every weekend.

I was at the PX with Bob "Red" Ewing and we were whiling away the time. I happened to look up on the shelve and saw a bottle of hydrogen peroxide. I remembered the girls had used this to bleach their hair so, just on a whim, I decided that I would too! I told Red that I knew of no army regulation against it and inasmuch as we were restricted, why not?

As you might guess, after my hair turned from jet black to red, the fad spread like wildfire! Everyone, or nearly everyone, joined in the foolishness and soon we were a company of blondes and redheads. Captain Stuhrman heard about the stunt and someone told him that we did it because he was such a decided blond.

I remember returning from the field one day and before we were dismissed, Captain Stuhrman ordered us to take off our helmets. He looked at the sea of predominately blond heads in the company, grinned and chuckled, shook his head and walked away. It was plain he was touched by this and that he got quite a kick out of it.

I mentioned <u>most</u> of us peroxided our hair. Sergeant Pierre was among the few that didn't. It occurred to us that if he would do it, our whole platoon would be blond. But, as he refused, if it was going to be done, it had to be done by force! I guess being penned up like we were, we were getting crazy because we decided that we were going to use force on him.

About six or seven of us with a perchance of living in the danger zone, decided that one night we would make a "commando" raid on Pierre in his private room and douse his hair good with peroxide. We knew he would struggle like a trapped bear, but we also knew he enjoyed a good free-for-all.

Dressed in dark clothes with our faces covered (not that it really concealed our identity) we staged our commando raid on him at about 0100 hours one night. Never in my life have I seen such a fight that he put up. It was like having a tiger by the tail. We couldn't hold him and we couldn't turn him loose!

We got the peroxide on his head all right, but he knocked us around pretty good. After our escape, he washed his hair so it had little effect. Nevertheless, old Pierre really enjoyed it, I know. He always enjoyed a good fight and this operation also showed him that we considered him "one of the boys".

I could recall a dozen more stories on Pierre. He always took up for the first platoon, but he never shirked the toughest tasks for us and we always excelled. We griped as all soldiers do, but we wouldn't have considered transferring to another platoon even if we had had the chance.

He took care of his men and we developed a healthy respect and love for him. On January 7, 1945, he was fatally wounded while rallying the platoon to charge a wooded area and the German positions therein. He went down fighting and died of his wounds the next day in the hospital. He is buried in the U.S. Military Cemetery near Luxembourg City.

Some years ago I visited the cemetery and his grave. It's located not too far from that of General Patton's. I think Pierre would approve of the location as a fit resting place.

CHAPTER 20
WEAPONS FIRING

I f you're going to be in an Airborne outfit, you must learn to fire a number of weapons. That includes many U.S. weapons plus many of those of your enemy. I was anxious to get started in this phase of our training as my mother was deathly afraid of guns and she never let me have even a BB gun. At last, I was going to get to fire all kinds of weapons and mother would not be there to stop me!

Once more anticipation was lots better than realization. Weapons firing in the service, like most other things, came only after a lot of hard, tiring work. We drilled with the M-l Garand rifle for days. We twisted our bodies into the different positions for countless hours, worked on getting the correct sight picture and did "dry runs" until we were sick of it. It seemed we would never go to the range and enjoy the actual firing.

Finally, the day did come and we started out for the firing range before daybreak for what would be the first of three long days. Half of us would be the pit detail the entire first day. That meant we would spend the entire day in the hot, stuffy pits behind the tall earthen mounds just in front of the targets. We would raise the large bullseye targets and the guys back on the firing line 500 yards away would bang away at them with their M-l's.

It was hot, tiring work with no recognition and definitely no fun. The guys firing usually hit everything except the bullseye. Then, we pulled the targets down, put markers in the bullet holes, ran the target up again and indicated their score by raising a signal pole. If we waved a red flag, which we called "Maggie's drawers", it signaled a complete miss. A few wise guys registered their disgust by firing at the signal poles. About the only benefit we got from working the pits was that we learned how a bullet sounded when it zipped a few feet over your head. We would hear that sound when we got in combat and we would wish we were back in the range pits!

Eventually, it was our time to fire and the other guys went to the pits. First, we did more dry runs. Then we zeroed in our weapons. That is, we set the sights so that if you lined them up properly, they would send the round directly into the bullseye. After that it was only a matter of getting into the proper position, lining up the sights and not flinching when you squeezed the trigger. It was harder to do than to say.

I never had perfect eye sight, but the rimless glasses I had brought with me into the service corrected me to 20/20 vision. I seldom wore them to the field, but I wanted to do good on the range, so I wore them when I fired. About halfway through the firing course, the rifle kicked back and smashed the right eye glass. I got a small cut on the cheek, but what hurt the most was I was left to qualify with only 20/40 vision. I barely made it as a marksman, the lowest qualification level.

I immediately applied for GI glasses and eventually received two pair of steel-rimmed glasses. When it came time to return to the range and qualify with the carbine—the weapon I was to carry as a mortarman—I was ready. This time I qualified as an expert. The M-1 was acknowledged to be much easier to fire than the carbine, so I always have wondered what I could have done had I been able to really see the target.

In the beginning days, the two gunners on the 60 mm mortar were to carry only .45 caliber pistols. This was in order to leave their arms free to carry the mortar. Fortunately, we later got the folding stock carbines and eventually, the canvas carrying cases to hang on our belts. This enabled us to have better personal protection. I sure would have hated to have gone into combat with only a .45 pistol!

At first, I was issued a .45 pistol and as it was light, it was nice to have during training. It lightened my load considerably! The only trouble was, I didn't know how to take it apart and therefore I couldn't clean it properly. In a few days I was in trouble.

When rust was detected in the barrel during an inspection, I was restricted and allowed no passes until I shaped up. I soon learned to take the pistol apart and clean it as I should have done before. I finally got it clean enough to turn it back in to the supply room and draw my carbine. That I could keep clean.

We then had some familiarization firing with the .03 Springfield rifle grenade launcher. We got to fire one round each, but that was enough. It wasn't much fun. By the time we left for combat, the .03 was gone and I never saw any rifle grenades while we were overseas.

I did enjoy firing the bazooka. We only got to fire one round each at a stationary target but it was fun to loop it up in the air and see it come down onto what could have been a tank or enemy machine gun. The "swoosh!" of that rocket-propelled round was exciting to hear. I figured I could fire that weapon if I ever had to.

Another exciting experience was throwing grenades. We practiced throwing dummy grenades at first and got to be pretty accurate. When we got to the live grenades, we all tightened up a little! I guess we were afraid we would drop them, but the training came off okay. When we got in combat, I noticed everyone was careful to wrap some tape around the handle after they had hung them on their web equipment!

Everyone also had the opportunity to fire a couple of magazines in the Browning Automatic Rifle (BAR). That was neat! The BAR was like a lightweight machine gun, but it was easy to aim and the weapon didn't jump around off the target. This was a good weapon and when we got in combat, it served us well.

I understand the majority of our company also got to fire the .30 caliber, air-cooled, Browning A-4 machine gun. Someway, I missed this training and as luck would have it, in combat I was transferred to a machine gun squad just before a big attack. I didn't even know how to load it, much least fire it at a human being. But that's another story.

Without any question, the most fun I had weapon firing in the army was with the 60 mm mortar. The "pea-shooter" as we called it, had good range, was accurate and could deliver casualties within a 25 yard burst radius. We could do some real damage with this weapon and I knew I wouldn't be able to help win the war with the way I shot a rifle!

Day after day while the rifle squads were pounding over hill and dale, we would set up our mortar in the shade of some trees and drill and drill on the firing technique. We got so we could set up in seconds, be on the base stake in a couple more seconds and have a simulated round on its way in less than a minute. We were good and we knew it. We got so we were itching to try it in a real live fire situation.

Those cool days in the shade were to end soon. We were running a live firing course one day and some other mortar squad in the division had a bad accident. Seems the squad set up and fired without making sure they had mass clearance. The round arms itself after traveling about 30 feet out of the tube and this round hit an overhead tree limb and detonated. One of the squad was killed and a couple of others were wounded.

After that, we were more closely supervised and the "goofing off" time all but disappeared.

As much as I liked being in the mortar squad of the First Platoon during those days, I always wondered about the concept of having a mortar squad in a rifle platoon. Since then, I have become convinced that it was not the best of ideas.

The idea of having close support for the platoon was good in theory, but there were problems we encountered in the field that negated that advantage. It seemed like we were always displacing forward to keep up with the platoon. We seldom had time to properly dig in before the rifle squads were on the move. Remember, we had to dig a pit for the mortar and then dig individual holes. In combat, with the ground frozen solid, it was never possible to give the weapon the proper protection it needed. We took a great chance of getting our gun put out of action from artillery fire if we fired from an unprotected position.

Communications was another big problem. We had no radio link with the platoon and it was hard to keep up with where they were in front of us. They could easily run off and leave us! During a fast-moving situation, it also was possible our rounds could fall on our own troops. On the other hand, if we stayed close enough to them to know where they were, it might keep us from being unable to fire at the enemy. At the minimum, we needed to be at least 300 to 500 yards away from our target.

The range table that comes in every cloverleaf of mortar ammunition and which was used to determine the range and number of charges, was only calibrated for 200 yards or beyond. Thus, any distance less than that had to be mostly a "guess" by the gunners. We didn't like making guesses when firing over the heads of our buddies.

Lastly, the mortar weighed about 42 pounds and every shell we carried was another three pounds. That was on top of our own personal equipment and every single pound we had to carry on a long march or up a steep hill took its toll on us. We were very aware of the load we had to carry. It was more than that carried by any of the riflemen in the platoon. In a combat situation we knew it could even mean the difference between life and death.

Later, when under fire we were forced to make a hurried withdrawal, I threw away a load of mortar ammunition and some of my personal gear. One of our squad members lost (or discarded) the bipod. As the squad had returned with only the tube and baseplate plus the casualties the company had taken in the action, it was decided to temporarily deactivate our mortar squad. The tube and baseplate were stored with the kitchen and supply truck and the other squad members were assigned to the weapons platoon.

This marked the end of the mortar squad, first platoon. Never again did we perform as a unit. The .30 caliber machine gun was the only weapon in the rifle company that I had never fired. I still haven't!

CHAPTER 21
MEMORIES OF DON WONDERLY

T he best I can remember, Don Wonderly was from Missouri. He was a bright, energetic young man about my age and built and got along well with his fellow members of 1st Platoon, D Company. I liked him and the rest of the guys seemed to as well.

During the days we were taking basic training, all of us stayed a little up-tight. They were working us pretty hard and the training was unrelenting. Up early, pounding the sand of Camp Mackall all day and many nights there were night problems and other forms of harassment that left us all with short fuses. The least little thing would often trigger a violent reaction.

That seemed to be the cause of the clash I had with Wonderly. We had come in from the field for the noon meal in our mess hall. The food wasn't all that good, but it usually beat the food we were served when we ate in the field. As was normal, we stood in line for 10-15 minutes and then had about 15 minutes to eat and rush back to our barracks.

This particular day we had the usual half-cooked fare and the usual hot-weather drink, Kool-Aide—or "bug juice" as we called it—to wash it down! Every day was near 100 degrees in North Carolina that summer, so ice-cold, bug juice was not totally disliked by the troops. It was the nearest thing we got to a cool, refreshing glass of iced tea.

The unwritten law at the large 10-man tables was that the man who emptied the aluminum beverage pitcher was obligated to go get it refilled. Sometimes, however, a trooper would leave a little in the pitcher in order to avoid having to go get it refilled. This caused many an argument, as you might imagine, and on this particular day that was no exception.

I poured myself another half cup of bug juice and left barely another half-cup in the pitcher. When Don attempted to fill his cup and found out what I had done, he slammed the pitcher down in front of me and demanded that I go get a refill. I replied that he had emptied it and for him to go and get his own refill.

Well, words led to more words, and finally in the heat of the argument, I picked up the pitcher and hit Wonderly over the head with it. The soft aluminum pitcher caved in and Wonderly was staggered momentarily from the blow and the shock of my surprise reaction. When he recovered he came at me with both fists flying!

We were immediately separated and hustled outside. The cadre loved this type of situation. It played right in hand with their program to toughen us up. At the slightest hint of disagreement between anyone, they would put boxing gloves on them and let them flail away at each other. It was great sport for the troops too, and it was a good way to tire the participants out and drain the last bit of aggression out of both.

So, behind our barracks Wonderly and I began slugging it out. The gloves were big and well-padded, so it was hard to actually hurt anyone with them. Naturally, a large crowd soon gathered and they began to cheer as they smelled blood! We responded with a flurry of punches that caused little damage.

The crowd formed a huge circle and that became our "ring." Some of the spectators climbed up on the large boxes that held the coal for our stoves in the barracks. I became aware that someone was throwing lumps of the coal at us. A couple hit me and at least one hit Wonderly. I figured it was the crowd trying to get us to mix it up more. In any event, the coal lumps weren't thrown too hard so neither of us were hurt.

As most of these type fights did, ours finally ended in a draw with both of us totally exhausted. Immediately it was time to fall out and resume our training. Both of us were really dragging as we had to struggle to keep up that afternoon. I remember being half sick and that Wonderly also looked about as bad as I did.

Of course, that fight drained the animosity from both of us and we became good friends after that. I must add that I also learned a good lesson. I never pulled the empty pitcher trick again as long as I was in service.

Later I found out that my good friend, Bob Pearce, was the culprit who had been throwing the coal lumps. He said he was trying to hit Wonderly and only hit me by mistake. I am not too sure I believe that. Knowing Pearce, he was probably trying to heat up the match and didn't care who he hit!

Wonderly figured in another incident after we got to England that might be considered humorous. One day we read in the Stars and Stripes newspaper where two GIs had been left overnight to guard an arrogant SS officer that their unit had captured. The devout Nazi had refused to give his interrogators any information and generally, had been quite defiant to his captors.

The two GIs, hoping to teach him a lesson, plied him with liquor that they had smuggled in and soon the Nazi passed out cold. Then they fetched a fellow soldier who moon-lighted as a tattoo artist and put him to work on the unconscious SS officer.

When the Nazi awakened, he was quite disturbed to find tattooed on his chest in full color, an American flag and the words "God Bless America"! The story didn't reveal what happened to the two GIs, but all of us, including the guys in Wonderly's tent, thought it was a great story and we roared with laughter.

I guess it was only natural when Don received a "Dear John" letter from his girlfriend back home, his buddies decided to take him to town and try to cheer him up a bit. But, when Don got too much to drink and passed out cold, the party turned ugly. His buddies took him to a tattoo parlor and had a couple of hearts and an arrow tattooed on his chest. The hearts bore Don's initials and those of his former girlfriend.

We found out about what had happened when early Sunday morning we heard Don wake up. Tearing off the bandage on his chest, he discovered the big surprise. He yelled, screamed and cursed so loud he could be heard all over the company area. Frankly, no one blamed him. He had the right to be upset!

There's no happy ending to this story. Don was killed on March 24, 1945, in Operation Varsity, the Airborne crossing of the Rhine River. His glider missed the LZ and came down far back within the German defenses. Don, along with two of my best friends, was killed. Many of the others in the glider load were wounded and all were captured.

In 1980, I took a tour back to the battlefields where the Division fought and we visited the Allied Cemetery at Margaten, Holland. Don is buried there, his family electing not to have his body returned to the States. I placed a small American flag on his grave. I couldn't help but think of the flag on the German's chest and, of course, the bug juice pitcher incident.

CHAPTER 22
A REDUCTION IN RANK

I never did tell my parents the truth about how I got "busted". That is, reduced in rank from private first class to buck private. Instead, I told one of those "little white lies" that you hear about. I was ashamed that I had gotten in trouble over a stupid, childish prank. I knew I should have been more mature. But it sure was fun!

It was while we were at Camp Mackall late in the summer of 1943. We had completed basic training and were into our unit training cycle. One day they told us we were going on a three-day tactical field problem and a new wrinkle was to be added. The Division I & R Platoon (Intelligence and Reconnaissance) was going to try to infiltrate our bivouac area one of the three nights we were in the field.

To add some reality to the operation, the I & R Platoon would be dressed in German uniforms and they were going to speak only in German. We were tasked with detecting them and if possible, capturing them for interrogation. It sounded like a lot of fun. We were kids again, playing cops and robbers!

We were not to know which of the three nights they would try this, but if our security was good and tight each night, we should detect them. Naturally, the officers were intent on not being one of the companies to fail this test. They were all worked up over it. We could tell that and that was what gave rise to this prank I conceived.

I explained my plan to my squad buddy, Orville "Hungry" Linrooth, and he thought it great and immediately agreed to participate. We would beat the I & R Platoon to their game by impersonating them and turning the bivouac area into a mad house! The officers would catch hell and we would have a great laugh at their expense!

We stored our fatigue caps in our musette bags as we planned to wear the caps as part of our disguise. We decided we would pull our big prank the first night as that seemed to be the night less likely to be chosen by the I & R infiltrators. We would carry our weapons, talk guttural gobbleygook and try to fool the guards into thinking we were the make-believe Germans.

That first night after everyone had gotten quiet in the bivouac area, we made our way out, completely undetected by the guards. We went down the road a short distance, took our fatigue caps from our musette bags, put them on and stored our helmets inside. Then we walked back up the trail being sure we were in full view, but appearing to be sneaking along.

It wasn't long before the guards spotted us and shouted for us to halt. With that, we began shouting to each other in our imitation German and dashed off into the bushes. Just as we had guessed, this caused a great deal of confusion with troopers running everywhere and a lot of shouting!

"They went this way!" someone shouted.

"There are four of them!" someone imagined out loud!

"They're heading for the CP," someone else guessed. "Head them off!"

After a while, we put our helmets back on and stored the fatigue caps away. We then melted into the confusion as we worked our way back to our squad area and to our tent. Arriving undetected, we literally rolled on the ground doubled up in laughter at the bedlam we had instigated!

Maybe our downfall was because we seemed to be enjoying the confusion so much. Maybe someone realized what had happened and ratted on us. And then again, maybe we were so proud of what we had done that we bragged about it to someone. In any event, the truth soon came out and we were found to be the culprits.

Lt. John Van Sycle, our platoon leader who already didn't like me, singled me out and asked if I was responsible for the uproar that had taken place. Well, I was a little proud that I had exposed our sorry state of preparedness on infiltration and also I didn't want to lie. So, I readily confessed.

Although everyone should have known there were two of us, Hungry wasn't mentioned as being involved, so I didn't bring up his name. Van Sycle then ordered me to report to Captain Stuhrman, tell him what I had done and to say that he recommended that I be "busted", or reduced in rank from PFC to PVT.

I went to Captain Stuhrman's tent and told him the whole plan that we had carried out. I even told him it was my idea as I knew our security was lax. Then, I told him Lt. Van Sycle had recommended that I be "busted".

Captain Stuhrman whom we all swore by as being the best officer in the division, proved to be just that. I think I caught the very faintest hint of a smile but he was not the kind of guy that would let personal feelings interfere with his duty. He had to support his own company officers. He looked down, shook his head and said, "Okay, you're busted."

I had made PFC on July 30 and now on October 2, I wasn't too happy about being reduced to private. It wasn't the loss of the stripe so much as it was the additional money it meant each month—about $6—enough to pay your insurance premium. And, for months after that, I caught every dirty detail Lt. Van Sycle could come up with.

I did one more immature stunt too. That next morning as we were moving out of our bivouac area, I spied Lt. Van Sycle standing at the corner just where our column was turning onto the main road. As we passed him, I reached up, tore the PFC stripe off my sleeve and threw it down on the ground right in front of him.

To his credit, Van Sycle ignored me and this childish act entirely. I have since regretted the whole incident, especially this last show of immaturity, but at the tender age of 18 years, I had a lot to learn about the Army, people and life in general.

When I wrote home the next time, I felt I should make some comment as to why my return address once again indicated me holding the rank of private. Already I was ashamed of the dumb stunt I had pulled, so I cooked up the story that I had been found asleep on guard duty and accordingly reduced a grade in rank.

I remember Mother writing how incensed she was that the Army would take such drastic action against me when she just knew her little boy was working so hard that he was not getting enough sleep! I prayed that she wouldn't write Van Sycle or Captain Stuhrman and give them a piece of her mind. You know how mothers are! Thank God, she restrained herself and didn't fire off a letter or I might still be on KP!

CHAPTER 23
GLIDER TRAINING

A s we sweated and gritted our way through basic training, we looked forward to the day when we would take our glider training. We were sick and tired of seeing the paratroops strutting around with their boots and wings. We also wanted something special to be proud of.

At that time, glider troops were not authorized wings, we had no boots and we did not rate extra hazardous duty pay. The number one thing we wanted right then was respect and pride for what we were going to be...a member of the Airborne team. Completion of our glider training in late November 1943, gave us that.

Later, in May 1944, we were given the opportunity to volunteer for jump school and those of us who completed the course in June got the boots, the wings and the extra $50 pay each month. However, in July 1944, Congress finally authorized glider wings and 25% of base pay as hazardous duty pay for glider troopers. Supply also began to issue everyone jump boots as replacements for GI shoes, but unless the soldier was jump qualified, he was not authorized to blouse his trousers in the boots when off duty!

Basic training was now completed. We had all been home on furlough and had returned to Camp Mackall. We were anxious for our next training cycle to begin. We were kept well aware of the fact there was a war going on when many of the officers and cadre of the division were suddenly pulled out and sent to join the 101st Airborne as they were shipping out to Europe. The 193rd Glider Infantry Regiment alone lost 11 of its best officers; one being from our company. It was time we "got on with it".

When glider training finally started, I believe we found it was not as exciting as we had hoped. Glider mock-ups were built in the parade field areas and the glider regiments took turns learning to tie knots and practicing lashing and loading of various equipment. It was mostly hot, boring work. We didn't know it at the time, but the glider program in the U. S. Army was just getting rolling then and most of the glider production and many of the pilots were being sent overseas.

For two or three weeks we split our days by working on the mock-ups for half of the day and doing unit training in the boonies for the rest of the day. It seemed we would never get around to doing the actual flying in the gliders. The paratroopers began to ask us if we were going to fly into combat in the mock-ups!

One day they loaded us in trucks and took us to the airport. Excitement ran high! Were we at last going to have our first flight in gliders? No. To get us used to flying (many of the guys had never been up) they took us for a hour-long ride in some old, tired C-47s. There was just enough turbulence that day to make many of the guys sick as dogs! It did very little to make us anticipate our first trip up in a glider.

I don't think our division had any refusals to go up in the airplane, but there may have been a few that refused to go up in the flimsy gliders. We heard that a 11th Airborne glider had crashed and six were killed. We also heard that a soldier in the 11th Airborne had refused to fly in a glider and he had received a Dishonorable Discharge and 25 years at hard labor. True or not, that rumor pretty well stopped most of the potential refusals.

You must remember we did not volunteer to ride in the gliders as the paratroopers had volunteered to jump! Some of the dissenters were persuaded by threats of punishment or other means, but a few just could not be coaxed into what they perceived as the risking of their lives. We heard these poor souls were promptly transferred out and sent to the nearest Port of Embarkation to become line infantry replacements.

It isn't easy to forget your first ride in a CG-4A glider. After about seven months of waiting and wondering how it would be, I found it a bit disappointing. First of all, it was scary. Second, you couldn't see anything out of the little tiny windows and third, everyone got sick, threw up and made a mess.

Maybe it had to be like that, but if I had planned it, at least I wouldn't have scheduled a two-hour flight for the first time. Maybe we could have become accustomed to the sensation if we had been treated to shorter flights. But, two hours was just too long and few stomachs could handle it.

Another thing was that the two-hour flight took almost all day. In true Army fashion we got up before dawn, ate a half-cooked breakfast and loaded on the duce-and-a-halves and were at the airport a good two hours before the Air Corps even got out of their beds. We marched to our assigned gliders, lay down on the cold, damp ground and waited...and waited...and waited.

We were briefed as to every screw and bolt on the craft and given all kinds of emergency instructions—none of which were anything that we could have used—and then we waited some more. If you ever thought they would have parachutes in the event the glider went down, forget it. No one had parachutes because you couldn't jump out of a glider if you had to. You just rode them down and hoped for the best. After all, a normal glider landing was nothing but a "controlled crash".

The CG-4A (the CG stood for Cargo Glider) that the American Airborne used, carried 13 men plus the pilot and co-pilot. There were seldom enough co-pilots to go around, so usually we flew with only one pilot aboard. Everyone just hoped and prayed that nothing happened to him!

The CG-4A could reach speeds up to 120 mph while on tow, but usually they cruised at about 100 mph. They frequently hit that 120 mph or more mark when in free flight. Then, when they came in for the landing, the pilot could pull down large spoilers on each wing that would slow the craft to about 80 mph. Sometimes when in the landing mode, he would yank back on the wheel and pop the glider back up in the air to miss a fence or a ditch. This always caused the passengers to gasp and gulp, but it seemed to give the pilot a great thrill!

About 15,000 CG-4As were built and they were the only glider the U.S. ever used operationally . A newer model, the CG-13A, was developed and 132 of these were built. They could be towed at 135 mph and carried about twice the number of troops. A number were delivered to the European Theater just prior to Operation Varsity, but as they were late in arriving, they were never used. I also heard they developed a CG-15A that could transport a bulldozer into the airhead, but fortunately, we never had to deal with this critter!

It was long after the war when I found out that many of the American glider pilots got part of their training at Bowman Field in Louisville. A glider pilot combat training unit was also set up there 20 March 1943. It just seemed funny I never heard about the gliders flying around Louisville. It wasn't a thing that could or would be hushed up.

The British Airborne used our CG-4As, but they also had a large glider called the Horsa. It could be towed at 160 mph and could carry a light tank or 30 or 40 troops. While our division was in England, men from C Company, 194th were being given a familiarization fight in a Horsa and it broke apart and killed all aboard. The accident was hushed up and I never knew about it until way after the war.

Finally, after we had waited most of the morning, our pilot for that first flight roared up in a jeep. We all blinked as a red-headed youth who looked like a truant from a junior high school stepped from the vehicle. He was a cocky little fellow with his hat, complete with a "50-mission crush", perched on the back of his head. We all sucked in our breath.

He was only a flight officer and couldn't possibly have been over 20 years old. I would guess 19 and would be willing to bet anyone he only had to shave once a week. We all expected pilots to be older, more experienced and to at least look wiser than us. Another scary thing—although we didn't have sense enough to know it at the time—was the fact we had no co-pilot. Fortunately, the boy wonder didn't have a heart attack during our flight.

Laughing and obviously getting ready to have a good time, the youngster checked out the glider. Then he really gave us something to think about. He said the ground crew had just put these gliders together this past week and it looked like they had done a good job on this one! Hooray! We were going to test-fly some kites that had just been put together! Let's all hope they did do a good job.

After more waiting while tightly strapped in our seats, suddenly it was time to go. The C-47s in the line began moving and when the tow lines had played out, the CG-4As slowly began to trail behind. There was a lot of stretch in the nylon tow line and when that was taken up and the line became taunt, the gliders suddenly began to race down the runway. Then, well before the tow plane lifted off, the little blunt-nosed gliders popped off the runway and soared 35 to 50 feet in the air! Then slowly, like they were in a terrific strain, the lumbering C-47s lifted off and the strange duos were Airborne!

"My God," we sighed, "these things really do fly!"

We craned our necks as we tried to see the ground and other gliders already in the air. We had the worse possible seats to really see anything. There were some tiny plastic portholes in the sides, but the best view was through the nose of the glider. All we could see there was sky and an occasional glimpse of the tow plane.

The first thing we noticed was the noise. It was impossible to talk. The wash from the tow plane made the glider shutter from nose to tail. The canvas fuselage beat a fierce tattoo against the aluminum frame and the wooden flooring rattled and shook. I looked at our boy pilot and he was no longer laughing and acting so carefree. In fact, he was dead serious with his hands locked on the wheel as he struggled to keep the small craft level.

I looked around at my companions. They were dead serious too, but when our eyes met, they gave a weak smile as if to say, "Hang on!" It was pretty obvious that all of us were trying to do just that. The only problem was, what do you hang on to?

Then we hit the first air pocket. This was an unexpected thrill. The glider seemed to fall straight down some 50 feet as if we had stepped off a cliff. Everyone lifted up off of the seats and had it not been for the safety belts, we would have been thrown around like rag dolls. Several helmets went flying off their owner's heads and banging around hitting the others. Fortunately, no one was injured by one of these steel missiles and we passed the word for everyone to be sure both their chin straps were tightly buckled.

The next pocket we hit, up to the roof went someone's M-1 rifle. It spun around hitting three or four troopers sitting in the immediate area. Now the word was passed to hold on to your damn weapon! I later heard cases of rifles poking holes in the glider's skin when held loosely by their owners.

We continued to "hang on" while we wondered what was going to happen next. Except for a few more dives where our stomachs threatened to come out our mouths, the rest of the trip was boring and without incident. They towed and we rode.

The first hour wasn't so bad. The novelty had now worn off and we were ready to come down. That's when the Air Corps went too far. We continued to pitch and turn and the time drug on. Slowly, we began to feel a new sensation—air sickness. We had not been offered any air sickness pills and the long flight was beginning to take a toll on us.

I tried to get my mind off the idea of being sick. I put up a good front, but down deep, I knew I was fooling myself. I was not far from loosing my breakfast but I was trying hard to fake it. One by one, at least half of my companions threw up into their steel pots and soon the aroma became too much for me. Ten minutes before we finally landed, I joined the club and surrendered my breakfast into my helmet.

I was totally disgusted with myself, but there was nothing I could do but laugh. It was amazing how much better I felt once it was over! We all looked at each other and had a good laugh. That is, all but the ones who were still hanging on. They were afraid to laugh!

Finally, the boy wonder reached up over his head and pulled the lever releasing the glider from the tow line. Then, like someone had suddenly closed a door, it was as quiet as could be in the glider. There was a faint whistle of the wind on the struts and some gentle flapping of the fuselage, but for the most part, it was like we had entered another world.

This part of the flight was great! The quiet and the view was wonderful! We circled slowly, seeming to just hang in the sky. Faster than we could judge, we raced toward the airport runway. Just before we reached that level, we became aware of our speed—around 100 miles per hour. It was great!

Our boy wonder pulled on the spoilers and we felt the glider slow and seem to hover as it kissed down softly on the runway at about 80 miles per hour. It was a perfect landing—hardly a jolt at all. We rolled down the wide, black asphalt strip and finally pulled off into the grass where we rolled to a stop.

We unfastened our safety belts, cheered the pilot on a good flight, and began to pile out. We still had the problem of the nasty steel pots holding our breakfasts and we wanted to get rid of that before we saw any of the guys from the other gliders.

This we did and washed them out with water from our canteens. We also agreed that this disgusting happening would be our secret alone. We would not tell the other guys, but instead we'd say no one in our glider got sick. I can't remember how well our little lie went over, but I doubt if we really fooled anyone. Everyone had the same problem!

That was the first flight. There were many others and finally we did get so we were not really seriously impaired by the tossing and turning of the gliders. One day I even tried to show my "macho" by writing a postcard to my folks while in flight! The glider was nick-named "Lillie Belle", no doubt after the pilot's girlfriend. We pitched and yawed so much you can hardly read the message!

For a short while a glider flight is not too bad. It is only in prolonged flight when the stomach is stretched beyond its endurance! I can't remember of ever flying over two hours in succeeding flights. Even the combat lift for Operation Varsity was only about two hours and air sickness pills were available for the troops.

The gliders were right for the era in which they were used. They cost the government only about $1,500 each back in 1943-45. That price looks pretty good when compared with the million dollar helicopters that eventually replaced them.

When the war was finally over, the country had thousands of these CG-4A gliders in inventory. With the advent of the helicopter in Airborne operations, it was plain that the gliders would never again be a tool of war and they were declared surplus. Still packed in their overseas shipping crates, they were sold for only $50 apiece. The buyers wanted the lumber in the crates, not the gliders. The gliders were junked and only three are in existence today. I have always felt this was a sad end for these gallant little birds.

CHAPTER 24
WHERE DID ALL THE "SCREW-UPS" GO?

Y ou might think that an Airborne outfit was filled with nothing but the finest of soldiers. Wrong! Just like every other outfit in the Army, we had our share of screw-ups too. However, before we went into combat most of them had been mysteriously transferred out or had shaped up.

In our company we had three Restored Prisoners (RPs) that we knew about. These were soldiers who had been convicted by courts martial in other outfits and sentenced to the army's prison at Fort Leavenworth. By volunteering to serve in a "hazardous duty" unit—such as the Airborne—they were given the chance to "soldier" their way out of their sentences. That meant, if they had a good record when the war was over, their record would be wiped clean and they would receive an honorable discharge.

One of these three was James Clancy, a gregarious, beer-drinking, crap-shooting Irishman! Naturally, we all liked him. We were also sort of proud of him as he was said to be the first man in the entire 17th Airborne Division to be absent without leave, or as we called it, go "over the hill"! While we were taking basic training, Clancy had his own personal prisoner chaser, a guard with an unloaded carbine!

Clancy had been in the army several years and had been through basic before, so he excelled over all us young fellows. Accordingly, Clancy was one of the first in the company to be promoted to corporal. At that time I didn't see anything wrong with that. Today, I question if it was the right thing to do.

Another one of the RPs was Paul Moffett. No one joked around with Moffett as he was menacing and unsmiling. He was quiet and kept to himself, but he knew more about a machine gun than anyone in the company. He also made corporal in a hurry and then soon was made sergeant and squad leader of one of the machine gun squads. He was a good soldier and did his job well. He "soldiered" his way back to a good discharge.

The other RP was John C. Riley and he was a real study of a round peg in a square hole. He was not much of a soldier. He did only what he had to do and he had to be closly supervised to see that he did that. In spite of himself, old Riley managed to make it to the bitter end of the war and I guess he got his clean discharge. As he was in our first platoon, we saw more of him than we really wanted to.

Riley's court martial was taking two-thirds of his pay, so he was on a very limited budget. He would buy a few sacks of Bull Durham Smoking Tobacco each payday and roll his own cigarettes all month long. And, each payday he would treat himself to a weekend drunk.

Riley would buy several bottles of Aqua Velva Shaving Lotion (high in grain alcohol content in those days) and then steal a loaf of bread from the mess hall. He would filter the shaving lotion through the bread and then mix the alcohol with a fruit drink and away he'd go! We always said Riley was one of the sorriest drunks we had ever seen, but he was by far, the best smelling drunk in the 17th Airborne!

We called Riley "the old guy" as he must have been all of 35 years old. You have to realize we were all about 18 or 19 years old ourselves, so he did seem old to us. He looked even older as he had false teeth and deep, weathered lines in his face. There was no doubt that there was a lot of mileage on old John Riley.

Robert Weitknecht, another member of our platoon, was trying to get a "Section 8" discharge—unfit for military service. To this end, he would wet his bed each night just before revielle. As everyone was convinced it was deliberate, the brass made him pitch a tent outside behind the barracks and sleep on the hard-packed, sandy ground.

"Whitey" continued to wet his blankets, get lost when we went to the field, not show up for KP, act hostile to everyone and any other adverse behavior he could dream up. He was put on every dirty, rotten detail they could find. Apparently he won the battle of wits as one day we returned from the field and he was gone, stinking bed, equipment and all. We never found out what happened to him and frankly, we didn't care.

Joseph Czubak or "Chulsby", was another first platoon member that was of little help to us. He was one of my "students" in the after-hours class I taught for awhile. He could not read or write or even sign his name and he was very difficult to get along with. One day he also vanished never to be heard from again. We were just told that he had been transferred. I feel sure the powers that be just gave up on Chulsby ever being a dependable member of the unit.

There was one soldier most of us hated to see go. He was Alwin L. Houghtaling and he trained in our platoon as an assistant BAR man. Old "Houghie" was a good sport and everyone liked him. He worked hard to do his duty. He just wasn't too smart and after awhile everyone realized we couldn't count on him in a tight situation.

Houghie was transferred to another outfit in the 17th Airborne—I believe it was the Service Company. In any event, we were all saddened to learn while we were in England, that Houghie had been accidentally killed one night in a truck wreck.

I remember another screw-up we had and he was of a different kind. He was bright enough, but he was a trouble maker for sure. His name was John Barnes and he was also in our first platoon as a rifleman. He was capable of soldering, he just didn't want to.

Barnes was another one of those who "went over the hill" early in our basic training cycle. He was brought back, did some time in the stockade and then was returned to the company under guard to continue his basic. He thought he was much tougher than he actually was and eventually, I was one of the guys who was provoked into challenging that idea.

We were on a field problem while we were in England. Everyone was tired and worn out as we climbed a long hill in the hot sunshine. We were trudging along maintaining five yard intervals on both sides of the road and Barnes was marching immediately behind me.

I can't remember what the argument was about, but we had been jawing at each other for the last few miles and I just finally decided that I had had enough. I stopped, turned around and as Barnes walked toward me with this head down and eyes on the ground, I completely surprised him with a sweeping uppercut to his face.

Barnes was taller and heavier than me, but I was much faster. Shocked by the sudden blow, Barnes was easy meat after that as I pounced on him and began to pound him in the face unmercifully. By the time he knew what was happening to him, someone pulled us apart and the fight was over.

I never got into any trouble over that as I feel sure all the men and officers were glad to see someone take it to Barnes. In fact, I think Sgt. Pierre, our platoon sergeant, was delighted and thought much more of me after that. The sudden attack worked wonders for Barnes and me too. He now knew he could not bully me and in the future he and I got along fine!

One other note about Barnes, so you can see what kind of guy he was. One day after we had entered combat, we captured a rather pitiful German soldier. He was a little short guy wearing an overcoat that came down to his shoe tops, a helmet that engulfed his beady little head and thick eye glasses that looked like Coke bottles. He was not the vaunted Superman that Herr Hitler pictured.

Barnes was given the job of taking the prisoner to the rear. He prodded him with his bayonet and cursed him as he led him down the road and through the snow-covered Ardennes forest. There was shooting going on in the area, so I can't be certain of where it came from, but we heard a few rounds fired that seemed real close to our position. Soon afterwards, Barnes reappeared and someone asked him what happened to the prisoner.

"Oh, he tried to escape," Barnes replied, "I got him though, before he could get away!"

We never went back down that road, so I don't really know what happened, but I can tell you one thing: That frightened, little German prisoner was not the type that would try to escape! If he was shot—as Barnes would have us believe—my opinion is he was murdered!

These were just a few of the wonderful people we had in our company. Most of the guys were real nice, but a lot of them were certainly not the type of people I had been used to running around with in civilian life. I doubt if my mother would have approved of any of them!

PART II:
Maneuvers and Camp Forrest

CHAPTER 25
TENNESSEE MANEUVERS

I'm not 100 percent sure why I was transferred to the third rifle squad in our platoon, but I feel it was in some way punishment for the prank I had engineered while we were on the problem in North Carolina. That was the one where my buddy Hungry and I faked an infiltration of the I & R Platoon and it resulted in my reduction in rank from private first class to private.

I really never regretted pulling the prank, however, I did hate to loose the extra $5 per month. And, if the transfer to the rifle squad was part of my punishment, then maybe it wasn't such a clever move after all! There were several reasons why I hated to leave the mortar squad and be assigned as an assistant on the Browning Automatic Rifle (BAR).

First and foremost, I calculated that a mortarman might stand a better chance of surviving combat. Mortarmen normally were not sent out on combat or recon patrols and they were never included in an assault echelon. In the defense, they were always located in a defilate position at least 100 yards or so behind the three rifle squads of the platoon.

During training this also meant that we normally had more time to lie around and take it easy. The riflemen always seemed to be thrashing around maneuvering through the area or working at keep-busy tasks. Many times it was like the maneuver units had forgotten about us. They would go off somewhere and we would lie around in the shade, take naps or shoot the bull.

When we went to the range to fire our mortar, we were all business and we did work hard at that. All mortar squads want to be the best and we were not an exception. Our live firing record was very good and we were proud of it. With a score of 94 out of 100, I had scored the highest in our squad on a test we all had to take for individual proficiency on the weapon. We were confident we could do our job when we got to combat.

The transfer to Sergeant Arthur Jastal's third rifle squad as a BAR man was punishment to me even if it was not intended to be. Coming just before we left Camp Mackall for Tennessee Maneuvers, it meant I would have to work much, much harder during that period of our training, and it would not be half the fun it ordinarily would have been.

Art Jastal was okay, I guess, but he was a Polish kid from Cleveland, Ohio and as a southern boy from Kentucky, we were just not on the same wave length. He was a cocky little guy who seemed to always be daring you to "go too far" with him. The three sergeant stripes with a rocker that he wore was enough to make most refuse to tangle with him, but I was never afraid of him and I think he sensed it.

Early on I decided that I was in enough trouble already. One more screw-up like the bivouac prank, and there was no telling what they would do to me. I was right on this score as later, after maneuvers when we were stationed at Camp Forrest, I saw our company mess sergeant, Sgt. Charlie White, "busted" from staff sergeant to private. Then the army pulled a real stupid trick. They put him in a rifle squad and ran him until his tongue hung out. We all thought he was going to have a heart attack. Finally, he was transferred out somewhere and we never saw or heard of him again.

I didn't want to be branded as a "screw-up" and have my fellow soldiers loose respect for me, so I resolved to show everyone I could soldier when I wanted to. I had too much pride in myself to tumble to this level.

Surprisingly enough, Jastal didn't seem to pick on me. If he did, I was not aware of it. He was fair. I even began to like him! He treated me just like the rest and we got along fine. One reason, I imagine, was the fact that I really worked hard for the good of the squad and Jastal liked looking good to Lt. Van Sycle. Whatever you can say about Jastal, you must admit he really "brown-nosed" the lieutenant.

On one problem during maneuvers our "Blue Army" force was ordered to capture and blow a bridge guarded by forces of the "Red Army". Our company drew the job and the first platoon was assigned the critical task in our plan. The third squad was to flank the bridge, get in position and when the rest of the company lay down a base of fire, we were to rush the bridge and plant dummy demolitions.

When we got in position, I suggested to Jastal that it might be easier to sneak down the river bank below the bridge and plant the wooden blocks that simulated the explosives. He liked the idea and as I guess I had volunteered to do it, he said he would hold up the attack to give me time to get down to the bridge.

I got almost to the bridge and then realized my way was blocked the last 35 yards or so. The only way to reach the bridge was by going into the water. Now, this was in the winter and it was cold in Tennessee! Nevertheless, I peeled off my heavy clothes and eased myself into the little river.

I planted the wooden blocks and got out of there. Then the attack broke out! That was just what we were trying to avoid. Some way the whole plan got messed up and everything went off as had been planned originally. We took the bridge but my cold swim was not even considered a factor by the umpires. In fact, I was laughed at and kidded by the other guys as I stood sopping wet and shivering in the cold.

I resolved right then I was not going to try anymore would-be heroics for the third squad. I would just bide my time until someway I could work my way back into the mortar squad. The squad was still one man short and I figured they were holding the vacancy for me. I knew I was a better gunner than any of the guys who were ammo bearers and that they knew it!

Finally, after Tennessee Maneuvers were over I did get back in the mortar squad, but I didn't get that PFC stripe back until December 1 while we were in England. There were still a few more adventures with Jastal and the third squad awaiting me until the day I was forgiven for my prank back in North Carolina!

As always, we lived for the weekends. The maneuver phases lasted a week each and then on the weekend we would clean our equipment and a certain percentage of the company would get passes. It meant going to a nearby town for a few hours of fun. My time came one week while we were near Portland, Tennessee. We got our passes and I took about 4 or 5 guys for a short visit to my home in Bowling Green. We were lucky to catch a ride in a 2 1/2-ton GI truck that was going there.

My mother cooked us a good meal, some of the guys lay down in a real bed and slept a few hours and soon it was time to go back. As we had exceeded our distance and the time was late, Dad and Mom had to drive us back to a spot near our bivouac area in Tennessee. It was a dark, rotten night and it began snowing soon after we got underway. To make it worse, the defroster and heater on our old family '37 Dodge didn't work too well. I'll always remember Mother crying when they stopped out there in the middle of nowhere and let us out.

I had one more interesting adventure with the third squad. On one maneuver problem, we got lost. There was no goofing-off, at least at the beginning. We were honestly lost. When Jastal saw the "Red Forces" had full control of the area we were in, he decided he would at least evade capture and led us back into a real remote spot in the hills.

We found a nice secure hilltop with good cover and with some farmhouses nearby. From the farmers we could buy eggs, bacon and bread, and get water from their wells. We planned to hole up there for the remaining days of the maneuver phase. Jastal seemed content to give us a break, so we were in great spirits.

We built a big fire against a rock outcropping and were sitting around one day drinking coffee, swapping tales and thoroughly enjoying ourselves. Someone got too carried away and as a prank, tossed a blank cartridge in the fire. In a few seconds it exploded and everyone leaped back in surprise.

We began to laugh at each other, but then we realized that one of our guys, Sam Jordan, had been injured by the explosion. The blank round had chipped the rock wall behind the fire and a sliver of that rock had spun out and hit Jordan on the wrist. The sliver of rock was as sharp as a razor and it slashed Jordan's wrist, opening up the main artery.

Blood from the cut began to squirt in all directions and all over us until we were able to settle Jordan down and get some pressure on the wound. Realizing it was a serious injury and that he would need some medical attention, we were forced to come out of our hiding place in the hills.

We found an aid station and got Jordan some medical care. There we learned the phase was over by this time, so we got transportation and went back to our unit. This mishap was a sign of things to come. When we went into combat, Jordan was one of our first casualties. A German 88 hit dead center in his hole and literally blew him to bits. Jastal and Ernie Stull were also showered and wounded by the shrapnel.

There was another bad accident during these maneuvers that changed things for me in the 17th Airborne. Izzie, my friend from Bowling Green who had gone into service with me, was in a bad jeep accident and had to be hospitalized in Nashville. He ended up having his spleen removed, was transferred from the Airborne, given limited duty and eventually given a medical discharge. I really hated to see him leave. Our old Bowling Green fivesome was now down to one: me.

On April 2, 1995, I had a long telephone conversation with Joe Miller and he dredged up some memories of Tennessee Maneuvers that I just can't remember. We were in the same platoon, so it stands to reason that the experiences he had, I had too.

For example, Joe talked at length about the night we paddled across the Cumberland River in rubber assault boats. The river was up and near flood stage and the night was dark and cold. Such an adventure should have been so scary, I can't imagine forgetting it...but I have!

Somewhere in the back of my mind, I do have a dim memory of hearing about an accident that did occur to some unit. In crossing the river a boat capsized and several men were drowned. As was the custom during those days, I assumed the whole thing was hushed up. Joe said the accident happened okay, but it was reported with big headlines in the Nashville papers.

Another story he recalled was that we got flooded one night in our bivouac area and had to abandon most of our equipment and move to higher ground. I can't remember anything about this either. I just remember maneuvers were a real test for us and ideal training for the combat that lay ahead for us.

On 19 February 1944, during Tennessee Maneuvers, the 17th Airborne lost some of it's top units. The 517th Parachute Infantry, the 460th Parachute Field Artillery and Company C of the 139th Airborne Engineer Batallion were suddenly gone and no one knew the details at that time, As it turned out, the units were shipped to the European Theater in anticipation of the coming invasion. Among the replacement units the 17th received, was the 513th Parachute Infantry which was transferred from the 13th Airborne Division.

We left Camp Mackall and arrived in Tennessee on 10 February 1944. From then on until we moved from the maneuver area to our new station at Camp Forrest on 27 March, I know it either rained or snowed every single day. It was the worst winter I could ever remember. Maybe learning to live this way in such horrible weather helped us when we found ourselves thrust into the Battle of the Bulge, but as for me, I would rather have skipped the whole experience!

It was certainly a happy day when the last phase ended and we were told we were going to be moved to Camp Forrest as our next duty station. I was especially happy as I knew being only four to five hours from Bowling Green, I should get to go home frequently.

To celebrate our successful completion of this part of our training, the cooks prepared a feast for us that last night we were to sleep in the field. They cooked all the goodies they had been holding back. In fact, they had been holding them back too long, as it turned out.

About four o'clock in the morning the whole company bivouac area was alive with guys suffering from a bad case of "GIs", or diarrhea as it is known in civilian circles. The company latrine (slit trenches dug in the ground) was crowded with guys and dozens of others were out in the woods digging cat holes with their entrenching tools.

Time soon came for us to be trucked to our new home, but the "GIs" continued. Several pit stops had to be called en route and guys poured over the tailgates and hardly got off the roadway before dropping their pants. We were reduced to completely ignoring the passing traffic—this was an emergency!

In the trucks between stops, the men were forced to use helmet liners or hang their rear ends out over the tailgates. It was an embarrassing and demeaning end to what had been a successful maneuver by an elite fighting force. If nothing else, it brought it home to each of us that we might be the vaunted Airborne, but when it came to food poisoning, we were no different from line infantry.

CHAPTER 26
THE PARTING OF THE RANKS

I have always remembered that Bible story of how Moses, while leading the children of Israel to the promised land, parted the Red Sea to lead them to safety. Mostly, I remember the excellent acting job Charlton Heston did for MGM in the movie. I also will remember the day I engineered a similar parting.

Our division was now stationed at Camp Forrest, Tennessee and it was in those months early in the summer of 1944, that this historic event took place. It all came about when I decided to take my buddy's motorcycle for a spin. This was also the last time I rode a motorcycle.

Near our billets, in the center of Camp Forrest, there was a large parade ground. Bordering each side was a long, straight, paved road. It was an ideal location to "open up" a motorcycle as you could see a long way to determine that no MPs were in sight. We would abide our time and when it was clear, we'd zip down the road at 50 or 60 miles per hour. That was well over the post speed limit!

Ray Crabtree had a big hog Harley that he would let his friends ride. Like an idiot, I borrowed it one day and took it over to the straight-away and prepared to open it up! My plan was to slow up when I got to the street on which we lived. I would turn there and go up to our barracks where someone else was waiting to take a ride.

All the streets on the post looked alike, but it was easy to recognize our street as there was a movie theater on the corner where you turned. Our barracks was only a block from the theater.

It was early evening when I prepared to take my dash down the road. A big crowd of soldiers had begun to gather in the area in front of the theater, waiting for the movie to open. Although they didn't know it at the time, they were in dire danger from a inexperienced motorcycle rider.

I looked down each side of the parade ground and the roads were both clear. I eased the throttle up and up and the big Harley really began to roll. Soon I was flying down the pavement and enjoying every second!

Then, before I had expected it, there was the theater and the road where I intended to turn. I feathered the brakes and felt the rear wheel begin to slip in the thin cover of sand that had accumulated in the road intersection. Instinctively, feeling that the bike was going to slip out from under me, I cut the wheel to bring it out of the skid.

The front wheel caught traction for a second, enough to straighten me up, but also enough to flip me into the area in front of the theater where the soldiers were waiting for the movie to open. Still going at least 30 miles an hour, I headed right for the sea of humanity.

I was horrified! There seemed to be no way I could miss the mass of GIs. Instantly I realized that at best, I would kill only 10 or 12 of the poor souls. I tried to steer as best I could and to miss as many of them as possible!

That's when I did my Charlton Heston act. Like magic, that sea of kakhi parted as I slipped and slid through without even touching a shirttail! Suddenly, I had done it! I had made it through!

I had pulled a dumb trick, but I wasn't so dumb that I was going to stop to apologize and get beaten to a pulp! I gunned the Harley and plowing through the sand, got back on the road and out of there as fast as I could! The curses and yells of the near victims were ringing in my ears as I drove up the street toward our barracks where several of my friends from the company had observed the whole thing.

"Don't stop here!" they shouted, "Keep on going like you don't know us! Don't come back for an hour!"

It wasn't hard to understand why they had "disowned" me so quickly. If I had stopped, no doubt a mob from the theater would have come after me and all my friends as well.

As I said, that was the last time I ever rode a motorcycle. A fact, no doubt, that everyone always appreciated. After all, how many times can you expect the Red Sea to part?

CHAPTER 27
THE GIRLS WE MET!

S oldiers live for the weekends. The Monday through Friday training schedule is just something to be tolerated and endured. Come Saturday, a soldier's mind turns to the weekend and the day and a half of fun it promises. A weekend without an adventure in the civilian world is a whole week lost!

In the Airborne it seems we had to do things differently from the "leg" troops. Instead of being able to head for our weekend of fun on Friday night, we had to work a half day on Saturday. Although it was usually "Group Sports" or "Care and Cleaning of Equipment," it still meant we gave the "legs" a half day head start each weekend.

That may not seem like much, but it was often enough to guarantee they had first shot at the best hotel rooms or the limited number of beds at the USO, or what's worse, the pick of the available girls! Whatever you did over the weekend, it usually meant you got a late start at it.

There was another weapon the brass hung over us: The Saturday morning inspection. If your personal equipment did not pass inspection, you could be restricted and not receive a weekend pass. It could be morale-shattering after a week of hard training to find yourself stuck on base all weekend.

As tough as that punishment could be, there was another threat that hung over us that was even worse. If any portion of the barracks was found to be dirty and not pass inspection, the whole platoon or the whole company could be restricted. What made this so tough was the fact that everyone could be punished for the failure of just one careless individual. The person or persons who caused this to happen was a very despised party and usually suffered severely at the hands of his fellow soldiers.

Memory, however, is a funny thing. You tend to remember the good times and forget the bad. Such is the case when I recall the weekends I spent in the army and the fun that I did have. I tend to forget those weekends we scrubbed the barracks floor or cleaned our rifles instead of going on weekend passes.

I especially recall the trips I made while in North Carolina to see football games. They would have free tickets for soldiers and we went to Chapel Hill and Durham several weekends to see games. Most of the universities did not field teams during the war, but the air corps and naval programs which were on many of the campuses often sponsored "Pre-Flight" teams and they played pretty good ball.

Of course, the other main attraction while on weekend pass was the availability of girls! They were in short supply as most mothers saw all soldiers as sex-starved monsters and they kept their little darlings in over the weekends. I know this was not the universal truth, but it seemed that way.

It was tough to meet a nice girl when you were a soldier. There were the usual bimbos hanging around the bars and beer halls, but to meet a really nice girl was really tough. As Georgeanna and I had split up most of the time before I went overseas, I was interested in meeting a nice girl. I wanted to be treated as a decent person and it irked me to be regarded as the stereotyped soldier on a weekend pass.

My desire to have a normal relationship with a nice girl ran into some weird consequences. Some were complete strikeouts and some were on the scary side and are best forgotten. Like Mary Vaughty, the girl I met from High Point, North Carolina.

I had sat next to her on a bus one weekend when I was traveling back to camp from one of the football games. Naturally, we struck up a conversation and in addition to being very attractive, she seemed very nice. She lived in High Point and had been visiting friends. When I said I had never been to High Point, she suggested I come up the next weekend and she would show me around.

The next weekend, after riding a bus for several hours to get to High Point, I arrived late Saturday afternoon. I registered for a bed at the USO, then called her and she arranged to meet me. We walked around town some, had dinner and went to a movie.

I then walked her home and when we arrived there it was only about 10 o'clock. We sat in the living room and listened to the radio and talked. I was certainly no "monster" and although I might have had in mind some kissing and tender caresses, nothing—absolutely nothing—had happened when I heard her father scream curses at me from upstairs!

Mary quickly explained that her father was an alcoholic and this was a regular ordeal she had to endure and I shouldn't be afraid. I really wasn't afraid, but I had no wish to get involved in a complicated family problem like this. I began to think about leaving and suggested that maybe I should.

She reassured me all was okay and that he often raved on like this and would eventually quiet down and go to sleep. Uncomfortable as I was, I had traveled several hours to get here, it was the weekend, and I hated to give up so early. So, I sat back and soon we were in each other's arms and exchanging kisses.

Somewhere about this time, "Daddy" screamed at me from the top of the stairs. I sprung to my feet and to my horror, there he stood in his underwear and of all things, he had a shotgun in his hands! That was enough for me. I didn't stop to say goodbye. I was out that front door and off the porch before he could get down the stairs.

I sprinted up the street without looking back. Then, to top off a memorable evening, I heard that shotgun blast into the night! Maybe he fired it in the air, but I will always wonder if I didn't outrun the buckshot!

Needless to say, I never went back to High Point and that girl was history. I did get a letter from her, apologizing for her old man's action and urging me to write her and plan to come back and see her. I never replied. Although I felt sorry for her and her situation, I wanted no part of it. There were too many "fish in the ocean" to take a chance on getting shot over a weekend pass.

I left another North Carolina girl rather abruptly, but I wasn't shot at this time. Instead, I was nearly bored to death.

The Aberdeen USO had a program where a family would invite a soldier to their home for a Sunday. The family picked you up at the USO on a Sunday morning, you went to church with them, had a home-cooked Sunday lunch and spent the afternoon with them in some planned activity. As you can tell, it was not meant to be a wild event. The idea was to offer the lonely soldier an opportunity to be in a "real home" again.

A friend of mine had done this and met a nice girl and had a nice time, so I decided I would try it. The family, consisting of the father, mother, kid brother and teen-age daughter, picked me up one Sunday morning and away we went. The church service was fine, the lunch delicious (I still remember we had fried chicken, just as we used to at my home on a Sunday), and the teen-age daughter was not bad looking.

I was not prepared, however, for the "family activity" that had been planned for that afternoon. The daughter, it seems, was an accomplished pianist and she started playing everything she had learned from age three until the present. I was amazed at her stamina. After two hours, she was still going strong.

Somewhere about this time, I began trying to think up a decent excuse to let me make a polite exit out of there. It was obvious she was prepared to play on into the night. I was torn between demonstrating the good manners my parents had taught me and the reality of the fact I could not stand much more of this.

All thoughts that I might have had about romance with this young lady quickly vanished. All I could think about was getting out of there and stopping that pounding in my head. Finally, I had had enough. It was time I had to make a move.

I looked at my watch and then jumped to my feet. "Good grief," I exclaimed, "It's almost 4 o'clock! I have to be back at the USO by four to catch my ride back to camp. As much as I am enjoying this, I really must go!"

I hurriedly said my "thank yous" for their hospitality and moved toward the door. Once outside I was so relieved, I broke into a run. Not as fast as I had run that evening in High Point, but in some sense, I felt I was in just as big a hurry to escape!

A postscript here might be the fact that soon after that the USO dropped the "Spend the Day with a Family" program. I don't think they were getting many takers. Maybe too many guys were ending up with the same family I did.

I spent a lot of my spare time in the small village of Aberdeen, so this was where I met another girl whose name is long forgotten. This meeting could have gotten me in real big trouble. I met this girl in the bus station. I was on my way back to camp and she had just arrived on another bus from Fayetteville.

While I was waiting for my bus, it became quite evident to me that the party that was to have met her had not showed up. We began talking and I learned that she was to meet some paratrooper that she had met the week before. We waited and waited but still he didn't show. I even let my bus leave without me, determining I could still catch a later one.

Finally, I devised a daring plan in my head. I asked her what outfit her trooper was in. When she told me, I said something to the effect that I had heard that that particular outfit had been alerted for a special night problem that night and no doubt her trooper would not be able to come in to town to meet her!

That big, fat lie seemed to turn the table in my favor and I guess the girl decided that I was better than no date at all! So, we walked around town for awhile, had a Coke and then found a nice secluded spot and spent a couple of hours together. Apparently, she didn't find me too unattractive when compared to a "no-show" trooper!

The time for the last bus back to camp was rapidly approaching so I began thinking about breaking away. The trooper had made a reservation for her to stay at a local rooming house, so I walked her there and quickly bid her goodbye. I had already been smart enough not to give her my right name and unit because I didn't want that trooper to come looking for me!

I had to run to get to the bus station in time for that last bus back to camp. Miss it and it would be a 10-mile hike back to camp, plus I would probably end up AWOL. It seemed like I was always running away from women instead of after them!

I reached the bus station just as the last bus from camp pulled in. On it was one lone paratrooper. He got off, looked all around the bus station and then began talking to the station agent. I was sure he was inquiring of the agent if he had seen a young lady waiting around there earlier.

I couldn't hear their conversation, but as fast as I could, I boarded the bus which was heading back to camp. I hunkered down in my seat and began praying that it would leave as soon as possible! The paratrooper left the station—presumably to go to the boarding house—and after an eternity, the bus, with me aboard, pulled out for Camp Mackall. I never was so glad to go back to camp.

I recall two more weird encounters with young ladies during those strange days of World War II. These stories are thrown in just to prove that not only were the guys crazy in those days, but the gals also did some stupid things.

While stationed at Camp Forrest, Tennessee, I was able to get a pass to come home to Bowling Green almost every weekend. I would arrive here via bus at about 6:00 p.m. Saturday night and I had to leave Sunday night on a 10:00 p.m. bus. This was the last bus and it would get me back to Camp Forrest about 4:00 a.m. Monday, tired and sleepy, but happy!

I still knew a lot of young ladies going to college in Bowling Green, so it was easy for me to get a date at the last minute and to "fix up" any of my buddies who came home with me. There was a girl named Kathie Hunt that I dated several times. She and I and one of her friends and my buddy, Gerry Quick, would often go out together during the weekend.

One weekend I had come home alone for a change and for some reason, long forgotten, I did not have a date with Kathie. Sunday night when I boarded the 10:00 p.m. bus to go back to camp, I was surprised to see her friend also on the bus, so I sat down beside her. She had recently graduated from the Bowling Green Business University, and was on her way back to Nashville where she had taken a job.

Before the bus was 10 miles down the road, that girl was all over me, confessing a secret love for me and urging me to stay overnight with her in her Nashville apartment. All that is pretty heady stuff for a young soldier, but I managed to keep my wits. I also did not wish to be court-marshalled for being AWOL! I resisted her strange behavior, declined the offer and returned to camp.

The next weekend I returned to Bowling Green and called Kathie. I wasn't going to mention my adventure of the past week, but one of the first things she told me was the news that her friend had gotten married the past week! I guess I had been selected to be the "last fling". Now who in the world can understand women who act like that?

The other dumb thing happened as a result of a chance meeting on the bus going from Bowling Green to Nashville. I sat down by an attractive young blond named Ruth Graham who lived in Whitehouse, Tennessee. We struck up a conversation and before she got off she urged me to come to see her the next weekend.

I was unable to make it that next week, but I wrote her and asked her to write and to send me a picture of herself. I wanted to remember how she looked and writing the letters would let me keep the invitation open until I could get back to see her.

She wrote a very sweet letter back and included a very nice picture of herself. The only trouble was, she was sitting out in her yard cradling a framed picture of some Air Corps officer in her arms! That was all for her. If she would send me a copy of the same photo she obviously had made for her officer boyfriend, she wasn't for me!

P.S. I still have the photo, so I guess I might be a bit goofy too!

CHAPTER 28
JUMP SCHOOL

B efore I entered service in April 1943, I don't think I had considered for a second about becoming a paratrooper. I know I had never even heard of glider troops until our troop train pulled into the station at Hoffman, NC and I looked out the window and saw a sign reading "Glider Infantry"!

All of us looked at each other and wondered what that sign meant. In the months to come we certainly learned the answer. Some would love this new branch of the army, but some would hate the sound of the words and do most anything they could think of to get a transfer out. It didn't matter where—just anywhere except the Airborne!

There was one thing we learned fast. The Airborne was composed of paratroops and glidertroops and the two didn't mix too well. If we glider troops didn't stay in our own area at Camp Mackall and out of the paratroopers' way, we were likely to end up in a fight. The troopers I saw in those early days of 1943, were all at least six feet tall, weighed about 180 pounds and were lean and mean. As a matter of fact, that was basically the physical requirements for the paratroops in the beginning and only later were these standards eased somewhat.

As the months rolled by, we glidertroops began to gain more confidence in ourselves and our abilities. Most of us were away from home for the first time and we were slowly changing from boys to men. Before long the paratroopers no longer held any real fear for us. We realized that we were as good a soldier and as good a man as any one of them. The only thing they did that we didn't do was jump out of a airplane! Big deal! Were they man enough to ride in those flimsy gliders?

Almost from the day we arrived at Camp Mackall, rumors kept popping up that the glider troops were going to be cross trained as paratroops. All the early rumors proved to be just hogwash. I even told my folks not to worry about me becoming a paratrooper as my eyesight would hardly meet the physical qualifications. After all, they kept me from getting in the Navy. Surely the paratroops were more demanding physically!

Finally, the showdown came early in April, 1944 at Camp Forrest. The two glider regiments were given the opportunity to volunteer for parachute training. The division would establish and operate a division jump school and all glider regiment soldiers who wished to, could volunteer for jump training. Qualification carried with it the privilege of wearing jump boots with our pants legs bloused, the much-admired jump wings and an extra $50 pay each month!

The physical was a snap. I weighed 168 pounds, was only five feet, eight inches tall but this didn't matter. They were taking everyone who volunteered! My eyesight was 20/40 in the right eye and 20/70 in the left eye. Although both were correctable to 20/20 with glasses, the minimum was 20/30 without glasses. That worried me. I solved it all by memorizing the 20/30 line on the eye chart as we filed in the room! I wrote home that it was P-C-T-E-D! No problem!

About 2,500 volunteered from the regiments and after three weeks of intensive training, about 2,200 qualified. The 300 or so who were "washed out" were judged as not having the proper fortitude—or "guts" for the job. This rate of successful qualification was unheard of for that many who volunteered. There remained no doubt that our Airborne training had prepared us for the ordeals of leaping from an aircraft in flight!

Jump school is normally four weeks in duration, but our division school was cut to three weeks. Our year of Airborne training had whipped us into good physical condition and the first week of physical conditioning was omitted. We were ready to handle the rigors of parachute training. The people who washed out—or signed "quit slips" as we called it—did so not because of physical reasons. Mostly, they could not put up with some of the harassment or realized they could never take that first step out of the door of a C-47.

Those in our company who volunteered for the training, were issued a pair of jump boots when they turned in a pair of worn shoes. But, the shoes still had to be worn and ready for salvage. When the word of this new policy spread, we immediately took bayonets and hammers to our shoes. In no time it was astonishing how many pairs of GI shoes needed salvaging!

Out of our platoon of 44 members, 31 volunteered. There were 17 or 19 in the 2nd platoon and only about nine or 10 in the third platoon. Once again, the first platoon set the pace for the company! I know some of the company dropped out during the three weeks of training that followed, but best of all, no one was injured. And, jump qualification did not cause a division among the guys, either in the platoon or in the company. We still got along fine with each other, jumper or not.

The discipline, or actually the harassment that we incurred, was easy to handle. No matter what they said or did to me, I was determined that no one was going to run me out of the program. I practically laughed to myself when I was given pushups or was screamed at by a "Black Hat" from about six inches away! It would not have been so easy if I hadn't had those 10 months or so of Airborne training.

First we jumped off low platforms and made rolling tumbles into sawdust pits. These "PLFs", or Parachute Landing Falls, were to learn to distribute the shock of landing over all of our body and not just on our feet and ankles. Then, the platforms got higher and we tumbled some more. We hung in suspended harnesses which we called "suspended agony" and learned which risers to pull to turn a decending parachute in a certain direction. Between classes in these procedures, we ran and ran and ran until we were ready to drop!

Then it was to the mock-ups. These were wooden structures built to resemble the fuselage of the C-47 aircraft. We donned dummy parachute harnesses, hooked up to a wire cable in the mock-up and practiced exiting an aircraft. We landed on our feet, counted to three thousand and then tumbled into the sawdust.

Next we moved to the 40-foot tower and this was beginning to feel like the real thing! The rough part of this was climbing a ladder 40 feet straight up to the platform from which we jumped. We made five or six jumps from here and why someone didn't loose their grip and fall backwards off that ladder, I'll never know. We had a number of quitters here on this one station. Better here than later, I thought.

When you reached the platform at the top, the instructors would hook your harness to risers leading to a pulley that was attached to a long, steel cable. It lead down on a slant to a huge sawdust pit where other instructors waited. The secret to this training device was to never look at the ground. It was so close that if you let yourself think, fear would take over your mind.

The student simply obeyed the jump commands given him. He moved to the edge of the platform and when given the "Go!" command, he leaped forward off the platform into space. Next came a sudden stop and a shock that was to be similar to the opening shock in a real parachute jump. The risers grew taunt and the student began his ride down the wire on the pulley to the sawdust pit. Other instructors graded your every action. If you didn't do it right, up you went again.

This was for many worse than jumping, especially if you looked down at the ground. From this low height you were acutely aware of the height and the inherent danger if that cable broke! I had no trouble whatsoever with this station as I had complete confidence in the cable and I really enjoyed the ride. I didn't, however, enjoy climbing that tall, tall ladder.

Although we continued to run, do pushups and other tiring calisthenics, we eventually were taken to the packing sheds to learn to pack our own parachutes. The sheds were shaded from the hot Tennessee sun, so these sessions were welcomed. Riggers pack all the chutes now, but in those days, the troopers packed their own. You can be sure we listened carefully to the instructors and proceeded with caution and care.

The T-5 Assembly used at that time called for a long static line to pull the parachute canopy out of the back pack when the jumper exited the aircraft. It would fill with air and practically come to a stop in mid-air. The jumper would continue to fall at about 100 miles per hour until he reached the length of his suspension lines-some 20 feet—and then he too, would come to an abrupt stop!

This action was called "the opening shock" and it gave us a real good jolt. If your leg straps were not tightened almost to forcing you to walk stooped over, you could receive a painful mashing of the family jewels! And, if your head was not bent forward with your chin touching your chest, you could receive a cranium-cracking blow to the back of your head from the adapter buckles on the risers as they snapped up.

Finally, on Monday, June 12, 1944, only four days after we had learned about D-Day and the Airborne jumping into France, we were scheduled to make our first jump. The night before some had trouble sleeping. I wasn't concerned at all, but I was excited and couldn't wait to go! I feel sure many were wondering if they could actually do it when the time came. There was no question in my mind. I knew that when the time came I was going to blast out of that door!

In my plane I was the last man in the second "stick" of 12 jumpers. When the command was given for the first stick to stand up, one guy failed to stand. He was just opposite me a few positions and I could see how pale he was and there was fear written all over his face. The jumpmaster came back and screamed obscenities in his face, but he clutched the seat and wouldn't stand up.

The other members of his stick jumped and the plane circled around to make another pass over the drop zone to drop us. As our stick stood up, we urged him to hook up and go with us. But, he wouldn't, or couldn't, move. Then we also cursed and taunted him while he sat frozen on the empty row of seats. He took the abuse silently and without any expression.

I have often wondered about that poor fellow. What an ordeal he suffered. I wonder if he has ever been sorry he didn't conquer his fear and jumped. Maybe he still feels he did the right thing. In those days we were not very understanding of anyone's feelings.

When my stick jumped we were practically on each other's back as we went out the door. I know we did well. There was no hesitation on the part of anyone. I counted loud and I heard others counting. Some guys say they grit their teeth and never count as instructed! The important thing is to hurry. One second's hesitation in the door can mean 100 yards on the ground. This means you could cause the last men in the stick to end up in the trees that always seemed to be at the end of the drop zone.

When the chute opened it was time for celebration! We had done it! Even if we broke a leg when we landed, we could always say we had made a parachute jump! We yelled at each other in the air and whooped and cheered! We were a happy bunch of guys at that moment.

It didn't last long. From 1,200 feet we were approaching the open field where we were to land. We were also now within yelling distance of the ever-present Black Hats, the instructors. We were cautioned to assume a landing position and we did. My landing was like stepping out of bed. I was so charged with adrenalin that I felt like nothing could hurt me!

I rolled up my chute, put it in the kit bag we carried, hooked my reserve on the handle, threw it over my shoulder and began to double-time to the turn-in truck. I was so pleased with myself that I could have run all the way back to camp! After turning in the chute and getting my name checked off the list, I climbed up in one of the trucks with some of my buddies to await the trip back to camp. We were all high with excitement at what we had accomplished and we swapped jump stories all the way back to our company area.

Five jumps were required for qualification so we had four more to make! The next day, Tuesday, June 13, we went up for jump number two. Already we were getting pretty cocky and had begun to think this jumping was routine. It was a hot day and everyone came down pretty hard because of the heat, but we were all pumped up and we hardly gave it a thought. We were pretty full of ourselves and what we had accomplished by this time!

On the morning of Wednesday, June 14, we were raring to go for jump number three! We soon cooled down when we learned that we had had our first casualty. It was a cook in the 194th Glider Infantry. He got a streamer and for some reason did not pull his reserve, but rode it in.

If that wasn't bad enough, one of the instructors formed us in a column of two's and doubled timed us to the trucks—right past the body of the dead trooper. Most of the guys looked at him as we ran by, but I didn't. The motive here, as before, was to force out the weak, the ones who didn't have the stomach for jumping. The theory was that it was better that a man should quit here in training rather than when we got in a combat situation.

During these first three jumps the instructors worried a lot of us by not giving us the chute that we personally had packed. We were ordered to just take a chute out of a big pile and we had no choice over who had packed it. There was that fear that the one you got was packed by some nut that goofed it up. We did hear reports of shot bags that had been left in the parachute and that went hurdling through the air when the chute opened. Nevertheless, outside of a few sprained or broken ankles, no other mishaps were recorded.

On Thursday, June 15, we made two jumps: one in the morning and one that night. We really didn't sweat the morning jump, but we were a bit concerned about the night jump. One night jump with field equipment was a requirement. We would also wear steel helmets instead of the clear plastic, football-type helmets. To make it worse, many of us received camouflaged chutes that night. These had been packed by the riggers and none of us had ever seen a camouflaged chute. We were afraid that at night the camouflage canopy would appear to have blown panels. We also wondered if at night we would be able to see the ground and land properly.

Our worries were needless. The morning jump was a piece of cake and at night the camouflaged chutes proved as easy to see as the white ones. In addition, the moon and stars lit up the ground like day and a light rain that afternoon left puddles and softened the earth of the drop zone.

Once again I was to jump in the second stick. I was in the number eleven spot and my buddy, Ray Crabtree, pushed the stick at number twelve. We jumped at 1,000 feet and Ray and I celebrated all the way down! Returning to our barracks we were a happy group and it was hard to settle down and go to sleep!

After all we had accomplished that week, the army had its own way of bringing us back to reality. Friday was a work day and we resumed our normal training schedule! We were qualifying for the Expert Infantryman Badge. It was worth $5 more per month in our pay!

The next day was Saturday, June 17, 1944, and that morning we had a battalion formation and those who had qualified were presented their jump wings. We were so proud! It was a happy, happy day for us! We hadn't heard about the heavy losses the 101st and the 82nd Airborne Divisions had taken during D-Day. I rather believe the top brass figured they were going to need a lot of Airborne troops before this war was over.

CHAPTER 29
THE DIVISION SHIPS OUT

While we were stationed at Camp Forrest in Tennessee, I had a good deal. As long as I did my job and kept out of trouble, I was usually free to go on pass most weekends. In about five hours, I could be home in Bowling Green!

As Bowling Green was a two-college town in those days and most of the young men were in service, there were plenty of available young ladies running loose! I still had some good connections around campus, so I knew how to operate! I regularly had guys in my outfit practically begging to go home with me. Most of the time, Gerry Quick accompanied me and he and I had a ball.

Years later, I asked Jerry Stuhrman if he hadn't favored me a bit when it came to setting up the roster for weekend details. I cannot remember getting weekend duty all the time we were at Forrest. Jerry completely denies that he showed any favoritism. I did work hard and really toed the line, so maybe my good behavior paid off!

Eventually, the string ran out for us. We finally got our orders to be shipped overseas. Officially, the orders to the division arrived on July 3, 1944. On the next day, the Fourth of July, we were restricted to the post and with that everyone knew that the time had come. We had trained now for about 15 months, had completed our glider training and many of us had completed jump school. It was time.

The next couple of weeks at Camp Forrest were filled with care and cleaning of equipment, show-down inspections, turning in worn equipment and drawing new, getting shots and going to lectures. One of the things we hated was the order to remove the "Airborne" insignia on our outer garments. I guess the idea was to keep the enemy from knowing that another Airborne division was coming after them!

Soon the pay phones on post were disconnected so no one could call out. The men who had cars were given three-day passes to take them home or sell them. Some unit equipment had even started its move to our new destination by July 11. This routine was all part of our "Preparation Of Movement", or P.O.M. as it was called. We got the feeling that the fun was all over and everything from now on was for keeps.

Just before all this started, we had sensed it was near. In fact, I told my parents one weekend late in June when I was home, that this would probably be my last pass home. Dad and I decided on a personal code so that I could tell them exactly where I was when we arrived overseas. He later completely forgot everything we set up, which was just as well! The news kept them informed of the division's general location.

About the second week of August we closed out our barracks and loaded our bags on waiting trucks. Then we were trucked to the train station where we boarded coaches and waited. Finally, we pulled out for parts unknown.

Although once again we were aboard a dirty, steam-driven train with it's "no-frills" coaches, it was not quite as bad as it had been when we reported in to Camp Mackall for basic training. This ride seemed shorter as we moved right along and didn't stop and start and back up as we had done on that first train ride. And, unlike other troop movements I heard about, we made no stops for Red Cross coffee and doughnuts.

In addition to a few rest stops out in the open countryside and to take on water or food supplies, our only stop was when we reached Camp Miles Standish near Providence, Rhode Island about August 12. This was not far from Boston, which was to be our Port of Embarkation, or P.O.E. as it was called. No one got passes, or at least, that's what I thought. I later found out some officers did, but no one in our company was permitted to go farther than the Post Exchange.

While at Standish, we continued to swap old equipment for new and to polish and clean every item we had. Sometime during this frenzy, we received a new 60 mm mortar. We hated to give up our old "pea shooter". As it seemed we had carried it a million miles, it was like saying goodbye to a member of the family.

One of the wonderful things they did for us while we were at Standish was to give each of us a Yellow Fever shot. They were something else! It was a hot summer afternoon when they marched us about a mile to the dispensary to get them. Many of the fellows needed other shots too, so they got them all at one time. And, rather than take the time to check the records to see who needed what, they just gave everyone all the shots again. But, it was the Yellow Fever shot that was the real doozy.

First of all, the shots hurt. The Army used their usual "square needle", but the worst part of it was the fact that the shot contained a lot of serum and it hurt going in! Then, in the hot sun, we began the mile hike back to the area where we were billeted. That turned into a real fiasco.

The guys started getting sick and many were throwing up as we marched along. Some staggered out of ranks and passed out cold in the ditch along side the road. It was almost like the Army had expected this to happen as an ambulance followed us and picked up those who passed out. I made it okay, but I'll always be surprised we didn't loose some guys for good.

A little rest revived us and we quickly snapped back. Then it was lectures. They tried to give us some idea of what we would face living with the people of Europe. England was never mentioned as our actual destination, just that it was one of the countries where we might be heading.

Inspections assured that no Airborne tabs were on our outer garments. There were more show-down inspections, our insurance coverage was reviewed and everyone was given the opportunity to declare a next-of-kin and prepare a will. We got the picture. Things were really getting serious.

In a complete contradiction of all the super-secret moves we had made so far, we were called together one day for a drawing to determine those among us who would receive nine free passes to a major league baseball game in Boston! Of course, I won one of the passes. It was the only time I had ever won a drawing for anything. However, before we could be trucked in to the ball park, the area was hit with a cloudburst and the game was rained out! I knew it was too good to be true. Things were truly SNAFU at this point!

I was amazed at how long this whole shipping out process lasted. It seemed like we were going to be there forever! Finally, about August 19, we put on our packs, shouldered our barracks bags and weapons and donned our steel pots and boarded another train. It was a short ride to Boston Harbor where the train pulled right up on the pier. There most of us saw the biggest ship we had ever seen: the U.S.S. Wakefield.

Struggling under the overload we carried, we climbed the gangplank. As we went up, someone called our name and we yelled back "Ho!" From here on it was follow the leader. The leader, unfortunately, kept going down a series of steel stair steps until I felt we must be in the very bottom of this big ship.

When we finally reached the level that they told us was to be our "stateroom", we were exhausted. No one was happy about the space designated for us. The air was hot and stale and smelled of body sweat and the adjacent latrine. The canvas bunks were stacked five deep and were so shallow that a person could hardly turn over. We were not happy but there was nothing we could do about it.

When we dropped our equipment, there was hardly room to move around. It was then that most of the men made the decision that they would sleep topside on the deck. A lot of guys had that same idea and as a result, you could hardly walk on deck at night for the men trying to sleep. It was one thing to have your ship torpedoed and be cast into the sea, but we damn sure didn't want to be trapped down below and go down with the ship.

Another regulation also caused a lot of grumbling. The showers piped in salt water during most of the day. Soap just wouldn't lather in salt water. For an hour each day, they spewed forth soft water in a weak little trickle. It was almost impossible to take a shower in this trickle with 100 other guys having the same idea. We solved this problem by just not bathing, which added to the lovely aroma coming up from the bowels of the ship.

I heard about one prankster who devised a good trick for the row of toilets. The 12 or 15 seats were all situated over a trough that carried a steady stream of sea water which in turn, carried away the waste. The prankster poured lighter fluid on a spare roll of toilet paper, set it afire and let it float down the stream under the row of toilet seats and the bare behinds of their occupants! I understand the seated GIs got quite a surprise.

Our seven-day ocean trip was mostly boring. We read, we slept, a great many of the GIs got seasick and all of us longed to be on land again where we could exercise. We were not used to all this inaction. And, of course, we often wondered if those dark waters were hiding a German submarine that was watching and stalking us. It was not a fun trip. It was a scary time in our lives.

PART III:
OVERSEAS AND ENGLAND

CHAPTER 30
CROSSING THE ATLANTIC

Most of our division embarked from Boston and crossed the Alantic on the U.S.S. Wakefield. The speedy ship was the converted luxury liner Lafayette and was on loan to the Coast Guard for troopship duty. She carried over 8,000 of us and crossed the ocean in only seven days. The division strength was only about 10,000 at this time as the 507th Parachute Infantry, already in the ETO, had not as yet been assigned to the 17th Airborne. Other division personnel either came in an advance party or in a later echelon.

We traveled alone without the protection of a large convoy as was common in those war days. We were told this was because of the ship's speed. We traveled a zig-zag path changing our direction every four or five minutes, a maneuver said to prevent an enemy U-boat from computing the range to launch a torpedo at the ship. I was just young enough to believe the story.

Our trip was rather uneventful. We had a few scheduled life boat drills where we assembled at assigned stations and learned how to inflate our life belts. Generally, we just went about any duties we had and most of the troops spent the rest of the time sleeping or glazing out at the endless ocean. Unless a person was seasick, this was a vacation compared to the routine we were used to.

One day—we were just off the Azores Islands— we were shocked to hear the alarm calling us to assemble at our life boat station. There had been no scheduled drill for that time and the alarm had a sense of urgency about it. A large lifeboat had been spotted and the ship was slowing to investigate.

One of the sailors assigned to an anti-aircraft gun near our lifeboat station, told us it might be an old Nazi trick. A U-boat would lurk around a lifeboat carrying survivors until some ship stopped to pick them up. Then they would torpedo the rescue ship.

Maybe they just wanted to scare us, which they did. I said a quick prayer as I wanted no part of a submarine way out here in the ocean. Everything turned out okay, as the lifeboat was empty. A machine gun crew sunk it to eliminate it as a hazard. We breathed a sigh of relieve and plowed on.

My company, as a whole, drew no details on the trip over. However, all the privates in the first platoon, were assigned KP duty in the troop officer's mess. At first, this sounded like we really had been shafted, but it turned out to be a real break. Had they known what a good deal it was, we probably would not have gotten the call!

The troop officer's mess had about 12 tables, each seating 10 officers. In order to serve all the officers three meals each day, they were scheduled in three separate seatings for each meal. Each seating of 10 officers was allocated 30 minutes during which they had to eat their meal and leave.

As KPs, we were all assigned specific duties. Mine was to care for one of the tables. This included setting the table for each seating, bringing in bowls of food from the galley and always keeping them full, then after each seating carrying the dirty dishes to the galley where the mess stewards took over. Then I would put on clean linen and set the table for the next seating. All in all, I worked about four and a half hours total each day. When compared to the eight to ten hour days we usually had when on dry land, it was a snap!

In addition, the KPs were allowed to use a smaller room just off the galley for our own private day room! We played cards there and lay around and read. Adjacent to that room was a room where the ship's quartermaster sold ship's stores to the troop officers. It was like a small PX and we were allowed to buy from that facility as well. Elsewhere on board, the troops had to stand in line for hours to make PX purchases.

The best deal we got was the fact that we got to eat our own meals there. We feasted on meals of steak, chicken, fresh vegetables and fruit and choice deserts served on the ship's fine tableware. Meanwhile, our fellow troopers stood in line with their metal trays for an hour to wind down into the bowels of the ship for meals of spam, weiners and spuds!

If that wasn't enough, the biggest surprise came at the end of the trip. At the last meal, the officers at each table for each of the three seatings took up a collection and left us a tip! As I recall, mine totaled in the neighborhood of $70 or $80. In those days, we found it hard to believe we were getting tipped just for doing what we regarded as our duty!

I enjoyed our trip over. The salt air was refreshing and I liked to stand on deck in the evening and look out over the water. I wondered what dark mysteries lay hidden below those waves. It was a beautiful scene with the moon on the water.

As peaceful as it looked, sooner or later, weird thoughts would come into my mind. Could a submarine be tracking us at that very moment? Would my life belt inflate properly if I had to squeeze the two little bottles that were attached? Could I swim the remaining thousand or more miles to Europe?

Seasickness was common amongst the troops. In spite of the fact we were on a large ship and not subject to this problem like if we had been on a smaller vessel, it laid a lot of the fellows flat, literally. The sick bay was said to be filled to overflowing with the really bad cases. There were dozens of guys lying on deck that should have been there. Some never ate or went below deck the entire trip.

I never got seasick, although on the third day out I began to experience some repeated dizzy spells. About every 10 minutes I could feel it coming on. My head would go swimming around, things would nearly go black and this dizzy spell came over me lasting for only about five or ten seconds. This went on for about two days and then I was fine.

I was afraid I would get one of these dizzy spells when I was carrying a full bowl of food to the table I served. I could imagine what would happen to me if I dumped a load of gravy in some colonel's lap!

I got so I could anticipate when these dizzy spells were due to hit me. I would stop, grab the handrail on the nearest bulkhead and hold on until it passed. Then I would hurry to the table with the food before it was time for another spell!

Finally, one day we were surprised by a big bomber flying over our ship. Some of the guys thought we were in trouble, but soon we realized that it was a British patrol plane. The sighting of a "friendly" at this point could mean only one thing: we were nearing land!

This fact cheered up everyone and went a long way toward curing our seasick passengers. It was very plain we were soldiers, not sailors. When we sailed into Liverpool, England, on August 26, it magically healed a lot of seasick soldiers.

They didn't have to tell us to ready our gear to move out, but for some reason, no order came and we lined the railing as we waited at the dock for almost an hour. We began worrying about German bombers and what a juicy target we'd be! Finally, a train pulled in nearby and the reason for our delay became evident. If we had disembarked earlier, those guys would have been scattered over half of England!

From the rail of the ship, we watched the sailors unload all of the garbage we had accumulated during our trip. It was rapidly becoming a small mountain. Nothing had been dumped overboard enroute and we had been cautioned not to throw trash overboard. We were told the U-boats often followed "garbage trails" to track down troopships.

English dock workers were picking through the garbage looking for whatever they could salvage. Soon they were joined by a number of the biggest rats I have ever seen. They were a foot long with tails of another foot. They were huge!

The dock workers then amazed us. They would sneak up behind one of the rats, grab it by it's tail and swing it around over their heads. Then they would slam it down on the deck, either killing it or leaving it kicking in it's death throes!

The GIs, watching from the ship's rails cheered their approval and tossed coins to the dock workers. This sport entertained us until finally, the order came to disembark. This was it—England at last!

We moved directly from the ship and loaded on the train. The passenger cars, divided into compartments, were clean, well-kept and far superior to what we had ridden in back in America. We were then treated to a pleasant ride through the English countryside skirting around London toward what was to be our home for the next four months.

Soon, we arrived in a town called Swindon. We would soon become well-acquainted with this interesting town. From here we went by truck winding through several clumps of English houses to a small village named Chiseldon. Just outside this village was Camp Chiseldon, named for the score of so of old World War I British barracks located there. We were home at last!

Not all the division's units were located there at Chiseldon. We were scattered all over the nearby countryside, but located close enough so that control was not a problem. Some of the units were lucky enough to be billeted in old English army barracks, but the 193rd was doomed to occupy a muddy, hastily-constructed tent city. For what it was worth, our cable address was AMKIDY.

Someone had set up the tents, but that was all. The area included walkways, but they were mud holes. We set to work immediately, setting up canvas cots, stuffing straw into sack mattresses and trying to get some kind of heat going in the pot-bellied charcoal stoves located in the tents. We had a lot to do before we could be comfortable in our new home.

CHAPTER 31
"THE WAR OF THE FLOORS"

I t was early in the morning of August 26, 1944, when we landed in Liverpool harbor. After we got unloaded and transported through the countryside to our new billets, it was almost dark. By the time we got moved in, set up our cots and filled our mattresses with straw, we were pretty tired. We slept well our first night in merry ole England.

During the next few days, the company area underwent some big changes. Gravel was hauled in and the company street changed from pure mud to half mud. Keeping a shine on our beloved jump boots became almost impossible.

Water pipes were hooked up to an outdoor sink and this gave us a quick place to get water. We could now heat water on our stove and shave in our tents. It also afforded us a quick way to wash our hands and fill our canteens. We still had to go about 75 yards to a Quonset hut to take a shower or use the toilet, but unlike aboard ship, this was soft water, there was plenty of it and it was hot!

Later, the guys in our tent pitched in and bought an English radio. That is, it operated on direct current (DC) unlike alternating current (AC) as they have in America. This was great entertainment for us as now we were able to hear some war news and listen to some big band music.

The number one tune on the Hit Parade in those days was "I'll Be Seeing You" and every time I heard it, my eyes would get all misty! Some of the favorite English songs were "I Leaned Across and Kissed You" and "There'll Always Be An England". They also liked to play a song called "Choclate Soldier From The U. S. A."

Our favorite program was "Duffel Bag" on the American Expeditionary Forces Network (A.E.F.). The GIs would write letters bitching about everything in the world and the announcers would read them and talk about it for awhile and, of course, nothing ever came of anything! At least we got to hear the Glenn Miller Orchestra, led most of the time by Sgt. Ray McKinley.

After a few days when we had settled in, we began to explore the area around us. A vacant tent area immediately adjacent to our Company D area naturally attracted our attention. This area, we were told, had been occupied by a company of the 506th Parachute Infantry of the 101st Airborne Division.

These brave troopers had parachuted into France on D-Day, June 6, 1944, and as far as anyone knew, were still fighting on the continent. Now that we had moved into the area and occupied most of the available space, we thought they would never be returning to this deserted area.

Accordingly, we helped ourselves to the wooden floors that the 506th troopers had fashioned for their tents. Made from discarded lumber from old packing crates, the floors offered some relief from the mud and cold ground. The floors fit our tents as well, and there was no reason to let the floors just lay there and not be used, we reasoned.

Everything went smoothly for a week or so and then an unexpected turn of events took place. To our surprise, one day the 506th troopers returned to their former billets at Camp Chisledon. They had been relieved in France and sent back to England to refit and retrain. It only took them a few minutes to realize what had happened to their floors.

Flush from 33 days in deadly combat, the 506th troopers came screaming and yelling into our area. All hell broke out! "The War of the Floors" had started!

Many of the 506th troopers still had live ammunition, smoke grenades and flares. They ran through our area firing their weapons in the air and tossing the smoke grenades into the tents. A few heads got cracked, but our guys fought back and an attack that was planned mostly to scare us, accomplished little.

Nevertheless, officers from both units were running around like mad trying to stop the mayhem! Commands and orders were ignored as total war seemed to have broken out. Nothing seemed to have any effect. The entire scene was a madhouse and completely out of control.

Those of us who bunked in my tent grabbed our rifles and stood in front of the tent. Sgt. Pierre was at the door and he was some hunk of man. No one challenged him and no one tried to enter our tent. If they had, I doubt we could have stopped them, but they would have had to kill Pierre and I think they realized that!

Finally, after what seemed like an hour, but was probably no more than 10-15 minutes, everything began to simmer down. The 506th officers got their men under control and moved them out. Some had recovered their floors, but most hadn't and they left vowing they would return for the other floors.

After that, the regular company area guard was beefed up both day and night to protect our property from another raid that everyone expected sooner or later. In the days that followed, our company became an armed camp. Every man had a club, blackjack or knife beside his bed ready for the call to defend his floor.

The next great battle never came about. On September 10, 1944, General Lewis H. Brereton, Commanding General of the newly-formed 1st Allied Airborne Army—of which the 101st as well as the 17th were a part—alerted his forces for a new Airborne operation. By September 15, the 506th departed for their marshalling area and two days later they were jumping into Holland.

History records that because much of the 17th Airborne's equipment and records were still at sea enroute to England, the 17th was not deemed operational and thus, was not chosen to participate in the operation. There are a few, however, who maintain the brass didn't know for sure that the 506th and the 193rd wouldn't fight each other instead of the Germans!

"The War of the Floors" probably served as a means for the 506th to "blow off some steam". At the same time it demonstrated to all that although the 193rd was as yet "combat-untested", they could be counted on to stand their ground. And, that we did.

CHAPTER 32
EVE AND HER APPLE

Not that anyone might get the wrong idea, but not all the Airborne troopers were clean-cut, wholesome types that you might imagine as the kid living next door to you. There was plenty of sin around and the opportunity to trip over the line was ever among us. I have often wondered how I managed to stay as straight as I did.

I will always remember a weird experience I had while we were billeted at Camp Chiseldon in England. It was a Sunday morning and that week I had decided to stay in camp rather than making the usual foray into London. This week I would sleep late and then write some overdue letters. You have to write them if you want to receive them!

Sunday morning was a good time to be in camp too. It was the one day the messhall served real, genuine eggs! They were scarce in England and they cost dearly. Only on Sunday, when most of the troopers were gone, did the cooks serve up eggs.

Rationing in England was tough. No one was starving, but most of the food obtained locally was bland and in short supply. Things like coffee, steak and sugar were just not to be found. Someway, they managed to get their precious tea, but it was scarce, expensive and heavily rationed. If you wanted to get the best meal available anywhere, the place to get it was not in town. It was at an American military messhall.

This Sunday morning I was walking up to our messhall with visions of a couple of real, honest-to-goodness, scrambled eggs with several crisp strips of bacon on the side. Maybe I'd also have a stack of buttermilk pancakes with maple syrup and a glass of cold milk. Boy, that sounded good!

As I neared our messhall, I chanced to glance up at the tent area that adjoined our own tent area. This is the area that had been occupied by a unit of the 506th Parachute Infantry of the 101st Airborne Division. At the present, the 101st was still in Holland where they had jumped during Operation Market Garden and their tent area was completely deserted.

To my surprise, I saw a crowd of soldiers gathered around one of the vacant tents. Wondering what was going on, I decided to stroll up to the area and see for myself. As I got closer, I could see that there was a line formed outside the tent. Whatever the attraction was, I wanted to find out, so I walked up and asked one of the troopers what was going on.

The answer I got rocked me back on my heels! He told me some trooper had been to town the night before and had returned early this morning with a "lady of the evening". Now he had gone into business and opened his own branch whorehouse!

I noticed all the guys standing in the line had some type of foodstuff in their hands. There were candy bars from the PX, cookies apparently mailed from home, and canned fruit which no doubt had been stolen from the messhall! The trooper explained that in addition to a pound note (worth about $4 at that time) the fee for the lady's services also required some type of foodstuff!

This I had to see for myself, so I walked up to the head of the line to peep inside the tent. Cries of "Get to the back of the line!" were hurled at me as apparently, the waiting customers standing in line thought I was trying to buck in ahead of them.

Disregarding the yells, I peeped inside the tent. At first I laughed at what I saw, but then it all but turned me sick. There was one lone cot set up in the tent and it had a straw tick mattress on it. Lying on the cot was this old bag of a woman and she was presently employed in "servicing" some young trooper.

The young trooper was kicking and scratching away and paid no attention to his audience. He seemed intent on getting his money's worth. And, I guess, his food's worth. The old bag likewise paid no attention to either the young trooper or any of the others that were peeping in the tent entrance and urging him to hurry up!

Stacked by the side of the cot was a pile of foodstuffs. It looked like a private supermarket! Her cupboard would certainly not be bare in the days ahead! And there, standing at the entrance with a wad of pound notes in his hand, was the boss trooper! It looked like he had robbed the paymaster!

All this was bad, but as I watched in amazement, it got worse. The old bag had a half-eaten apple in her hand and slowly, she put the apple to her mouth and took a huge bite and began to chew. That was more than enough for me. I left with my vision of womanhood shattered to smithereens!

CHAPTER 33
LONDON: A CITY READY FOR WAR

I 'll always remember London and how its people were prepared for war. The resolve of the English people was a major lesson to all of us Yanks. As Churchill said in his oft-quoted speech, "We will fight them in the fields, we will fight them in the streets and we will fight them from the rooftops; we will never surrender!" I believed him when he said that and I know the people did. Everyone was ready to fight to the last person.

Throughout this book I have made a number of references to some of the conditions that existed in wartime London. However, I feel a special chapter is in order to adequately express the attitude and fighting spirit that became their way of life in those days. If you ever had the idea that the English were "stuffy" or even a bit effeminate, forget it. They were tough and a real opponent to be reckoned with!

Most everyone carried a gas mask, but by the time we got there, the threat of a gas attack had diminished and a lot of Londoners had given up the habit of carrying their masks wherever they went. Still there were others who continued to carry them because they had been told to do so by the government and Londoners did what their leaders told them to do.

Most men of military age were in the uniform of the Royal Army, the Royal Navy, the Royal Marines or the Royal Air Force! The older men also wore various types of uniforms, but these were either those of the Home Guard, air raid wardens, firemen or policemen. It seemed everyone had some extra duty to do in addition to their occupation.

In addition, many of the young women were also wearing the uniforms of the various military services. Some wore the uniform of what was known as the Women's Land Army. This was a special force that moved from place to place just to help harvest the farm crops. London was a sea of uniforms!

There were many other signs of the war in London. I was struck by the mountains of sandbags that surrounded many buildings. St. Paul's Cathedral was protected by bags stacked 20 to 30 feet high. Most of the cathedral's finer art pieces had been removed and stored in the countryside to protect them from the bombings.

Other buildings had their windows boarded or bricked up and some merchants had built 8-foot brick walls out on the sidewalk. This was not only to protect their store fronts, but to protect pedestrians from flying glass during air raids. These walls also had peep-holes—or they could have been gun ports—located every few feet. You really got the feeling they were preparing to fight for every inch of real estate if indeed, the Germans did come.

I got a big kick out of one sign I saw posted outside a bombed-out men's shop. It read: "Jerry prefers we return to our old address on Old Bond Street—but we'll be back!" The whole country had the attitude that they might be a bit down just now, but they just couldn't be whipped.

There were large, portable roadblocks standing ready at strategic locations and they could be rolled into place in moments should an invasion come. They were made of large steel pylons laced with barbed wire and each roadblock was covered by nearby concrete pillboxes bristling with gun ports.

Spotted throughout the parks were large gun pits with the black snouts of their anti-aircraft weapons pointed skyward and their crews always on the alert. You could see more AAA on the roofs of some of the buildings. Nearby, giant searchlights stood with crews manning them during the evening hours.

Probably what impressed me the most was the provisions that had been made for air raid shelters. The most common of these were the subways, or "the tube" as the English called them. Officially designated as the Underground, they doubled as excellent protection for the majority of Londoners.

During the height of the bombing raids, people often spent the entire night sleeping underground on the concrete walkways. This practice was no longer necessary by the time we arrived in England. The Luftwaffe no longer was able to send over their hordes of bombers and the only need now for protection was from the periodic buzz bomb attacks.

Many Londoners chose to ignore the buzz bombs and went on with their work. It was one way they had to thumb their noses at Hitler. And, as they loved to say, "if it has your name on it, it'll bloody well find you no matter where you hide!" I must add I did not subscribe to this attitude and when the sirens screamed their warning, I looked for shelter!

In the areas not served by the Underground or located far from a terminal, concrete bomb shelters had been built. These were long, low buildings about eight feet high and some 15 to 20 feet wide. Some were a city block long. The entrances were heavily banked with sand bags.

Inside, the shelters had a double row of canvas bunks separated by a narrow passageway down the center. The GIs quickly learned that this was a handy place to take the "ladies of the evening"! Consequently, it was best to stay out of the shelters except during an authentic air raid alert!

In my mind, I can still see the little "S" signs. These were small signs mounted on the blacked-out light poles. The signs had a large white "S" and the word "Shelter" was printed below. Each had a little roof over it to shield a small dim light from the bombers above. Usually there was an arrow that pointed in the direction of the shelter.

Other places also were set up to serve as shelters. These included below-ground restaurants, park rest rooms, basement stores, storage areas and even bank vaults. If anyone wanted to find shelter, they could find it without much effort. I remember one Sunday afternoon when the streets were filled and we had a buzz bomb alert. In a matter of minutes the streets were totally deserted.

Another thing we got used to seeing was barrels and buckets of sand and water placed along the sidewalk. The GIs often tossed their cigarettes in them, but their intended use was for dousing incendiary bombs that might be dropped. Other fire fighting equipment was often stationed at key locations.

London was very much alive at night, but you had to know how to find it! The blackout really worked. It could be as dark as pitch out in the streets, but if you listened, you could often hear music and laughter behind blacked-out doors. Most of the pubs had double doors with a little entrance foyer where the first door closed behind you before the second one opened, thus preserving the blackout.

We Americans had a rough time getting used to the time until we finally got adjusted. We lost six time zones coming across the ocean and during the war, Britain was on double daylight saving time. France was one hour earlier and Nazi occupied Europe was on Berlin time and the Germans didn't use daylight saving time! We were always struggling with the time, even if it didn't really mean much to us. We weren't going anywhere far!

When you knew your way around, there was plenty of night life and it went on until the wee small hours. The mood was very much eat, drink and be merry, for tomorrow you may die. There were plenty of love-starved English lasses and an acute shortage of eligible males. The Yanks were doing their best to fill the shortage!

The Brits sometimes took a dim view of the Americans and many just tolerated their stay in the country. Fortunately, most of the English lasses paid little attention to this viewpoint. The Yanks had plenty of money it seemed and they were out to spend it on anything that promised to relieve the boredom of their lives. Many of the English lasses were hot on the trail of husbands and what it promised—a trip to America, the land of plenty!

Rationing was a way of life in England. The people had all the bare necessities and no one seemed to go hungry, but sugar, coffee, cigarettes and their beloved tea were among those items in very short supply. The GIs, because they were able to supply some of these items, were very much the heroes.

Civilian clothes were among the items really hard to get, so a lot of the civilians were getting a bit shabby. However, they patched and darned and kept everything immaculately clean. It made you feel good to see the pride they had. I think they all won our respect with the spirit they showed as they "made do" in order to further the war effort.

The Brits had another custom that I admired. We would frequently go to the "cinema", as they called it. I remember two of the theaters were named the "Regent" and "Marble Halls".

Then, when the movie was over, the lights would come on, everyone would stand and they would all sing the national anthem, "God Save The King". It was plain they sure loved their country.

Until years afterwards, I really never realized how close England had come to loosing the war. I don't want to sound like the smug American, but had The United States not entered the struggle when we did, England may well have fallen to Hitler. And, that would have been the tragedy of all mankind.

I know England never would have surrendered. You could sense that. It would have been terrible. The English people – and Londoners in particular — would have resisted until the bitter end. Their resolve was unwavering and to them the idea of England loosing the war was inconceivable.

CHAPTER 34
THOSE PARATROOPER BOOTS!

I've heard a lot of wild and funny stories about paratroopers and their shiny boots. They're all probably true. Any paratrooper I ever knew could usually tell you a story or two about how at times he had to do battle to defend his honored right to wear this special item of uniform.

There is no telling how many fights started because some non-jumper was discovered wearing paratrooper boots. Just as the beret is today, in their day jump boots were a highly sought-after item of military dress. Many times paratroopers were unable to obtain jump boots through normal supply channels, so imagine how they felt when they spied some "rear-echelon commando" wearing them!

Even while I was in jump school and although jump boots had been officially issued to me, when I went into Tullahoma I did not dare blouse my trouser legs in the boots. That privilege was reserved for the trooper who had completed his five jumps and had his wings. Several glider troopers failed to obey this unwritten code of conduct and came back to camp with their pants legs cut off at the knees!

This code continued even while we were in England. The 17th, the 101st and the 82nd Airborne Divisions all combined to enforce it. I recall hearing about a terrible fight that a group of 17th Airborne paratroopers had in London with a crack recon unit from Hawaii. The Hawaiians had always worn boots similar to jump boots and they had no plans to change. It got quite bloody with knives coming into play.

As a result of that fight on Saturday, November 25, the city of London was placed "off-limits" to the 17th Airborne for two weeks. This was the first and only time London was ever declared off-limits to any division during the war, a questionable distinction that was thoroughly relished by the troopers.

All this fuss was because those boots set the paratrooper off from the thousands of other soldiers in the U. S. Army. They showed at a glance that he was something special, a cut above the average. It was true back during World War II and to a certain extent, it's still true today.

In today's army, almost everyone now wears boots. But, if you look closely, you'll see there is a difference in the type of boots and a marked difference in the type of man who wears them. There is a certain cockiness you'll notice in the jumper. He walks with a different gait and an air of confidence. He is still something special.

Back in January of 1945, when I was wounded and entered the hospital chain, I was acutely aware that there were dozens of "rear echelon commandos" that were just itching to get hold of my boots. At that time, paratrooper boots were the most sought-after item on the GI black market!

At the evac hospital where I was sent, an orderly came to remove my boots. This was for my own comfort as well as to check my feet for frostbite. I knew if I was put to sleep so they could work on my arm, my boots would be easy prey. Lying on the stretcher I was rather helpless, but this orderly turned out to be a good guy. He tied the laces together, passed them under my upper body and tucked each boot in tightly at my side.

When I arrived at the main hospital they came to take me in for an operation. Another trooper in the ward volunteered to look after my boots while I was knocked out! I was lucky. No one stole my boots and today, they are on my desk serving as bookends! They remain a proud keepsake and reminder of those terrible days in combat.

I remember a funny story about paratrooper boots that involved my buddy, Ray Crabtree. We were in London on a late Sunday afternoon and were walking around Picadilly Circus. We had just remarked that we should go somewhere and eat. Our train back to camp left Paddington Station at 1:45 a.m. early Monday morning, so our weekend was just about over.

As we waited to cross the street, Ray struck up a conversation with an attractive girl waiting there. He asked her where would be a good place to eat. She mentioned a nearby restaurant and said she was on her way there and she would show us the way. In the London blackout, that was a big help.

This girl was not the typical "Picadilly Commando". As we learned later, she worked in an office. She was going to the restaurant to meet her girlfriend who worked as a waitress there and would get off work after the evening meal. Then they had planned to go to the cinema. Suddenly we had a foursome and we had plans other than the cinema!

The girlfriend, who would be my date, also turned out to be nice looking. So, after we had eaten, the four of us went pub-hopping. At about 10:00 p.m. we ended up at the apartment of Ray's girl. The idea of a little love-making was surely on the minds of all four of us!

The apartment was one of those "shotgun" types; an entrance into a living room, a long hallway running to the rear with a bedroom off each side and a kitchen at the end. After a while in the living room, Ray and his girl retired to one of the bedrooms. Later, the other girl and I went into the other bedroom across the hallway.

During the London blitz, many children and old people had been moved out of the congested areas for their protection. The mother of Ray's girl was one of those and she had been living with relatives in the nearby countryside. It was, therefore, a complete surprise and an unfortunate twist of fate that she chose that particular evening to make an unannounced visit back to the city to visit her daughter!

I heard the front door being unlocked and the mother call out for her daughter. I sprung to my feet and peeped out the bedroom door! I knew who it was immediately! I also knew I had to get Ray out of that bedroom across the hall and the two of us had to get out of that house as fast as we could!

Within a few minutes I heard a loud gasp and a muffled cry outside the door and I knew the mother had walked into the other bedroom. I rushed out into the hall with the idea that maybe some way I could save the situation.

I met the mother storming out of the other bedroom. She was highly excited as she hurried back to the kitchen. I dashed into the other bedroom and I'll never forget the sight I saw. The mother apparently had yanked the sheet back for there lay a stunned Ray with not a stitch on except his highly-polished, white-laced paratrooper boots!

As the daughter went back to the kitchen and tried to console her mother, I began grabbing Ray's clothes and shoving them into his arms. I then opened a window and once Ray had pulled on his pants, we climbed out and dropped to the gound. With Ray holding his pants up and both of us with most of our clothes in our arms, we went tearing down the street!

The absurdity of the moment overtook us and after we had run about a half block, we both began laughing so hard we could hardly stand up! There on the dark streets of London at midnight, we finished dressing properly and squared away our uniforms. Then we hailed a cab and set off for Paddington Station. We caught our train back to camp without further incident!.

We never saw those two girls again, but in my mind's eye, I can still see Ray lying there on those clean, white sheets naked as a jaybird with only his jump boots on! Later I asked him why he hadn't taken them off. I said I had never heard of anyone going to bed with a woman and keeping their boots on! Know what he said? He said he was afraid someone might steal them!

Well, I think he was just making a joke, but it does give you an idea of how we prized and jealously guarded "those paratrooper boots!"

CHAPTER 35
ALERT AND STAND DOWN

B y the time we got overseas, we had already trained longer than any straight leg infantry division. It was not unusual for regular infantry to head for a Port of Embarkation within a few months after individual unit training. Infantry replacements were often rushed overseas soon after they had finished basic training. Some poor fellows found themselves in a "live or die" situation after less than six months in the army.

In addition to Glider Training and Parachute School, it took a lot more time to train an Airborne division. What we never realized was there had been extra time factored in so we could be trained to fight while outnumbered, out-gunned and surrounded. Such is the fate of Airborne troops!

When we reached England, our training went on as usual. We were elite troops, highly trained for a specific need and it was obvious there were no plans to waste us in a conventional infantry role. Although the Bulge changed all that, we were being held back until the ideal opportunity presented itself.

Had we arrived overseas two or three weeks earlier, we may have been committed to the operations in the Netherlands. Monty surely would have liked to have had us at Arnhem to assist the hard-pressed British 1st Airborne. Who knows, that might have been the help that they needed to have turned that operation around. Instead, sadly, it was a "bridge too far".

What is so strange to me is the fact that we never dreamed Operation Market Garden was ready to happen. A unit of the 506th was billeted right next to us and one day they were there and the next day they were gone. And, we never knew how close we had come to going with them.

Many years later we learned that although the high brass felt we were ready for combat at that time, part of our division "tail" was still somewhere on the Alantic Ocean enroute from America. That included most of our records, a lot of our equipment and no doubt, some of our personnel. To have committed us at that time would have meant the division would not have been able to operate at peak efficiency. In addition, there was an acute shortage of airlift capability. The decision was made to hold us back.

I've often wondered if maybe it was also a bit of the fact General Eisenhower was having his problems with Montgomery then and was reluctant to commit more U.S. elite troops in an operation he had some doubts about. With the 82nd and the 101st committed, we were the only Airborne force of any size that he had left in his reserve.

While the 82nd and 101st were still engaged in Holland, we had our own alert. The 17th was alerted for a possible operation into Belgium. It seems that General Patton's tanks had pushed the Germans back so far so fast that Patton had outrun his supply lines. Running out of gas, the tanks had been formed into a defensive position sort of like the old western wagon train forming a circle to fight off the Indians.

The plan we heard that was being considered was that we would jump and ride gliders right into Patton's position and then fight our way back to open up the supply route. Although I have read in various military histories where the 17th staff worked on several possible Airborne operations, I have never read where this particular operation was one of those considered. But this was no dream or rumor—we were actually awaiting the order to move.

Years later, when I was attending Command and General Staff College during my days in the West Virginia National Guard, I met a young officer who was an NCO in those days and assigned to the planning section of the 17th Airborne Division Headquarters. He confirmed that they did indeed make a complete plan for the "Patton rescue mission". Incidentally, he also told me that among other missions they had planned, they had completed a possible operation for the 17th Airborne to drop into Berlin. Thank God for the Russians, that one also was not necessary.

If it was deemed so insignificant to the top brass that the Patton mission doesn't even rate comment in the division's history, be assured that to us it was mighty important. We were told to pack our musette bags with a clean pair of fatigues, an extra set of underwear and a pair of socks and leave it under our beds. Everything else we owned, except our individual combat equipment and the clothes on our backs, went into our barracks bags and was locked up in a vacant building.

The payoff came when we moved out of our area and into the area left behind by the 506th unit. We were living a real Spartan existence there for a couple of days! Training went on as usual only we didn't stray far from the company area. We were told not to write any letters to anyone and to clean our weapons until they glowed. They limited us to one blanket and told us to make sure we had a full canteen at all times.

One day we were notified that allied forces had broken through to Patton and with gas, his tanks were rolling again. The alert was over and we moved back into our regular company area. As we cheered Patton, they returned our barracks bags and life resumed where it had left off about four days before!

Now, maybe that was a practice alert and maybe it wasn't. The only thing I know for sure is Patton apparently did run low on fuel and was forced to halt and regroup. Whether they ever intended to actually commit us in this situation, I doubt anyone will ever know. It might have been just training to see how fast we could be ready to move out in an actual situation. But, to those of us who thought we were going, it was for real and it was also a bit scary!

Back in our regular area, the six of us that shared the tent had pitched in and bought an English radio. After the alert, we listened to it carefully for hints of coming situations that might involve us. The news from the BBC (British Broadcasting Company) and the AEF (American Expeditionary Forces) was interesting, but we knew it was all censored and would reveal little.

Another pastime our radio afforded us was listening to a program called "Jerry Calling". It featured "Axis Sally", or "The Berlin Bitch" as we called her, on German radio. She came on each night at 8:00 with a special program directed at American forces. Here we heard the Nazi propaganda machine operating at its very best.

Sally was an American woman named Midge Gillars from Ohio. She was a small-time radio personality and a would-be actress who married a German and got herself cut off in Germany when the war broke out. In Germany, she found the stardom that had evaded her in Ohio and became the ace propaganda voice on German radio.

We laughed at her attempts to destroy our morale, but mainly we listened because we enjoyed the music. After the war, poor Midge was convicted of treason and did 12 years in prison. She was released in 1961, taught music in Columbus, Ohio, and died in 1988 at the age of 87. May she rest in peace!

The BBC was constantly sending messages to clandestine forces operating on the continent. Many were weird messages. The announcer might say something like, "The green goose flew over the purple pond." Or, "The fox is now in the chicken house." You can read all kinds of secret messages into those phrases and probably none of them would be accurate!

Many did serve to deliver important information to those who received them in France. For example, the FFI (Free French of the Interior), were alerted to the fact that D-Day had started when a strange message went out saying "The dice are on the carpet". The message was then repeated and the FFI knew it was time for them to join in the attack on the Germans.

In mid-November, the rumors were flying again. The story being circulated was that we were going to move to the continent to be "closer to the action". A mass truck movement to Chilbolton Airport for a division-wide review was set up for Wednesday, 15 November 1944. Many said this was only a cover story for the division's move to the continent. Then, when the uniform of the day was announced as Class A, and we were not ordered to pack our gear, we finally realized it was just that: a division-wide review. It went off smoothly.

When the time came for us to actually go into combat during the Bulge, the alert and the actual moving out of our area was quite different than we had imagined. There never was any doubt that it was for real. If any enemy agents had been anywhere near, they could have hardly failed to recognize that the 17th Airborne was on it's way! The sense of urgency was everywhere. Everyone knew that this time it was for real.

CHAPTER 36
BARBARY CASTLE

W hile we were stationed at Chiseldon, our company was assigned a training area a mile or so away and designated on the map as Barbary Castle. At first, we thought the name was just another quaint example of the way the English liked to name villages and homes after their historic past. It wasn't long before we learned the true story about our training area.

Barbary Castle was actually a real castle, or at least it used to be. The giant stone walls, the massive drawbridge and moat were gone but a few remaining stones and the depressions in the earth traced the outline of what had been a place seeped in history. The history also lived on in the folklore the people in the area told us.

I have forgotten most of the facts that I was told, but I recall the castle dated back to the days of the Norman Conquest and it had, according to the stories we heard, been the scene of several bloody battles. All this served to awaken us to the fact that England went way back in history. Our United States was a youngster in the family of nations.

The scenery in the area itself was spectacular. Lush, green, rolling moors and countryside surrounded by thick, dark green forests studded with towering old trees with a virtual carpet under their boughs. The place reeked of English history and I could close my eyes and almost see Sherlock Holmes gliding through the early morning mist!

As much as we dreaded each day of training, I couldn't help but feel inspired when we marched out to our historic training area. Even the most calloused members of our unit had to admit this area was beautiful and better by far than the sand and scrub pines of North Carolina and the red clay dirt of Tennessee.

We usually got another thrill as we would march to the Barbary Castle area. Our camp was near a Royal Air Force airfield and it was one of the bases that formed the screen protecting London from German bombers. This airfield had fighter aircraft— Spitfires and Hawker Typhoons—and they were really fast! Although by that time the threat of London bombings had pretty well diminished, the air bases still put up their patrols and the air jocks still zipped around throughout the area.

One of the favorite tricks of the Typhoon fighter pilots was to get below the horizon and the surrounding hills and then zoom up and make a mock strafing run on our column marching down the road. You could seldom hear them coming and then all of a sudden they were on top of you!

For the purpose of our training, at first our officers had us disperse and dive into the ditches to each side of the road. Then, after an "all clear" and we had reformed on the road, here they came again. I could just see those fighter jocks laughing their heads off on how they had scattered the Yanks! This game soon got old, so finally we took to ignoring them and went on our way cursing them under our breath, but glad on the other hand that they were up there and on guard.

Once we reached the Barbary Castle area we would run tactical problems for the better part of the day. Generally, it was either mock attacks or setting up defensive areas. The attack problems involved a lot of walking, but the defensive problems involved some digging and that was always hard work.

If we were on defense and dug foxholes, we had to refill our holes before we left to return to camp. After awhile the area began to look like an old graveyard as I guess our "filling in" was done pretty haphazardly. It was a shame too as the filled-in holes certainly didn't improve the beauty of the moors. For more than one reason, we were glad to get the order one day that in the future, we would only "simulate" digging in.

For a mortar squad, going on the defense now became the best of news. It meant that we would not have to dig a two-man mortar pit and individual holes which is a lot of digging! Mainly we liked it because this generally gave us more time than the rifle squads to lay around and soak up the sunshine and "shoot the breeze"! It was nice to take it easy and not constantly be pounding over the hillsides.

Brownie, our squad leader, enjoyed laying around shooting the breeze as much as any of us but, because he was responsible for the squad, he was always worrying about some officer coming up and catching us goofing off. He was always pacing around and trying to keep an eye peeled for someone who might chew him out if they caught us loafing.

We soon learned—as all privates will—that as long as he was keeping such a keen lookout, there was no reason for us to do so. Consequently, we usually flopped down and either went to sleep, made coffee or had a good bull session. It drove Brownie crazy, but there wasn't much he could do about it, so he made the best of the situation.

We called him the "Old Mother Hen" and joked about him looking after his "little chicks"! Sometimes it really got comical. He was always checking to see if we had all the things we were supposed to have and had done all the things he had told us to do. Sometimes he could be like a nagging wife!

The one thing Brownie counted on was that when we had to perform as a mortar squad either on the firing range or in doing our job as a unit of the platoon and the company, we would do well and he would come off looking good. Thinking back now, I don't know how we did it, but we always did well and Brownie never had to take any guff about our abilities or performance.

I often think about the Barbary Castle area and the days we spent walking over the moors there. England really is a beautiful country and I found that the way to appreciate that fact was not by visiting the cities, but by walking in the countryside. We got to do plenty of walking in the Airborne!

CHAPTER 37
FUN AND GAMES IN LONDON

N ot all our combat training took place on the hills and moors of Merry Ole England! We worked hard all week and looked forward to a pass and spending a weekend in London. What a fun place it was! There was Buckingham Palace, Westminister Abbey, Big Ben, London Bridge, all the places we had read about in our history books. And, of course, there were lots of girls!

Competition, however, was quite keen in London. Not from the Brits, but from our own American forces stationed in the vicinity! England had pretty well drained their manpower resources and almost every able-bodied English male was in the King's service. Many were scattered over the globe so there was a distinct shortage in the United Kingdom itself.

Everywhere you looked there were American Air Corps and service troops. The "fly-boys" were the darlings with the British. Maybe it was because the average English citizen saw more of their combat activities. England was one big airfield with thousands of bombers and fighter bases everywhere you looked. The pet saying was that if any more Yanks and planes landed on England's shores, the island would surely sink!

I don't mean to minimize their contribution because it was their action that had saved Britain. The Battle of Britain was won in the air and it was not won solely by the RAF. They had a lot of American help. Every day American planes took off from England and clashed with Hitler's forces and when they did get some time off, they came to London and they played hard!

The Americans were the best paid troops in the war and paratroopers seemed to have more cash to spend than any other U. S. troops. And, boy, did they spend it! Consequently, they had little trouble making out with the young ladies, a fact the British were well aware of. The saying went around British circles that the "Yanks were overpaid, oversexed, and over here!"

To this, the Yanks replied, "The British are underpaid, undersexed and under Eisenhower!" This seemed to rankle every Brit as they knew Ike had the say-so over Montgomery even to committing British troops. This fact was blown out of all proportion by the press and by Monty himself.

All of this heated competition for the English lasses, caused no end of conflict between the forces of the two counties crammed together on the small island. It also led to some sorry tactics in dealing with the matter. Some of those tactics I would have never stooped to in ordinary times, but in war time, as they say, "all is fair in love and war!"

One time when my buddy Ray and I had picked up two girls that we later determined were duds, I recall the cruel way we got rid of them. At the time we were strolling around in the area known as Picadilly Circus where the public rest rooms, or WCs (water closets), were located underground. We suggested that we all make a stop. The girls went into the ladies' entrance and we ducked into the men's entrance. We then quickly emerged from the exit located some 30 yards away and disappeared into the crowd. We never saw the girls again. The question, however, still remains: who dumped who?

As cruel as this might seem, such tactics were not judged too harshly in those times. One must remember that these were unusual times. There was precious little time for anyone to waste and manners sometimes tended to be overlooked. Actually, it was typical of the times as everyone seemed to live for the moment with a shrug of the shoulders to the future!

There were nice places to meet girls and there were rough places to meet girls. Your could always go to one of the big USOs in the city like the American Eagle Club or the Rainbow Corner Red Cross Club at Shafenbury Avenue. They even broadcast programs from here back to the States. The girls you met here were sworn not to make dates with GIs, although they did so sometimes.

I remember eating in Dunker's Inn at Rainbow Corner. More than that, I remember the gigantic crap game that was holding forth downstairs in the men's latrine. There were privates and captains shooting dice together and the stakes were BIG. It was too rich for my blood!

And then, there was Picadilly Circus. A lot of girls came there to meet GIs. One weekend in London, Ray and I picked up two girls in Picadilly on a Saturday night and thought we were set to go with them to their home. Arriving with them at Liverpool Station, they suggested that we have a "nightcap" at a nearby little pub called "The Ship". This was in an area seldom frequented by Americans and all eyes were on us when we entered. We thought it was the shiny paratrooper boots and wings, but I guess we were being carefully looked over for what followed.

After 15 or 20 minutes, the girls said they were ready to go and we all left. Outside it was dark as pitch and with the blackout regulations and unfamiliar surroundings, we were forced to following the girls like sheep. Suddenly, out of the dark came more British soldiers than I could count. They pounced on Ray and I and down we went.

I remember one on each arm and one on my legs and another pounding my head on the sidewalk. A few feet away, Ray was apparently getting the same treatment. I couldn't move and I couldn't get away, so I began yelling for help! I hoped there would be an MP or a Bobby around that would save us.

The next thing I remember, I was trying to collect my wits and the attackers were gone. So were the girls. And, so was Ray's hat, a fact that would cause us all kinds of problems before we left London that weekend. Every MP in the city stopped us and threatened him with being out of uniform. Yet, there were no MPs around that night when we really needed them.

I never knew what really had happened to us. Maybe the girls had arranged this little party and led us into a trap, but our billfolds were not taken which usually happened when you were "rolled". Maybe the Brits just wanted to get even with some Yanks—any Yanks. Could be the girls were not in on this and fled in fear. We never saw them again, but we did revisit "The Ship" and never had any further trouble there.

The first time I visited London brought on an interesting experience. One Saturday night about 9:00 p.m., my buddy Gerry Quick and I met an English girl and her companion who was French. We accepted an invitation to go with them to their home and were enroute when the air raid sirens began wailing. Actually, it was not German bombers, but our first experience with a German "buzz bomb". This one had gotten through the net of Spitfires and Typhoon fighters that protected the city.

We ducked into a couple of doorways where we were somewhat sheltered and shunning a trip to the air raid shelter, we awaited the "all clear" siren. As we huddled in the doorways—Gerry with the English girl and me with the French girl—we began kissing and embracing. I was enjoying my first air raid!

Suddenly, I became aware of the engine on the buzz bomb. It was really chugging along and as folks said, sounded like an old Maytag washer! Then, the motor stopped and it was dead silent. We realized the bomb had shut off and was diving to earth. God knows where it was headed, but it was sure to be close by.

Within 10 or 15 seconds it hit. The explosion was loud, the ground shook and the brick dust from the old building where we had taken refuge showered down on us and the street. It was thick enough that we coughed to clear our throats. The bang had been like a lightning bolt and it was very, very close. In fact, it hit about three blocks away, but the concussion was very real.

I hung on to the little French girl and she hung on to me. I tried to act brave, but the bomb had scared the devil out of me! The buzz bombs were set to fall on London, but that was as close as they could be set. They couldn't be zeroed in on a specific target. We could see the red glow in the sky, so we headed for it to see what damage had been done.

It had hit in a commercial area and completely demolished what had been a three or four story building. There was a big crater some 15 feet deep where it had buried itself. The fire brigade was on the scene putting out some adjacent fires, but everything seemed to be under control. We were told there were no casualties as those who worked there had gone home hours before. This time London got lucky.

Each weekend when it was time to go back to camp and face the week of training ahead, we would catch the very last train out of London. It left Paddington Station at 1:45 a.m. and if you missed it, you were going to be AWOL at Monday morning's formation. I still wonder how it was that we never missed that train!

Even though the weekend was over, we were always thinking about the next weekend or even the remaining hours before our passes expired. Accordingly, we would board the train and before they turned out the lights and pulled out of the station, we would check the scene out carefully. We did this by walking the length of the train, peering into each compartment to see if any interesting opportunities existed to meet unescorted young ladies!

Two females traveling alone presented an opportunity to get acquainted during the two-hour trip to Swindon where we had to detrain. If no such opportunity presented itself, we would look for two bench seats and hope to catch some sleep during the trip.

When we got to Swindon, we had to catch a cab to Chiselton and then walk to our area at the nearby camp where we were billeted. Then we would put on our fatigues, lie down on our bunks and get about an hour of sleep before it was time to fall out for duty. We would be dead all day Monday, but all agreed it was worth it!

One early Monday morning, Gerry Quick and I caught the train and proceeded to go through our "checkout" procedure. This particular trip, there were no eligible females available, so we decided to settle down near a compartment occupied with some American sailors. They had several quart bottles of Sterling Beer, the first we had seen since we had left the States.

We learned that one of the sailors had married a London girl and the other four sailors were his buddies who had come along to wish him well. Now they were all returning to the Portsmouth area where the sailors were land-based. The beer was flowing freely and the wedding party was feeling no pain!

We accepted their offer of some of the American beer and sat down in the aisle by their compartment. Soon, before we were an hour out of the station, all were asleep, including the new bridegroom. Gerry was napping out in the aisle and I was soon nodding off as I sat in the compartment doorway.

After a while, I became aware of someone feeling my leg. It was dark in the blacked-out passenger car and the only light that filtered in was from a star sparkling outside in the sky. I finally realized that the hand on my knee was that of the English bride who appeared to be asleep like all her friends as well as her new husband!

I was awake immediately and my heart began beating like mad! I moved away, but her hand followed my leg. I guess it was curiosity that kept me there as I knew I should move further away. However, I didn't and the hand moved higher and higher and finally it reached the "never, never" zone!

The bridegroom and his four sailors buddies were all snoring and appeared to be dead asleep—or dead drunk. Nevertheless, I knew I had to get up. I arose and went out into the aisle and told Gerry what had happened. We moved a distance down the aisle and were talking about what we should do, when "here comes the bride"!

I have heard of women attacking men and I never believed the stories, but before I knew what was happening, this woman grabbed me and began kissing me and was all over me! It was plain what her intentions were and it was me she was after and not her new husband. I was totally shocked!

She said her husband and his friends were all passed out and she wanted sex with me right there in the aisle! She said that they'd never know her secret as to the trick she had pulled on her wedding night! Well, that was more than enough for me. I pulled myself away from her and Gerry and I started moving down through the coaches toward the engine as fast as we could!

I feared it was some kind of set up and that the sailors would come piling out of that compartment any minute. Gerry and I kept moving through car after car until I was afraid we would be in the locomotive soon if we didn't reach the Swindon station! I was seriously considering whether a jump from the train could be made without serious injury.

We seemed to make good our escape as there was no sign of the sailors or the amorous bride when the train pulled into Swindon. We got off the train fast and headed for the taxi stand. It was comforting to disappear into the darkness and head for the relative safety of the camp!

I have often felt sorry for that poor sailor. He certainly had poor taste in women and the one he had married was a real looser! That marriage had little or no chance to last. That bimbo just wanted a ticket to the U.S.A. She didn't care a bit about that sailor. He probably found it out sooner or later. I was just glad I didn't have to jump off that train!

CHAPTER 38
YOU'RE NEVER FAR FROM HOME

One of the most rewarding things that could happen to a guy while in service was to be able to get to see and talk to a friend from their hometown. We had uncles and nephews get together and even brothers meet for a brief visit. It was like getting to go home for a few moments.

I guess I got my share of this, but I sure could have used more! To begin with, Bob Pearce, Robert Isbell, Tom Uhl, Ken Holloway, and Dick Lacefield were all Bowling Green friends and we were all in the 17th Airborne Division at the same time. Later, Jimmie Spencer and Joe Petty also joined the 17th.

Pearce, Izzie, Joe and Tom were Bowling Green natives and had been friends of mine for years. Ken and Jimmie were friends from college days. And, although I hadn't known Dick Lacefield before I went in the service, he was also a Bowling Green native. He knew my family and they told him to look me up. He did so and we became good friends then and after service.

Pearce and Izzie enlisted with me and we kept together all the way to Camp Mackall. Shortly after we finished basic training, Pearce obtained an alternate appointment to Annapolis and was discharged from the army. Although he failed to make it into the academy from the Baimbridge Prep School, he remained in the navy and served the rest of his time in the fleet.

Izzie was in the 155th Airborne Anti-Aircraft Bn. and went to Tennessee with us for the January-February 1944 maneuvers. While there, he was critically injured in a jeep accident and after a long hospitalization and several operations, he was assigned to limited service and finally medically discharged.

Tom Uhl, unlike me, accepted the chance to go into the Army Specialized Training Program (ASTP) soon after we arrived at Camp Mackall. He was sent to Georgetown University in Washington. When ASTP was closed down, he was transferred to the 13th Airborne Division and completed jump school. He went to Europe with them, but the division was never committed.

Ken Holloway, who married Ruby Nell Jones from my high school graduating class, also seized the opportunity to go to ASTP. After the program closed, he was accepted into OCS, made a career out of the military and retired as a major.

Jimmie Spencer, who was from Grayson, Kentucky, had been a friend of mine during my abbreviated college days. Jimmie had also been in ASTP and was assigned to the 17th Airborne's Quartermaster Company shortly before we left Camp Forrest for overseas. I just happened to spot Jimmie on the train as I returned to camp after a short furlough at home.

Jimmie married a girl named Mickey McQuire who had also been a student at the

Business University. I got with Jimmie several times both at Camp Forrest and then while we were in England. The first weekend in December 1944, Dave Phipps, another old BU friend, came to see us. Dave had been in the 491st Armored Field Artillery Battalion and had been wounded in France. We went to Swindon and had our picture taken. I can't believe I did this, but I wore a British battle blouse that day and managed to avoid the MPs! We enjoyed a great day together talking old times.

Joe Petty was an old friend from Bowling Green, but I never got to see him while we were in the division. We had played football together at Bowling Green High School and he was one hell of a competitor. He was a demolitions man and had joined the 513th while we were in England. By the time I found out he was actually in the division, we were moving into combat and it was too late for us to get together.

I had never met Dick Lacefield before going into service, but the name was familiar. Someway, he was advised I was in the division and one day at Camp Mackall, he walked in my barracks and introduced himself. He was in Division G-2 and his duties included responsibility for photography. He offered to try to get me transferred to Division Headquarters if I was interested. Like a fool, I declined!

Later, while we were in England, he had me come over to his work station where he took some great photos of me to send home. It was a rainy night and I rode a GI bicycle over to his shop. I was in fatigues from the waist down and Class A uniform from the waist up! You sure can't tell it from the photos!

We both knew the reason for taking the pictures, but we never mentioned it. I truly thought it might be the last thing my parents got to remember me by. After the war was over Dick and I became even better friends. Until his death in 1983, we enjoyed telling and retelling stories about our days in the 17th Airborne.

One day while on pass in Swindon, England, I saw the name of John Hanes, another Bowling Green friend, in the USO register book. I left a message for John and in a few days we managed to arrange a meeting. That night, December 15, 1944, marked the last time we were given passes before the division headed for combat. The details of that meeting are related in another chapter of this book.

I tried to set up a meeting one weekend while I was in England with Morris Henderson, a friend of mine from Bowling Green, but it turned out to be a big disappointment. Morris and I had met the previous September in Charlestown, S.C. and had a fine time, but this meeting failed to come off as planned.

We agreed that we would meet at the Paddington railway station in London. Apparently we should have made more precise arrangements because as it worked out, we were both there at the correct time, but by some fluke, we failed to find each other. We each waited for an hour or so, then left thinking the other had failed to show.

One weekend while on pass from Camp Forrest to Bowling Green, I did manage to meet my old best buddy, George "Butter" Williams who was home on leave from the Navy. We had a great time seeing each other, but the time just flew.

One other good thing came from that brief meeting, I met Butter's date, Kathy Hunt, a student at BU, and on future weekend trips from Camp Forrest I dated her. She was also able to line up dates for any of my Airborne buddies who came home with me! They all thought I was quite "an operator" in Bowling Green! Believe me, they were all eager to come home with me!

I also enjoyed brief meetings at Camp Mackall with Paul Ankeny, another former student at BU before the war, and Pete Egbert, who was from Bowling Green. Paul was a paratrooper assigned to XVIII Airborne Corps and Pete was a trooper with the 11th Airborne. I was in the throes of basic training, so our ways parted before we could spend any real quality time together.

All these meetings were like little mini-visits back to Bowling Green. Add to them the fact I was so lucky to be stationed at Camp Forrest and be so near home. I'll always be grateful for this stroke of good luck and the time I got to spend at home.

I am also grateful that I was able to bring so many of my buddies home with me. I know my parents enjoyed getting to know some of the fine young men that were my friends in the service. When Gerry Quick and Red Ewing were killed, it really brought the war home to them and they grieved right along with me.

CHAPTER 39
RAYMOND CHARD: THE LAUNDRY BOY

Rustic Camp Chiseldon in merry ole England lacked many modern facilities, but we seemed to be able to "make-do" almost everywhere we landed, and this location was no exception. Before very long, our engineers provided electricity to each tent, hot water showers in the bath house, a convenient water tap in our company area where we could get water to wash and shave in our tents and charcoal heating stoves that kept the tents as warm as toast.

The radio we bought helped make the tent a little more like home. We would listen to the news on the Armed Forces Network and we really enjoyed the music of Maj. Glenn Miller! Our favorite show was "Mail Bag" and it featured Miller's right-hand man, Sgt Ray McKinnley, directing the band. It was mainly a talk show with gripe letters from GIs, but we also got a lot of that smooth Miller sound!

The last piece of the puzzle seemed to fall in place when we finally found a way to get our clothes laundered and pressed at a price we could afford to pay. It was an overcast, rainy day (most days were in England) when a young lad of about 12 years of age ducked in our tent and greeted us with a smile. Our last prayers had been answered!

He introduced himself as Raymond Chard and he said his mother was interested in taking on a limited number of customers for weekly washing and ironing. The price was right too. He only had to make one sales pitch. All six of us in our tent jumped at the offer and the Chards were in business!

Raymond, or his younger brother Dennis, made the pickups and deliveries. They were always on time, rain or shine. The Chard family also included a 17-year-old sister and another two-year old brother, but we never met them.

Mrs. Chard did excellent work. The clothes were always spotless, neatly ironed and folded. I can't remember the rate she charged, but it was very reasonable and we figured we had a really good deal while paying a fair rate.

As time went by, Raymond and Dennis did a lot of other jobs for us. They were our personal valets! They brought in coke and kindling for our stove, swept out our tent, carried out the ashes and shined our boots. Raymond was saving his money to buy a "wheel", or a bicycle as we called it. He even wrote a note introducing himself to my parents and I mailed it home. Mother loved it!

We also gave the young boys a few goodies we could buy at the PX. The English people could get very little sugar during the war and candy and chewing gum were a real luxury for the kids. Soap was near impossible for civilians to obtain, so we bought soap at our PX and provided it to Mrs. Chard for our laundry.

Mr. Chard was a farmer and that, plus his sizable family, had excluded him from full-time military service. Nevertheless, like most other Englishmen, he was a member of the Home Guard. As such, he drilled a couple of nights every week learning to use an old, bolt-action rifle. I have no doubts the English were ready to stand to the last man to repel the Hun if he should dare land on their shores!

About this time the U. S. Army approved the wearing of the "Ike" Jacket. We looked at this as a great improvement over the old, ill-fitting, issue blouse. But, as might be expected, we were probably scheduled to be the last ones to be issued the new garment. The fighting troops never seem to get these new issues until everyone in the rear echelon got theirs. I also think that the Airborne came last on the Army's list as they thought we had enough special items of issue already.

One day when Raymond was delivering our laundry, we were discussing how we would like to have some of the new Ike Jackets. Always an entrepreneur, Raymond spoke up and said he could get us some jackets. Well, he admitted he didn't have a supply of the new Ike Jackets, but he did have a pipeline to obtaining British battle jackets!

We were game for anything, so we "contracted" with Raymond for some British jackets. I got one and after the old GI blouses, it felt pretty good! I wore it in to Swindon a few times on pass and although I avoided any close contact with the MPs, I experienced no trouble. Encouraged by this, I wore it to London one weekend. Although I avoided the "Snowballs" (the MPs in London all wore white helmet liners and that was our nickname for them) I managed to get away with it!

Dave Phipps, an old friend from college days back in Bowling Green, was on hospital leave and over one weekend came to our camp to visit with Jim Spencer and me. During the weekend we went in to Swindon and had our picture made. I still have that photo and that British blouse could hardly be mistaken for an Ike Jacket! Dave said I hadn't changed a bit from college days except he noticed I had joined the Limey Army!

I have often wondered what happened to our laundry that the Chards had when we were suddenly alerted, sent to the continent and into combat. Not that the loss of the clothes made any difference to us, but the Chards were so conscientious, I feel sure they worried themselves to death about not being able to deliver our things back to us. We also felt bad about it because they had done all that work and we'd never be able to pay them.

It is hard to realize that the 12 year-old lad who used to come for our laundry, if he's still alive, is a man about 64 years old! I wonder if he had children of his own and if they were the hustling businessman their father was. Raymond Chard was a fine lad and I feel sure he was successful in life.

CHAPTER 40
THE REPLACEMENTS

I think one of the toughest jobs in the Army was to be a replacement. Replacements were treated like so much meat by the people in the supply system. They were tossed in with a group of fellows who all knew each other and as newcomers, they were usually completely ignored.

Replacements were usually left to fend for themselves, told nothing and given all the dirty details. Even worse, if one was killed, seldom did anyone remember his name or feel any deep sense of remorse. Mostly, the veterans seemed to feel that if they got too close to the new guys they would jinx them or themselves.

I had only a few occasions where I came in contact with replacements. Had I returned to my company before the Rhine operation, I would have had an opportunity to be one myself. Due to taking so many casualties, all units had to be completely rebuilt and restaffed. In fact, the entire 193rd Glider Infantry Regiment was deactivated and the survivors of the Bulge combat absorbed into the 194th as replacements.

The first experience we had with getting replacements was in mid-September, 1944, in England when the Table of Organization and Equipment (TO&E) of the Glider Regiments was changed. One of the changes saw each of the rifle squads receiving two additional men to serve as a Bazooka team. The Bazooka was the shoulder-fired rocket tube which served us as an anti-tank weapon. These guys were really additions rather than replacements, but it had the same effect. The majority of us had been together for over a year and now about 12 new faces suddenly joined the company.

Another change saw us get two additional machine guns in the weapons platoon. These were the A-2 version of the .30 Browning A-1. They were equipped with a shoulder stock and had a bipod which was attached. They resembled the Browning Automatic Rifle, but were capable of firing continuously with belt ammunition. I would guess this added another eight or ten new men to the company.

Soon after we arrived in England we were assigned 2nd Lt. Bill Rudicel as our new platoon leader. Bill was a nice fellow and treated everyone very fairly. We became good friends after the war and when he died in 1995 of cancer, we were really saddened.

We also got an extra officer while we were in England. I guess this was backup in anticipation of combat losses. He was 2nd Lt. William A. Millerich and he became a casualty himself during our first week on the continent. He had to be evacuated when a German grenade he was fooling with accidentally exploded.

We also had received two or three new people just before we came off of Tennessee Maneuvers or before we left Camp Forrest. They were overflow the Army had when the

ASTP program was shut down. Most of these people were assigned to the Headquarters section as over-strength or with rather vague duties. I think they were beefing-up our strength as they knew we would take a lot of combat losses.

I will admit that I hardly knew these people had joined the company and today I find it impossible to remember their names. I do remember one guy named John Bengiovanni who had been a tailor in New York City in civilian life. He made a lot of extra cash in England by altering and tailoring our uniforms. His specialty was to cut down the regular GI blouse to resemble the newly-introduced "Ike" jacket.

Another one of the new guys that joined us in England was Don "Ike" Eckholt. I don't recall him from those days, but from our attendance at post-war 17th Airborne Reunions. I have become quite fond of the big, gentle giant who is now an Iowa farmer! It bothers me that back when I know he must have needed friends in the strange company to which he had been assigned, I didn't think to make the effort to become acquainted with him.

One other sad incident looms in my memory. We were in England and had just received our November pay. That night in the tents the crap games went on until lights out. I won my share at dice and this month I was hot! So, the next day, I was still wanting to keep the game going. We were scheduled for a glider flight that day and there was the usual two-hour delay while we waited for the Air Corps to arrive on the scene.

As we lounged around the glider, I got another crap game going. As was true the night before, I was still hot and one by one I broke every guy in the game. This one particular replacement, whose name I can't recall, hung with me and seemed determined to beat me. I was too hot, however, and the game ended with me taking every cent he had. In all, I had pocketed several hundred dollars and I sent it home in money orders.

A few weeks later we were on the continent and in combat. One day someone told me about the guy that I had cleaned out in the crap game. Seems like almost the first day after we had been committed, an 88 landed near him and a big chunk of shrapnel hit him in the head like an axe. He was dead before he hit the ground.

I felt bad about it, but then someone told me the guy was married and had two young children. He had volunteered for the military and volunteered for the Airborne. Then I really felt bad. Why did he have to volunteer for that crap game? I decided I would send some money to his wife, but like now, I couldn't remember his name. As good as my intentions might have been, they were lost in the confusion and terror of the combat that followed.

I had one more occasion to sense how replacements felt. This came after my first hospitalization and on the way back to my company. I was sent to a Replacement Depot (Repple Depple, as we called them) from which I was to be trucked up on the line to the location of my company. Here I was thrown with dozens of other guys who were joining companies as completely green replacements.

Most of the time those of us who were rejoining our old units just lay around sleeping or writing letters home. It was pretty plain that none of us were in a hurry to get back to the war. The new guys were all excited and continually pumped us as to what was it like. They wanted to know such things as how it felt to kill someone, how many of our guys had been wounded, or did we have to sleep out in all this snow and cold!

I remember some of the guys told them bare-faced lies and delighted in seeing their eyes nearly pop out at their wild tales of horror! I didn't engage in any of this, but I do remember how young they looked and how green they were. I wondered just how long most of them would last. At this point, I didn't want to know their names. I didn't want to get too close to any of them.

Since those days several of the guys who joined us as replacements have become friends of mine in the 17th Airborne Association. Today there is no distinction between those of us who were with the division when it was activated and those who joined it later. And, that's as it should be. We all shared a common goal, suffered together and as survivors, we are all brothers.

CHAPTER 41
I REMEMBER LILLY

It was a cool, Sunday afternoon late in October, 1944. My buddy, Ray Crabtree from West Virginia, and I were passing the day window-shopping and girl-watching in London. Soon it would be time to head for Paddington Station to catch the train back to Swindon and from there go by bus or taxi to our camp. Another weekend of "R and R" was about to come to an end.

It was a four-hour trip from our tents outside Chiselton to the big city, but the trip was always worth it. We never seemed to get free until noon on Saturday and by the time we got cleaned up, caught a ride into Swindon and then waited for the train, it was nearly dark when we arrived in London.

We would get something to eat first and then start hitting the pubs. Most of the time we'd "score". Somewhere there would be a couple of pretty, young English lasses who were attracted to two young paratroopers in shiny boots and cocked caps. Then, we tried to make Saturday night last as long as we could!

Most of the time, after we had spent a lot on them, we'd end up taking them home and it all ended there. Sometimes they'd even excuse themselves to go to the "WC" and then, when we weren't looking, they'd take off. However, frequently we would hit it lucky and they would take us home with them! Our average was just good enough to make us eager to come back to London every weekend that we could get a pass!

This particular trip to London wasn't one of our best efforts. We had "struck out" the night before, so Ray and I had spent the night at the Union Jack Club. Actually, the place was like a USO Club, but only for members of "His Majesty's Forces". However, if you got there real late, the clerk on the desk was usually sleepy or drunk, or both, and he never looked at you too closely. It was the best and cheapest place in London to sleep and the breakfast they served was super!

Ray and I had ridden the Underground to Hyde Park. We liked to walk through there and listen to all the crackpots that came there to preach on their own special hate. Standing on their soapboxes, they were self-proclaimed experts on everything from weird religions to how the Americans were a pox on their soil. It was a real zoo.

We were on the Underground escalator moving upward toward the street exit when I saw her. Lilly and a friend were on the down escalator heading for the lower level where the passengers could board the "tube". She was blond, with a "peaches and cream" complexion and moist lips that smiled when our eyes met.

I really don't know what got into me, but I felt that if I didn't act instantaneously, she would be gone out of my life forever, and I knew I couldn't let that happen. Without saying a word to Ray, I scrambled over the space separating the two escalators and onto the stairs heading down with them.

Lilly and her friend were quite surprised, as was everyone else in the immediate area. The British were hardly used to such goings on! But, I'm sure they must have tossed it off as "just another crazy American" and sighed at the price they had to pay in return for our help in beating the Hun.

When we reached the lower level, I was talking fast, trying to find out where they were going, and could we go with them. I knew I had to delay them until Ray reached the top of the stairs and could come back down to our level. This took a few minutes, but before too long, we had talked ourselves into a guided tour of London.

Although I guess this started out as just another pickup, it began to be something more than that almost immediately. At least it was for me. I was smitten by the beauty and sweet, gentle personality I found in Lilly. I really didn't know how genuinely lonely I had been until I met her.

We saw all the sights in London that Sunday. From Westminister Abbey to where the latest buzz bomb had landed. I could hardly take my eyes off Lilly. Her voice was soft and like music. Her British accent captivated me and I strained to hear every word she whispered.

We took them to dinner that evening and soon they said they had to go home as they had promised their "Mums" they would not be out late. These were definitely not the type of English girls we had been used to meeting on our trips to London!

Ray wasn't too excited about the date I had found for him. He had been looking for something—well, a little different. I had been too, but after seeing Lilly, I imagined that I was in love and I couldn't wait to see her the next weekend.

Several more weekends I came to London to see her and I even met her mother. I would make arrangements to meet Lilly on Saturday night and then again all day Sunday. She fixed us picnic lunches and we walked in the parks. We ate fish and chips and we had dinner in different little restaurants she knew about where the GI's didn't go. We held hands and we kissed, but Lilly was a lady and I was well aware of the fact.

I was beginning to think of Lilly as "my girl" and I wondered what would happen if one day I took her back to the States as my wife. Of course, that was out of the question for now. We all knew it was only a matter of time until we would be alerted to go into combat and many of us would not survive. It was no time to take a wife.

It was turning colder now. It had moved into December and Christmas was just around the corner. I had plans to spend Christmas weekend with Lilly. I had purchased a number of items from the PX that were in short supply to British civilians and I planned to take them to Lilly and her mother. As it turned out, I couldn't even call her that I wouldn't be coming.

Unfortunately, that weekend the situation on the continent went out of control. Von Rundsted's forces broke through in the Ardennes and the Battle of the Bulge was on. The 17th Airborne was alerted and we moved to a nearby marshaling area and began preparations for our entry into combat.

I never saw Lilly again. Even when I was wounded and sent to hospitals in England, I did not try to contact her. I was in a hospital in Wales and then in Scotland and I knew it was too far for her to travel to see me and I couldn't travel. And, to be truthful, I don't know if I really wanted to see her. I began to realize that she really didn't mean that much to me and I didn't want to lead her on.

Lying in bed all day I had a million things to think about and I was very confused and upset. Those days were a real low spot in my life. After seeing your friends blown apart right before your eyes, I don't think anyone could ever be quite the same again. We all grew up fast. We had to.

I was encased in plaster of Paris from my neck to my waist, except for my right arm, and I felt miserable. Later, after I had been told I would be shipped back to the States, I envisioned a boring stay in more hospitals and then either a disability discharge or being shipped to the Pacific as more cannon fodder for that theatre. I was not a happy camper.

Then, lying there in the hospital, a strange thing began to steal into my thoughts. I wondered what might have happened to Georgeanna, the girl back in my home town that had broken up with me some two years before. We had been sweethearts since we were sophomores in high school, but we had had a bitter parting and had both said we never wanted to see the other again.

There was more hospital time when I got back, but I mended pretty well. I went home and I married my former girlfriend. We have been very happily married now for over 52 years. We have four smart, productive grown children and eight wonderful grandchildren.

Somehow, I was able to make the right decisions about my life as I stumbled through it and today I am a happy man. But, sometimes I think about the pretty, young English girl that befriended me at a time in my life when I needed to know that the world hadn't gone completely mad.

Yes, I will always remember Lilly.

CHAPTER 42
THANKSGIVING DAY, 1944

H ow do you describe an incident in the course of your military career that was very memorable, yet deals with a delicate personal subject? I really don't know for sure, but it seems this story once recalled should be recorded. I'll try to do it in an acceptable way.

Winter was not far off. It snowed a little on November 10, 1944, but it didn't stick. No one paid it much attention. We were completely unaware of the fact Europe's worst winter in 50 years was on it's way. It was just as well we didn't know what was ahead for us. We wouldn't have liked it at all.

We were comfortably settled for the cold winter months in our tent city home at Camp Chiseldon, England. We had a wooden floor in our six-man tent, a pot-bellied stove with an ample supply of kindling and charcoal, an English radio and running water just outside our door. A foot soldier could hardly wish for more!

It would soon be Thanksgiving Day, and we would have the day off. It meant no training for that day and passes for those who wished to visit the small towns in our area. There would not be any passes for London, however, as the world's largest city was "Off Limits" to our division for the time being. It seems some of our people got in a big brawl there the week before and there would not be any London passes that week for anyone in the 17th Airborne.

But, this didn't seem to dampen the troopers' anticipation for the holiday. The messhall had received a truckload of turkeys with all the trimmings. We all had visions of sleeping late, having a fantastic meal and then maybe going in to town for a few milds and bitters—those terrible types of English beer! Ah, life was going to be so sweet!

The meal served up that day really was a fine one. Among other goodies, the 17th Airborne consumed seven tons of turkey, 1,407 pounds of candy, 93 bushels of cranberries, 703 pounds of sweet potatoes and 1,128 number 2 1/2 cans of pumpkin made into pies. There were seconds and even thirds for the hungry men.

Unfortunately, several things went wrong when that long-awaited day rolled around. The first thing was the fact I found my name on the roster for KP. Even that was not too bad, however, as it afforded me an opportunity to steal a couple of large #10 cans of fruit cocktail for my tent. That was almost a requirement for anyone on KP. He was expected to take care of the guys in his tent. Everyone did it—it wasn't even considered dishonest.

The only other thing that went wrong that day went really, really wrong. In fact, on Thanksgiving night our whole battalion practically turned into one big basket case. If the Germans had invaded England the next day, D Company and the whole battalion would have had to surrender without firing a shot. The entire battalion went down with the worse case of diarrhea that could be imagined.

The big Thanksgiving meal came off as planned. It was delicious and the guys stuffed themselves with all the goodies. I even got excused from KP that afternoon to play basketball with our company team. I made four points and my buddy Ray Crabtree, who was a good basketball player, made 10 points as B Company of the 1st Battalion beat us 44-33.

It was an easy day, as Airborne days went. We enjoyed the day away from the grind of training. Everyone went to bed that night well-fed and well-rested. It wasn't until about one or two o'clock the next morning that the entire battalion began to feel the problem.

I woke up because of all the talking outside in the company street and the moving around in our own tent. People were up and awake when normally they were sound asleep. I felt fine, but no one could sleep in all that confusion, so I got up to see what was happening.

The latrine was located down at the end of the company street and our company shared it with an adjacent company. There were only about eight seats and there was a long waiting line for each. The guys that were waiting were screaming to their buddies to hurry up and it was plain that things were getting tense.

Many of the guys never made it to a seat. Many sets of underwear were violated that night. Other troopers were seen heading over the elevated road behind the latrine with an entrenching tool in their hand. An adjoining farmer's field had many a visitor that night.

As strange as it may seem today, the English farmers in those days used human excretion as fertilizer for their fields. Maybe because it was impossible to buy fertilizer during the war years. In any event, the latrines were built over huge "honey buckets", as we called them, and on a regular basis some farmer in a horse-drawn wagon would come by, gather the full buckets and leave empty ones.

I can assure you that the farmer that came to our latrine the next day must have thought he had hit the mother of all jackpots. All the honey buckets did runneth over!

About 0900 (that's 9:00 a.m.) the medics finally arrived on the scene. By this time most of the guys were so weak and dehydrated that they had quieted down some. Everyone was in bed too sick to lift their head. Everyone that is, except me!

I couldn't believe this! I had been on KP all day, had eaten a ton of turkey, stuffed myself with dressing, downed cranberry sauce by the tablespoonful and really pigged out on pumpkin pies. I had a little growling in my stomach and felt a cramp or two, but I never went out of control like everyone around me. Was I inhuman or just mighty lucky?

The medics converted the big tent we used for a dayroom into a first aid tent. They moved in gallons of thick, creamy pink medicine and rounded up everyone and made them come to the tent for a dose of the disgusting liquid. The line that formed must have had over a hundred troopers in it. Others were too weak to line up and had to be treated in their bunks.

The medics in the first aid tent apparently had only two or three spoons, so as fast as one trooper got his medicine, they would dip the spoon in a glass of water and then fill it up again and poke it into the next guy's mouth. It was the assembly line in its finest hour!

I was getting pretty worried about this time. Everyone was sick and I wasn't. I was afraid something was really wrong with me. Thinking maybe "an ounce of prevention may be worth a pound of cure," I decided I had better get some of that medicine before it was gone. So, I got in line and took the medicine like everyone else.

This may sound funny at this time, but let me assure you it was not a laughing matter at that time. Guys would get a spoonful of the medicine and then go to the rear of the line and line up for seconds. Some troopers would have to leave their place in line to rush to the latrine.

Needless to say, they had to cancel the training program for the battalion the next day. The order read "care and cleaning of equipment" but for one time that was the honest truth. Never did our equipment need cleaning any more than it did that day.

Everyone laid around all day and finally, by late afternoon the misery subsided. The guys began to get up and walk around some, drink some liquids and maybe even by the end of the day, eat some light food. The emergency apparently was confined to our battalion as I later learned the 507 PIR beat the 513 PIR 20 to 0 in a football game that afternoon. Not a single trooper in our battalion could have played football that day!

I came through this whole incident with only a touch of the dreaded "GIs". For some reason, despite being on KP, it just never hit me like it did the rest of the guys. I was quite thankful to be spared, but I was smart enough not to show I wasn't sick like the others. I knew if I did, I would be put to work taking care of the sick and doing all the other company chores. You learn to take care of yourself when you're a private. If you don't, no one else will!

CHAPTER 43
THE LAST PASS

O
ne night about three weeks before Christmas of 1944, I went into the nearby town
of Swindon on an evening's pass. The battalion ran a truck in every night during
the week and the round trip gave the troopers about five or six hours to fool around
town.

One diversion was to go roller skating. It was a popular sport at that time and more
importantly, the skating rink was a gathering place for the young ladies of the area.
Outside of going to the cinema, lounging around the USO and patronizing the street
venders selling "fish and chips", there was little else to do. Nevertheless, it did offer a
break from camp life.

On this particular night, I visited the USO. There was really nothing to do there,
but I thought I'd look the place over. While there, I chanced to glance at the register. This
was a big book, divided into countries—and even states of the United States. The GIs
would register their names and addresses in hopes of finding someone from their
hometown.

Although I had grown accustomed to never finding anyone registered from
Bowling Green, nevertheless, I looked at the Kentucky section. Lo and behold, there was
the name of John Hanes, an old friend from home! His address listed was that of a hospital
very near Swindon.

I copied down his address and the next day wrote a letter to him, asking if we could
meet in Swindon at the USO at a set time. The evening we agreed upon to meet was
December 14, 1944. It would be nice to see someone from home and John and his brother,
Ed, were both good friends of mine. I looked forward to seeing John and "talking home"
with him. Besides, it was almost Christmas and it would be nice to see someone from home
at this time of year.

Although we didn't know it at the time, early on the morning of December 16, the
Germans would begin their Ardennes offensive. The Battle of the Bulge was about to start,
but I don't believe the top brass—and surely the troops in England—had really grasped
the seriousness of the situation. Our division had not been alerted, but we all had a feeling
things were heating up and it wouldn't be long.

The day of our planned meeting, our division was ordered on a semi-alert. Only
10% of the company was permitted to go on pass that night and these passes were limited
to six hours and to the immediate area. We didn't know it at the time, but that was the last
time passes would be given before we headed for combat. Fortunately, I got to be part of
the 10% that night and my meeting with John came off as planned.

We talked about home and other friends we had heard from and got "caught up"
on home events. Then we walked around town for awhile, stopped at a friendly pub and

had a beer and then walked some more. We went by the skating rink and for a while we put up with the din associated with that place.

John had been a squad leader for an infantry company fighting in France. A sniper had winged him and he had been evacuated to the hospital near Swindon to recover from his wound. At this stage of my young military career, I was all questions. How was combat? How did it feel to be hit? And, was it difficult to pull the trigger on another human being? I was showering him with dumb questions!

John was not very comfortable with all my questions. He was mostly content to say that I would find out soon enough and avoided any direct answers. To the contrary, I was "gung-ho" at this stage of the game and freely expressed my eagerness to "get at the Krauts" and to help end this war!

I will forever remember John saying "wait until you get in the middle of it and you'll wish you were back here in England!" Only later was I to learn how right he was. But, that evening I must have sounded pretty silly as I told him it would soon be over once the 17th Airborne got into the fight!

Soon it was time to be heading for the trucks and to catch our rides back to our respective billets: John to the hospital and me to Camp Chiseldon. John's truck was to load at one end of town and mine was to pick up its load of soldiers at the other end of town. We made plans to meet again a few nights later and I told John I would walk with him to his ride before returning for mine.

As we walked down the street, we passed two young ladies heading the other way and they spoke to us in a very friendly, "come-on" style. With that, I forgot all about walking John to his ride or even catching mine! I grabbed them by the arms and yelled to John to come with us as we headed down a side street!

To John's credit, he said no thanks, wished me luck and continued on to catch his ride. That was the last I ever saw of John until well after the war was over and we were back in Bowling Green, both civilians again.

When I returned to camp, we were alerted two days later and by Christmas we were in combat. I often thought about what John had said about combat and how when I got there I would wish I was back in England. He was 100% right on that score and I quickly realized how stupid my remarks about anticipating combat must have sounded to him.

That marked the end of my adventures in the British Isles! What, you may ask, happened to me and the two lasses with whom I disappeared into Swindon's blackout that night? Ah ha! That's another chapter I must write——someday!

Friends from home! My parents and my girlfriend, Georgeanna Banks, visited me at Camp Mackall during the summer of 1943.

You're in the army now! Four Bowling Green boys at Camp Mackall. Rear left: Tom Uhl, rear right: Bob "Izzie" Isabel, front left: Bob Pearce and front right: that's me.

A 10-minute break during basic training in North Carolina. Standing: cadre S/Sgt Andy Ondich; L to R: Adrian Test, Paul Moffett, Carl Royce and Dale English.

The best soldier I ever knew: S/Sgt Charles Pierre on leave with his Sam Brown belt and the glider pilot wings on his cap!

A large crowd gathered during the lunch hour to see Don Wonderly and me (that's me with my back to the camera) slug it out behind the 1st Platoon barracks.

That's me behind our 1st Platoon barracks at Camp Mackall, ready to fall out for another fun-filled day of basic training!

That's the 1st Platoon taking a break during basic training. We were in our hot and dusty training area at Camp Mackall. Basic was the toughest 14 weeks any of us ever had!

As second gunner for our mortar squad, I had to be ready to take over at any time. Here I sharpen my skills as gunner during a dry fire exercise at Camp Mackall.

Buddies Ernie Stull, left, and Ray Crabtree were frequent companions of mine when we could get passes. Ernie's old Dodge (background) sure came in handy in North Carolina!

That's me standing in front of Camp Mackall movie Theater No. 2, the only place on camp where it was cool! "Squadron Leader X" was showing this day!

This was our PX (Post Exchange) at Camp Mackall. Hardly compares to our present day malls, does it?

S/Sgt Gerry Quick, one of my best buddies, who was killed in the Rhine Airborne operation.

I was on duty as Latrine Orderly this day! It wasn't considered demeaning, but a nice break from a rough day in the field.

That's me in the gas mask, hamming it up! This was during basic training at Camp Mackall and those summer days were hot and dirty.

S/Sgt Leroy "Mac" McCaslin and I engage in a little roughhouse with a knife mostly for the benefit of the camera! Photo made in front of our barracks at Camp Forrest in June, 1944.

The sign puzzled us at first because we had never heard of glider infantry!

Camp Forrest, May 1944, in the area in front of our supply room. That's me joking with Sgt Henry "Brownie" Browning, "the old mother hen"! Directly behind me is "Mary" Ryan, then Roger Gardner, other members of our motar squad.

This was one of our company mess areas set up in a clearing while we were on a field problem in North Carolina. Sgt. Antonio Genovese keeps an eye on two KPs reluctantly peeling spuds!

Dressed in full paratrooper gear and just graduated from jump school! Photo made in June, 1944, at Camp Forrest.

The front stairs of our barracks at Camp Forrest. Back, left to right; Ernie Stull, "Mac" McCaslin, Ray Crabtree. Front right is Carl "Sonny" Gloor. As it was July, 1944, naturally I was cold and had put on my overcoat!

This was one of my good buddies: Robert "Red" Ewing. My short conversation with Red and his death only a few moments later, really shook me. I finally wrote his family how it happened.

This German tank, knocked out during the fighting in Houffalize, has been recovered and now serves as a monument in the center of town and a stark reminder for the people.

This is the glider we flew in. The CG-4A weighed 7, 500 lbs., had a wingspan of 83'8", was 48'4" long, carried 15 people and had a maximum towed speed of 150 mph. It was a scary craft to fly in.

Later, when the snow melted, many bodies were found in the mud and rubble of Houffalize.

There weren't many days when the fog lifted. When it did, it seemed like we were always caught in open terrain. This patrol plods through the foot-deep snow as they seek out the enemy.

The enemy lies dead. This SS trooper lies frozen where he fell. Seeing the first casualty of the war was a shocker for me. Later, we learned to ignore dead bodies.

The snow was 6-10 inches deep and the temperature hovered around zero. Tank support was seldom available and when it was, often drew artillery fire on us.

It was cold and miserable in Belgium and Luxembourg during the Battle of the Bulge. Digging in was near impossible. It was Europe's worst winter in 50 years.

Houffalize was a mess when the Americans and the Germans got through shelling the town.

During the summer of 1950, as a brand-new Second Lieutenant, I helped win the Korean War by handing out sporting equipment while acting as Recreation Officer at Fort Knox, KY.

When I finally got home, Georgeanna and I made up and life was wonderful again! See that plaster cast on my left arm?

The Army sure sent me on a paid vacation when they assigned me to the Redistribution Center at Miami Beach for 10 days! Loafing around the pool at the hotel was tough duty.

148

Service in the Army Reserve required attending a two-week summer camp each year. Here I emerge from a tear gas test room while training at Camp Gordon, GA during the summer of 1954.

That's me with no parachute and dangling 60 feet under a helicopter that eventually reached 1,000 feet! Special Forces use this method to insert personnel into deep jungle canopy.

April 1963; In the National Guard Special Forces and ready for my first jump in 19 years!

Joining the West Virginia Army National Guard's Special Forces unit in 1963, I resumed jumping after a layoff of over 18 years! I found out I was still good at it and that I loved it!

What every paratrooper wants: a full canopy! Photo taken on my way down!

In September of 1965, as a major in the Army National Guard Special Forces, I commanded some 50 troopers who attended the Mountain Warfare School in Alaska. Here I am in Fairbanks seeing the sights while on a weekend pass.

150

During the training in Alaska, we actually learned to climb up steep mountain faces like this using only ropes and petons. When we first arrived we all thought it would be impossible.

The "Slide for Life"! We constructed this line and rode some 100 yards down off of Black Mountain Glacier to the ground. We also learned to rig a litter to lower an injured person.

Here I am ready to board an Israeli CH-53 helicopter for a tour of recent battle areas along the Israeli-Lebanese border.

In Israel we were flown to Beaufort Castle, an Israeli outpost in the Golan Heights on the Lebanese border. The weapon belongs to the Israeli soldier in the center and it was for real!

Special Forces, July 1967; Annual Field training and my duty included supervising demolitions training! Fortunately, I had some NCOs who knew something about it!

At a 17th Airborne Division Association reunion in Memphis in 1983, I chatted with some old comrades. L to R; me, former Capt. Jerry Stuhrman, buddies Phil Recupero and Art Jastal.

On a trip back to the Ardennes area, in 1989, I stood in front of the monument at Bastogne and the panel honoring the three Airborne divisions that fought in the Battle of the Bulge.

PART IV:
COMBAT

CHAPTER 44
WE LAND IN FRANCE

While we were in England, I often wondered just how it would be when our company finally left for the continent and combat. When and how would all the training at last come to an end and the reality of combat begin? What would our reaction be? Would it be a dramatic moment or would it be rather routine? Would we be excited or calm? Would there be fear?

As we were an Airborne outfit, naturally I envisioned that we would be told one day that we were heading for the airport. We would be trucked to a marshalling area, briefed, issued ammo and then marched to our waiting gliders. We would be committed before we really had time to sweat it out.

Our division had been in England since August 26, and we had grown quite comfortable with the quaint English way of life. We had scouted out all the nearby towns and we knew where the good pubs and the pretty girls were. And, we looked forward to the weekends when we could visit London!

I had met a nice girl in London and with Christmas coming, I was looking forward to spending the holiday with her. In anticipation of this, I had purchased some gifts from the PX for her and her mother. I was literally counting the days until Christmas as it would be a long weekend for us.

It was about 1700 hours, Monday afternoon, December 18, and I had drawn guard duty. It didn't upset me at all because that meant I probably could count on being free of any duty on Christmas and nothing should interfere with my plans for a weekend in London.

I reported to the Regimental Stockade as ordered and entered upon my duties. I was a bit chagrined to find that my duty for the next day was to be acting as a "prisoner chaser" for Joe Miller, a trooper from my own platoon. He was awaiting a court martial for being absent without leave (AWOL).

Joe Miller certainly was not a trouble maker or the type of person you'd expect to find in a confinement facility. In fact, once we got into combat he even won the Bronze Star for valor. He was a capable soldier, well-liked among his comrades and just a nice fellow.

Joe had gone to London on pass one weekend, met a girl and thought he had fallen in love. He was just unable to tear himself away. One day became a week and that became two weeks and so on. When he finally turned himself in, the AWOL charge was a foregone matter.

That whole day I followed around behind Joe while he policed up Camp Chisledon. He had a big "P" on the back of his jacket and I carried an unloaded carbine at sling arms. We talked and he told me of the fun he had living in the big city and dreaming he was a civilian again. He almost had me wishing I could do the same. He was also smart enough to have a return train ticket in his wallet, so they couldn't charge him with desertion.

That afternoon at the proper hour, I returned him to the stockade. I was then surprised to be told by the guard commander to take Joe to his company orderly room and report to the Company Commander. I had noticed some frenzied activity in some of the company areas, but I was entirely unprepared for what I found when we reached the Company D area.

Everyone was running about shouting and giving orders and there was a giant bonfire going near the supply tent. We knew something was up, but it came as a surprise when they told me we had been alerted. Someone shouted that we were going into combat. At last, finally the day had come!

Anxious to officially discharge my duties as a guard, I took Joe to the orderly room as directed. Captain Stuhrman was not there and I was told to take Joe to the supply room. So, the two of us, me still carrying the carbine and Joe still in his prisoner jacket, reported to the supply room.

The supply sergeant ignored my explanation as to why I was there and handed Joe a M-1 rifle, several bandoleers of ammo and a half dozen hand grenades. There I stood like a fool, guarding a man who was better armed than I. It was plain what was happening; the balloon was going up! Wishing Joe good luck, I returned to my own tent to find out what I needed to do next.

Within a couple of hours, all of us had sorted through our belongings and arranged them in an "A" bag and a "B" bag. Only a few of us would ever see those bags again. We also drew ammunition and weapons and soon everyone was ready to move. Everything else—including any extra items that we were not authorized—went into a giant bonfire just behind the supply tent. Reluctantly, as I had two new pairs of boots, I tossed the jump boots I had worn in jump school into the fire.

Soon a column of deuce-and-a-halves pulled up and the company loaded in. We were off to the airport where we fully expected to load into gliders for a long, bumpy ride to France and into the combat zone. We were only half right. We went to France, but not by glider. This time we would travel by C-47s and eventually enter combat by jumping out of a GI truck.

It was early in the evening of December 19 when the 193rd reached the airfield. It could have been Aldermaston, but to me at that time it was just another airfield. Our division would move to France from seven different airfields: Ramsbury, Welford Park, Greenham Common, Membury, Aldermaston, Chalgrove and Chilbolton. All were within 30 to 50 miles of London.

We moved into a tent city which was to serve as our marshalling area. We had hardly dropped our gear before we were called out to go to briefings. This is when the whole thing began to make sense. It also put to rest a dozen rumors that had been making the rounds.

By this time, we'd all heard of the new offensive the Germans had launched on December 16th, but as yet the phrase "Battle of the Bulge," had not been coined. We were told that the enemy had broken through and was headed for the Meuse River and we were to be a blocking force. We would have the almost-impossible job of defending an 80 mile front running from Verdun north to Givet.

There was no hint of desperation or that the enemy might make it all the way to Antwerp. The picture I think we all got was that there was a shortage of troops and because of this situation, it was a good opportunity for us to have our baptism of fire and see some action before we were committed in an Airborne role.

I don't remember the briefing being very extensive or in great detail. Several companies—I don't think it was our whole 2nd Battalion—were led into a GI-type theater and some officer pointed to a huge map and told us where the enemy was and outlined in general, the line we presently held. I really don't recall it looking anything like a "Bulge." And, the way he talked it didn't strike us as being such a dire emergency and certainly not the beginning of the largest land battle of World War II.

We were given small invasion flags to sew on our jackets, but few of us did. I still have mine. What bothered me was the American soldiers walking around the area in German uniforms. I guess it was intended to get us used to seeing Germans. They sure looked frightening to me dressed in those uniforms as they strolled around the area. It shocked me to realize that after all this time, I was about to meet up with soldiers that looked like this. And, they would be trying to kill me!

Early the next morning we loaded ammo and other supplies into some trucks and climbed in for a ride out to where the C-47s were parked. Our truck had a load of cloverleaves of .60 mm mortar ammunition. As I was in a mortar squad, I supposed this ammo was for our tube. It was more ammo than we had fired throughout our training during the past 20 months.

We toiled and sweated as we loaded the ammo into the C-47 and lashed it to the floor rings. Finally, it was done and we left a guard at the plane as we were trucked back to the marshalling area. Here we set about getting our personal gear ready with a takeoff expected before nightfall.

After a few hours, we were ordered back into the trucks and returned to the planes. The C-47s, we were told, were to be used to make parachute supply drops at some place called Bastogne, a small Belgian town of some 4,000 people. Our mission had been scrubbed, so we had to unload all the ammo and pile it off the pavement near the edge of the field. The spot was located near the end of one of the long runways. It was good exercise, but we certainly weren't happy about the extra work.

Again we placed a couple of guards on our pile of ammo. This meant each member of our squad would pull two hours of guard duty. My shift came that afternoon just before dark. It proved to be an exciting two hours and I wouldn't have missed it for anything.

Apparently, this field could be used as an emergency landing field for bombers returning from missions over the continent. Several B-24s returning from daylight bombing missions over the continent landed right in front of us and they were all shot up badly. We could see big chunks out of the wings and pieces of the tail missing. Some had engines that were not working. All seemed to be landing too fast as if their brakes were out or the runways were too short. The crash trucks and fire trucks were running wild and it was very exciting and a little scary.

About 300 hundred yards from where we were, we could see a B-24 that had apparently crash-landed several days before. It had gone off the end of the runway and ended up in some farmer's field. The mechanics apparently had cannibalized the plane for parts, but I suspect the neighbors had carried off some of it. We explored the wreck and found chaff everywhere. Chaff is actually small strips of tinfoil that the bomber crews throw out to foul up the enemy's radar. I would see more of this when we got to Europe.

Finally, on December 23, we got the C-47s back and we re-loaded our ammo and stood by ready to go. Unknown to us at the time, our division's seaborne element was already in France. Our airborne element got the word to go about 0900 and before midnight we were airborne over the English Channel.

Aboard our plane the guys slumped in the cold metal bucket seats and tried to act "cool" about the whole thing. Some joked, some smoked and others appeared lost in their thoughts. Some went to sleep, either from exhaustion or in anticipation of what was ahead. I think I dozed some, but I'm not sure what my feelings were. Actually, I don't remember being too excited.

If I had known what was going on that very moment in the English Channel below me, I would have been quite anxious, but glad to have been in that C-47. After the war, I learned that elements of the 66th Infantry Division, also alerted for Bulge duty as we had been, were aboard two converted cargo ships and on their way from Southhampton to Cherbourg. A German U-boat torpedoed one of the ships and 800 troops were lost. It was the worst disaster to a troopship carrying U. S. personnel during World War II.

As we neared the airfield in the vicinity of Rheims, the crew chief came back and told our officers that they had been advised by radio that there had been enemy parachutists dropped in the area where we would land and that they were occasionally firing on the planes as they came in.

This report had been blown out of proportion when German Colonel Friedrich von der Heydte kicked off the offensive by parachuting in a force of some 1,200 men. Just as it had helped the Americans on D-Day when the troopers had been badly scattered, we were misreading the German drop as being much stronger and wider-spread than it actually was. The ill-fated German mission scattered the parachutists far north in the Ninth Army area, some even beyond Aachen. They were in no position whatsoever to jeopardize our operation.

We also were told that enemy aircraft had strafed the field earlier that day. German planes had been up that day and several airfields were strafed. Whether ours was, I am not sure. But, when that information was relayed to us, it got so quiet in that airplane, you could have heard a pin drop!

We were instructed that when we landed one squad would serve as security and the rest of us would unload the ammo. The pilot would idle the motors until that was accomplished. Obviously, the unloading had to be done with great haste as the fly boys wanted to get out of there. I didn't blame them.

We unloaded in a hurry with the thought in our minds the sooner it was done, the sooner we could get away from the plane. To us, it represented a big fat target. In record time, the plane was unloaded and the ammo moved to a nearby wooded area. Soon all the planes taxied away and we were alone in a dark, threatening new country with the idea that the enemy was observing our every move.

The best I can determine, it was Laon/Couvron Airfield, designated as A-70, where we landed at about 0100 Christmas eve morning. If this was true, we were just northwest of Rheims and about 75 miles west of the farthest German penetration. We might have been green to this combat thing, but we moved swiftly and did the job properly. Training came to our aid that night.

We took up perimeter positions in the woods and awaited the next move. Along about now we suddenly realized that it was beginning to snow. It was almost Christmas and

France was getting dressed for the holiday season. We didn't know it then, but Luxembourg and Belgium already had a fluffy coat of snow that had fallen three days before. Soon the word came to fall in on the road in a column of twos. It was still the same old army—we were getting ready to go on another road march.

After a short mile walk down the road, we came upon a column of empty trucks. We could hardly believe it. Were we actually going to get to ride into combat? The word came down: we were going to be trucked to a place called Moumellon where we would be billeted. We wondered how long we would be there.

My mortar squad was first on one of the trucks so we moved toward the cab. The seats were up, everyone had to stand, so Al Barclay and I stood at the very front overlooking the cab and watched the troopers load on the truck in front of us. You could just barely see with the truck "cat-eyes" and the moon being the only light.

As the trucks filled with men, I watched Bob "Arky" Golliver climb up on the tailgate of the truck in front of us. As he pulled himself up he planted the butt of his M-1 rifle down a bit firmly in the truck bed. The safety was not on and accordingly, the rifle fired a round straight up in the air.

The noise of the rifle firing broke the stillness and the relative quiet of the night. Then Golliver began yelling and we all thought surely he had been badly wounded and maybe he was even dying.

Strange at it may seem, the armor piercing round from his rifle went up between his helmet liner and steel pot. It broke a small hole in the steel pot several inches up, then traveled over the top leaving a furrow like a mole, split open another small hole and then dropped down his collar inside his shirt. The bullet was spent by this time, but it was red hot and that's why Golliver was yelling so loudly!

Well, after that scare, the officers and non-coms all began running around screaming for everyone to check their safeties. This meant, of course, for everyone to look and see if their safety was still off and if so to move it to the safe position. That command nearly made me the first casualty in our company.

Mortarmen had a large canvas carrying case hooked on their pistol belt in which to carry their folding stock carbine. This was to leave their hands free to carry the mortar and/ or mortar ammunition. The case was made like a large canvas pistol holster. It looked a bit awkward hanging at their side, but it was a handy piece of equipment.

As Barclay was standing to my left, his carrying case was hanging at his right side pointing down between my left foot and his right. Clearly excited and not thinking, Barclay reached inside the carrying case and in order to find out if his safety was on, pulled the trigger.

You can imagine what happened next. The safety was not on and the carbine immediately fired sending a round down through the end of the carrying case and into the truck bed. Luckily, it missed both our feet, hitting one of the wooden beams that alternated with steel beams in the truck bed. Had it hit a steel beam, it could have ricocheted around and hit several of us as we were packed in there tightly.

When I realized no one was hit, I exploded. I punched Barclay in the face as hard as I could. I screamed every cuss word I knew at him and the poor guy was so stunned he never uttered a word. I realize now how up tight and keyed up we all were at this time and later I was sorry for the way I had reacted. It had been a trying night and our nerves were on edge.

When we arrived at our destination, we learned it was called Camp Mourmelon. It was located near the village of Mourmelon-le-Grand which was about 30 kilometers from the cathedral town of Rheims. When the 101st Airborne had been withdrawn from the line November 25-27, it was here that they had been sent to refit and regroup. The breakthrough in the Ardennes had caused their hasty departure about a week before.

Mourmelon-le-Grand, having a population of about 4,500 people at that time, had been a garrison town for at least 1,998 years. Julius Caesar and the Roman Legions camped there in 54 B.C. and the French had occupied the barracks for 300 years. They still do today.

Locals called the camp "Napoleon's Barracks". It also had been an important location during World War I. Situated on the plain between the Marne River to the south and the Aisne River to the north, it was right on the traditional invasion route to Paris from the Rhine. In fact, the area nearby was still scared with old trenches left from 1914-1918.

Apparently, the 101st Airborne had admired the works left by the previous tenant, the Waffen SS. Many beautiful murals that the SS artists had painted on the walls had been preserved. In the messhall I remember there were 10-foot high majestic portraits of SS soldiers that seemed to glare down at us. They may have been works of art, but they bothered us knowing where we were going.

It was about 3 a.m. Sunday morning, December 24th—Christmas eve—when we finally got settled in. After about five hours sleep, we were up and set about getting our equipment squared away. I remember we had our first taste of "10-in-1" rations. It was mostly the terrible powered eggs I remember. The one "festive" thing that happened that night was when some Frenchman came around selling wine. It cost too much and was lousy wine but it was going to be Christmas tomorrow and the wine helped us to cheer up and for a moment forget what we knew lay ahead.

We turned in early that night and were asleep in no time. Those straw tick mattresses felt pretty good. The only thing wrong was the pre-dawn call we got the next morning. There were no gifts, no Christmas tree, and no Christmas meal awaiting us, only some more powered eggs and the word we were heading for the front. Before first light, we were loaded aboard GI trucks and headed toward what would be our baptism of fire.

It sure didn't seem like Christmas.

CHAPTER 45
COMBAT READY

T here was one distinct advantage in being an enlisted man; there was always someone ready to make all of the important decisions for you. You didn't have to clutter up your mind by doing much thinking! Usually, the decisions were okay so if you followed orders you got along okay. You had to be conditioned so that when someone told you what to wear, what to carry and where to go, you complied without question.

We were definitely well-conditioned to someone else doing our thinking for us when we left Camp Mourmelon in France at about 5:00 a.m. that Christmas, 1944, morning. Otherwise, we probably wouldn't have gone because this would be our first taste of combat.

The uniform ordered was long johns, O.D. shirt and pants, wool knit sweater, combat pants, combat jacket, overcoat, boots, the newly-issued artics and steel pot. That was a lot to wear. We knew it was more than we could comfortably run with, but the temperature had now dropped to around zero so we didn't gripe about the order. We had to let out our web belts and harnesses to allow for the additional bulk. Loaded down as we were, we felt a bit clumsy.

We were also told to carry our musette bags with a clean pair of socks and underwear, a mess kit and spoon and one GI blanket. On our web belts we all carried a canteen of water, a first aid packet and a basic load of ammunition. The riflemen also carried a bayonet. Everyone carried a gas mask, an entrenching tool, and their individual weapon.

Although those of us in the mortar squads who were armed with folding stock carbines had no bayonet, we did have the large canvas carrying bag for our carbine. This holster-like bag not only left our hands free for carrying the mortar and ammunition, but there was also room for a few other comfort items such as candy and extra smokes!

We wrapped our spoon in toilet paper and put it inside the mess kit. This stopped the rattle and also provided us with a supply of the needed paper! All of us had been issued a trench knife which most of the guys carried strapped to their leg at boot level. I had purchased a fighting knife while we were in England, not knowing the trench knives were going to be issued, so I had two knives! I hung the trench knife on my web belt and strapped the fighting knife to my boot. Armed to the teeth as I was with two knives, I prayed I'd never need either one.

We also were told to bring our wool knit caps, but I didn't. That never was a favorite item of uniform with me. Somehow it made my head itch and it always seemed that there wasn't enough room in my helmet for me to wear the cap. Instead, I brought a wool OD scarf. I figured if I really got cold, I could wrap that around my head and ears.

We were all given extra ammo and ammo pouches. Those who carried carbines were given extra magazines and the riflemen were given an extra bandoleer of M-1 ammo which they swung over their shoulder. I had about seven or eight magazines and even then I wondered if that would be enough. I had visions of being in a defensive position with hundreds of Germans charging and me fumbling around trying to load rounds into a magazine! Just to be sure, I scooped up a couple of handfuls of loose carbine rounds and dropped them in my pocket!

Then we were all issued two fragmentation grenades. Some of the riflemen were also issued smoke and white phosphorus grenades. Thankfully, all I received were the two frag grenades. Even then, I was half afraid to carry them. What if the pin fell out and I didn't notice it?

We hung the grenades on the hooks on the front of our harnesses. Then we took the tape from the canister and wrapped that around the handle and bent the pin way back. This gave us some feeling of safety even if it would make the grenade a bit unhandy if we were to need it in a hurry!

We all had gloves when we started out. The best kind were the mittens with a little trigger finger. This was the type I had. Mittens were much better than gloves with individual fingers. The fingers helped keep each other warm and if separated as they are with regular gloves, they could quickly freeze in this weather.

I mentioned we all had gloves when we started out. As you know, gloves have a way of getting lost and before long we had a lot of guys who only had one glove or none at all. This was a serious situation as the weather at that time was horrible. One day while we were in the Effel Mountains we heard it was 20 degrees below zero. A few minutes with bare hands in temperatures like that usually meant frozen fingers.

No one was too excited about carrying the gas masks and many of the guys vowed to toss them away the first chance they got. The general consensus was that long ago it had been decided that poison gas would not be used in this war. Besides, we had seen that German POWs were not carrying their gas masks. That seemed to tell us something. After a couple of weeks on the line, it was hard to find anyone who still had a gas mask.

I hung on to mine for some reason although I wasn't worried about a gas attack. In fact, I had even picked up another gas mask that someone had discarded. I dumped the gas mask part and was using the canvas container to carry my rapidly-growing souvenir collection! In addition to various items I had picked up, I had a large Polish sausage and some crackers and bread I had taken from a dead German. We were always hungry!

On January 7, 1945, the day of our first attack and our hasty withdrawal, I figured I had carried both my gas mask and the souvenir bag far enough. Besides, if I was captured, it would be pretty evident to my captors that I had taken various items from their dead. That could go hard for me. I dumped both souvenir bag and gas mask by the side of the road. I didn't want to carry any extra weight that would slow me down!

We had another piece of equipment that became sort of an Airborne trademark. They issued Airborne troops a special first aid kit which included among other items, a large dressing, some sulfur tablets, and a morphine syrette. We attached these kits to the netting on the front of our helmets. That was supposed to be a handy place if we needed to get to it, but it served another unplanned purpose. It gave our helmets a distinctive silhouette. This turned out to be a big help in identifying friendlies at a distance or when it was dark.

Before we had left the marshaling area in England, we were given a small American flag. We were told to sew it on our right jacket sleeve at the shoulder, but not many of us took the time to sew it on. I put mine in my wallet and joked with my buddies that I would save it and run it up a flagpole in Berlin!

As we moved out, we were issued about four "K" rations and one or two "D" rations. These we stored in the big cargo pockets of our combat trousers. The rations weighed about a pound each and banged against our legs at each step. Fortunately, we also had heavy suspenders to help hold up our trousers!

No one refused the rations due to the extra weight. We were always concerned with food. The K's were about the size of a Cracker Jack box and contained a skimpy, but passable meal. The D's were little more than a solid chocolate bar crammed with vitamins. These rations hardly compared with the canned "C" rations or "A" rations (the hot rations prepared by our cooks) but they would keep you going!

Depending on your job, there were other items you had to carry. Our squad leader, Sgt. Henry Browning, carried the sights and aiming stakes for our mortar. The first gunner, Pfc Orville "Hungry" Linrooth, carried the mortar when it was in one piece. It weighed about 42 pounds so we usually broke it down into two pieces and when we did, he carried the bipod and I carried the base plate and tube.

We never had to go into action so quickly that it took too long to assemble the gun. All those problems we ran during training when we tried to carry it in one piece were wasted effort.

In addition to helping carry part of the mortar, in combat I also carried a "saddlebag" of ammunition. This was a canvas carrying bag with a big pocket in front and one in back. It held eight rounds of high explosive .60 mm mortar shells. The shells weighed approximately three pounds each, so a full load was about 24 pounds. Each of the four ammo bearers in our squad also carried one of these saddlebags. Thus, we had a squad load of 40 rounds before the ammo bearers had to go back for more.

Although that about covers the required equipment and clothing, every man had some personal items. Generally, this included shaving items, toothbrush and soap, but some of the guys carried items that were rather surprising. Some carried writing paper and pen, framed pictures of their girlfriends, and other items they really didn't need.

I carried my soldier's paybook, a small address book and a small copy of the New Testament. The Bible was wrapped in a waterproof plastic bag designed to carry pipe tobacco. I carried it in the left breast pocket of my combat jacket. I had read in Stars and Stripes where some guy had carried his Bible there and his life had been saved when it deflected a bullet heading for his heart. Maybe I would be so lucky!

As our days in combat began to add up and the snow continued to fall, we began to see many changes in the uniforms of the men. The most obvious was for snow camouflage. We took sheets, curtains, pillow cases—anything that could be found in the houses that would help conceal us from enemy observation. We called them our "spook suits"! Almost everyone got some white cloth for their helmets. There was a real fear of sticking your head up and knowing that against the snow background the dark helmet would make a prime target.

The best thing that happened to me in the way of clothing was a swap I made at the "Repple Depple"—the Replacement Depot— on my way back to the company after my first hospital stay. I learned the supply clerk there was handing out jeep driver-style mackinaws to replace combat jackets turned in for salvage. I immediately took my knife and ripped up my jacket and salvaged it. These coats were waterproof, windproof, came down below the waist, and had a wool lining. My new coat was warm as toast and the envy of all my buddies!

In late January we were relieved from our positions near Houffalize and began a move south to the Wiltz area. We stopped somewhere along the way for a day of rest in some barns. Here we slept, washed and shaved and cleaned up our equipment. We also got some additional clothes. I acquired another pair of long johns and put them on over the old ones. I now was wearing a regular pair of cotton underwear, two sets of long johns, OD shirt and pants, combat pants, wool knit sweater and the jeep driver mackinaw. I was layered in warmth, I just hoped I could walk!

After we had been in combat a few days, I acquired a couple of handy items. One was a pocket knife I found on a dead German soldier. It had two blades, a punch, a screwdriver, a can opener, and best of all, a corkscrew! Such a tool was badly needed for opening liberated bottles of wine! It was a real Boy Scout-type knife and I still have it. It is, however, retired from wine bottle service.

The other item I found was also on a dead German. We were continually on the lookout for souvenirs, but we were also hoping to find items of intelligence such as maps and messages. On this particular dead German, I was delighted to find an OD-colored ski mask.

In the cold of that Ardennes winter, a ski mask was an ideal find. The German had it tucked in his blouse and was not wearing it when he was killed. As I was putting it on, I noticed a small tag sewed inside. The tag said it had been hand-knitted in Knoxville, Tennessee by a volunteer and was a gift from the Red Cross. My German friend had probably taken it from some luckless American. I figured some little old lady in Knoxville would be pleased to know that her ski mask had come back to our side.

When we made our first attack on January 7, 1945, we were told to drop our overcoats and artics so we could move easier. That was the last any of us ever saw of our overcoats. Fortunately, I ignored the order to remove the artics as did many others. I credit that for the fact my feet didn't freeze while I was in the line.

I also tried to change socks when I could. Even though I didn't do it as often as I should have, evidently I did it often enough. We would put the damp socks we took off inside our shirts and body heat helped dry them out. Then, when dry, although still dirty, we would swap back. I guess we smelled pretty raunchy all the time!

When I was wounded the second time and left the company, I had to leave my mackinaw hanging on a tree. To reach up and get it would have unnecessarily exposed me to more machine gun fire. As much as I hated to leave it, I couldn't take the chance. One of our guys got a nice, warm coat!

Although we all started out dressed as ordered and carrying the items ordered, we soon varied both to enable us to operate more efficiently. Our officers seemed to approve and were doing the same themselves. It was a long time until I came around to the realization that the dress discipline and routine orders we had accepted without question during our training had all been geared toward teaching us to adapt to a combat situation.

CHAPTER 46
THE ENEMY LIES DEAD

I t wasn't hard to know that we were in the combat zone. We could hear firing way off in the distance and every now and then we saw silent, burned-out tanks abandoned by their crews. And, of course, almost every building had been demolished or at least damaged. But, for me nothing was so shocking and as awakening as the day I saw my first dead body. This was the body of our enemy—a dead German soldier. Suddenly, the reality of the war burst upon me.

It sure didn't seem like the Christmas season and I thought to myself, "This is a hell of a way to wish a person "Merry Christmas!" It really didn't surprise us much, however, as our abrupt departure from England had been necessitated due to the breakthrough the Germans had made and we realized the time had finally come. The training was over. It was time to earn our pay.

They told us only the bare facts. The enemy offensive had punched a gap in the Allied line and the situation in the area of the Ardennes Forest had rapidly deteriorated. The 101st Airborne and some other support units had been isolated in the small Belgian town of Bastogne and they were in deep trouble.

Unknown to anyone at this time was the fact Kampfgruppe Jochen Peiper, attempting to break out of what had become a trap for his armored spearhead, had begun his retreat on December 24 in the northern part of the Bulge. At the southern shoulder of the Bulge, General Patton's Third Army was also on the move. On December 26th, the Third Army would break the siege at Bastogne opening a corridor to the surrounded Airborne troops. We never knew when this occured. It seemed we only got the bad news or no news at all.

Peiper, who would be convicted at the War Crimes Trials after the war for his role in the "Malmedy Massacre", lost 5,000 of his 5,800 Panzer soldiers during his failed attempt to drive to the Meuse River. By the time we got in the fight, the initiative had begun to swing our way, but the situation was so confused it was impossible for the common soldier on the ground to sense any progress being made.

The picture they painted for us was indeed grim. Our mission was to set up blocking positions to stop the Germans from crossing the Meuse River. If they crossed the Meuse, they would have a clear shot to head north to Antwerp. If Antwerp and its vital port fell, most of the Allied forces to the east of the Meuse would be cut off. It could be another Dunkirk.

On our way from Mourmelon we traveled through some small, quaint French villages but we were too cold to hardly notice. Half-frozen, we stopped in the middle of one village to take a break. We dismounted from the trucks and stomped our feet to try to restore the circulation. We had no choice but to urinate in the street. It had snowed hard all day

Christmas eve and it was still snowing. A heavy, dense fog covered the land and you could see only about 25 or 30 yards ahead. It would be the worse winter the Ardennes had had in 50 years.

Finally we reached another village which we learned was Charleville. It was located near the banks of the Meuse River. We were going to set up a defense line about six miles beyond on the east bank. This was where we were going to stop the German advance! The trucks took us as far as they could and then, strung out with a column on either side of the road we headed into the pine forests. We could hear the booming sound of artillery in the distance. The war was not far away.

As we moved through the tall trees, we passed by a clearing in the forest. It was two or three o'clock in the morning, but there in that clearing was what appeared to be an ordinance company working on disabled tanks. This might have been true, but an armored soldier I later met in the hospital told me this was about the time they were converting the Sherman tanks to use the new .76 mm cannon. The Shermans, called "Ronson Lighters" by the troops because they caught fire so easy, had proved far less effective than the Panzers of the enemy.

There were three or four tanks and mechanics were swarming all over them. The noise they were making and the lights they showed as they worked was upsetting to us, but I guess they knew what they were doing. Some of them called out to us to "give them hell!" They obviously knew where we were heading and it was almost like they were telling us goodbye.

When we reached the positions that we would occupy in the forest we had no idea of where the enemy was or for that matter, where we were. We found some old foxholes, but most of us had to dig for new positions. The ground usually was not frozen this solidly. If you could chip through the first two or three inches, you could dig. But this year a "Russian High" had blown in, and it was like trying to dig in concrete.

These forward positions did have one great advantage. Once they were prepared, we were able to move back to a group of farm buildings where we got to sleep in the barns. We kept guards on our positions so that if the Germans were reported to be coming, we could rush up to defend the line. If we had remained out in those positions in that weather, soon we would have been completely ineffective.

We had a tragic accident while we were in this area. Someone found a German "potato masher" grenade and got the idea we should know how it worked. We had received an extra lieutenant before leaving for France and he appointed himself as the expert on enemy weapons and prepared a demonstration.

With a group of the men standing well away, he prepared to throw the grenade over by a bombed-out building. He pulled the cord in the handle and then abruptly stopped and said it was not working right. He was wrong. The grenade then went off, badly wounding the lieutenant and S/Sgt Wilbert Springstubb, the company supply sergeant, who was standing nearby.

Soon a medical jeep arrived with two stretchers mounted on back. The lieutenant and the sergeant were loaded aboard. Before they left, I remember the lieutenant saying for us to take his artics off as one of the men who had none could use them. He said he wasn't going to need them where he was going!

That was the also the end of the war for Sergeant Springstubb. His lower legs were chopped up pretty badly. He didn't loose them, but when I saw him at one of our reunions in 1982, he was still having trouble walking and standing.

On December 27, about half of the 1st platoon, with attachments, was assigned to protect a road intersection along our front and we left the main body of the company. That experience of guarding the Franco-Belgian border is told in another chapter.

On January 2, after D company had been united again, we were trucked to the vicinity of a village named Neufchateau. There the 17th Airborne relieved elements of the 28th Infantry Division. Neufchateau was located about 20 miles southwest of Bastogne. The 193rd then moved northward toward Mande-St-Etienne which was about 15 miles southwest of Bastogne. The history books say the Bulge had turned in our favor about this time, but none of us could tell it. There were still plenty of Germans in the woods all around the city so we were on a tight alert.

One day we were moving down a small road. We were in a column on each side of the road with a five-yard interval between men. Suddenly, someone yelled "grenade!" In one second everyone disappeared into the ditches. Nothing happened and after awhile, the men climbed out slowly and it was determined that one of our own people had accidentally dropped a grenade. Fortunately, the pin did not come out and thus no harm was done. I knew right then that our company could move fast if they had to!

We continued to move closer toward the area just southwest of Bastogne and closed into positions in a pine forest adjacent to a lone railroad track. This marked our boundary between another company which was deployed on our flank. The track ran along a fill that raised it some 20 feet above the level of the intervening clearing.

Gazing out at the track, I saw that a supply parachute was draped across the elevated railroad track. This was no doubt one of the supply chutes dropped by the C-47 crews to the 101st Airborne the day before they carried us over to the continent. The canopy was lying across the tracks and the empty container hung down on our side of the embankment.

And then, I saw him. It was the first dead body I had seen of anyone—friend or foe—killed during World War II. He was a German soldier in full uniform, coal bucket helmet, personal equipment and all. His rifle even lay nearby. He was lying on his back next to the empty container.

I approached him carefully. Maybe he was playing possum and would suddenly rise up and shoot me! There was no chance of that as I soon realized he was frozen stiff and his eyes were glazed over with ice. There was a bloody wound in his chest and it was evident someone had probably nailed him as he went to retrieve the parachute bundle.

I stood there and I wondered if he had died quickly. I wondered what he must have thought when he was unexpectedly hit by that bullet that took his life. I wondered if he was married, if he had children and would they ever learn just what happened to him. I wondered how it felt to die.

Then, I did a curious thing that I have always wondered why I did it. I saw this beautiful gold ring on his finger. It had a pretty blue stone and was obviously an expensive ring. I said to myself he had no more use for it and I might as well have it, otherwise someone else would.

I tried to slip the ring off of his finger, but it was either too tight or was frozen in place. It wouldn't budge. So, I took out my trench knife and started cutting his finger off. I had cut the flesh all the way around and then I began to saw on the bone. The bone was a little more difficult to cut.

Suddenly, I realized what I was doing. I was cutting a dead man's finger off to rob him of his last remaining possession! The full impact hit me and I shuttered. This man meant nothing to me, but how could I sink this low? Even though he was the enemy, I owed the dead more respect that this.

That was enough. I stopped and returned to my position in the woods. I was ready to kill if I had to, but butchering and robbing the dead...I hadn't sunk that low...yet.

CHAPTER 47
THE CHILDREN

T here's nothing pretty about war and it sure isn't the wonderful adventure young people imagine. There are really three things that bring the tragedy of war into focus. At least, that's the way it was for me.

Naturally, the sight of your friends being killed or wounded becomes the primary awakening call when you enter combat. I'll also have to include the sight of enemy dead. It is a little easier to deal with this, but it is still trying to see bloody, mangled bodies regardless if they are enemy.

The second thing that shakes you up, is the devastation and disorder all around you. Perfectly good homes ripped and torn apart, dead farm animals bloated and lying with their legs pointed to the sky, vehicles overturned and burning, personal belongings scattered in the ruins and over the countryside. It looks like a world gone mad.

Then there is a third sight that seemed to spell out the tragedy of war even more sharply than the first two. That was the presence of children. They were totally out of place in this kind of environment. They did not seem to understand anything that was going on around them, yet there they were right in the middle of total chaos.

Being unmarried and barely 20 years old at the time seemed to help me deal with it. But some of the older guys, especially if they themselves had children, were really torn up to see some of the hardships these youngsters were undergoing. Years later, after now having children of my own, I can understand how they felt.

Many families fled the battle areas, but every now and then you'd find some the war had seemed to just roll over. Electing to stay behind and care for their livestock and personal belongings, they went into their underground food cellars to wait out the fighting and shelling. Then, when it quieted down, they would emerge wild-eyed and frightened to see if anything was still left of their home and belongings.

The children were always hungry, dirty and ill-clothed and seldom wore a smile. Their parents were usually there with them and they looked the same. Despair was written on their faces. Everyone seemed to be tuned to the idea of "making it one more day". That's all that seemed to matter.

I was surprised to see how many families had stayed with their homes and villages. I always worried about them when we had to clear and go through villages or farm buildings. The approved method was to throw grenades in the cellars and buildings and then rush in with weapons blazing. The thought that stuck in my mind was "what if there were civilians in there"? What if there were children in there?

Most of the time (thank God!) the civilians would flee to the rear or to the shelter of some wooded area if there was time. Then the military tore up their homes with artillery and tanks as they watched from afar. As soon as things quieted down and we moved on, they would filter back and try to pick up their lives.

I was amazed at how soon they would be back. Regardless of the war, a farmer had to think about his livestock. Cows had to be milked regardless. With snow on the ground, they had to have feed forked out to them and they had to have shelter even if only in some half-demolished barn. And, there were always a few chickens that the soldiers had missed and they were pecking around trying to find enough to keep alive. The farmers were actually risking their lives trying to keep their family possessions intact.

When we first left the barracks on Christmas day 1944, the mission we were given was to set up a defense line at the Meuse River. The breakthrough was in high gear and it appeared the Germans were going to be tough to stop. The Meuse River would be the last line of defense and if they got this far, it would be up to us to stop them.

Our truck convoy moved through the French village of Charleville. On beyond the village a mile or so into the countryside we stopped and dismounted. Half-frozen by this time, we marched off into the woods where we occupied some old positions that someone had prepared to defend the river line.

After a nervous night, we established outposts along the line and the majority of the company was pulled back a few hundred yards to a cluster of farm buildings. Our positions could be occupied in a few minutes if we received word that the Germans had broken through, but in the meantime, the weather made it necessary to find shelter for the troops in the farm buildings.

This was a terrible time to be living outdoors. The night of December 23, had seen what the French called a "Russian High" roll in and the mercury had plunged well below zero. Not only would this be the worse winter in Europe for 50 years, it would be 50 more years before it was equaled.

Except for the freezing cold, things weren't too bad up to this point. We slept inside the buildings we had taken over, pulled a turn or two of guard duty at the outpost positions and although we could hear artillery firing, the war seemed to be still some distance away. Our kitchen truck came up early in the morning and late at night and served us two "hots". They would leave C-rations for the noon meal.

The kitchen set up in a sort of courtyard where they served us the two hot meals. There was a stone wall about six feet high around the courtyard and we sat around on the ground and hay bales or various farm implements. We alternated so only about one-fourth of the company was being fed at the same time.

Breakfast was nearly always hot cakes and powered eggs, but there was plenty of hot coffee. For the evening meal we always had potatoes and possibly another veggie such as turnips or beets and maybe a piece of beef or pork. We would joke that it was whatever the artillery had hit that day!

The only flaw in this setup was the fact that they could not stop the children from coming into the courtyard. I doubt if they even tried. The children all wanted to see and talk to the "Amis". They knew we also had gum and candy and that they could easily talk us out of our goodies!

The youngsters, about 10 or 15 of them, ranging from four or five years to the early teens, soon learned when we would be receiving our meals. They arrived in time to stand around and watch us eat. For us, hungry as we were, eating under those circumstances was a hard thing to do. Hungry eyes could spoil your appetite.

The children hung around the garbage can and anything that a trooper dumped out of his mess kit was quickly scooped up and consumed. In fact, there was almost a fight to see who got each scrap.

At first, we would really load up our mess kits and then only eat about half of our meal and save the rest for the kids. This didn't work for long as the cooks started giving us less and no seconds so they wouldn't run out. As might be expected, the troopers—me included—soon got around to "sharing" our meals and then we were going around a bit hungry. You felt guilty if you ate everything you were given.

Funny thing too. There never seemed to be any children playing in the streets or around the houses. We saw very little of them until our kitchen truck arrived and then there they were, standing silently, staring at us and waiting for a handout. I wondered if they did that to the Germans when they were there.

A few children seemed braver than the others and would hang around our billets and even near our foxhole positions. The attraction here was the possibility of charming us out of gum, cigarettes and candy from the C-rations cans. They were usually successful!

There were also a few teenage girls who seemed to be attracted to some of us young troopers and they soon began to hang around our positions. I talked to some of them and they tried to teach me some French phrases. I'm afraid they thought me rather stupid as I seemed to be a rather poor student of their language!

I figured the adults would survive the war. After all, they had done it before...several times. It was the youngsters that troubled me. They were caught in the crush and there was little they could do about it. We didn't have long to think about it though. In a few days we were on the move again. This time heading closer to the shooting war.

CHAPTER 48

THE WATCH ON THE BORDER

On December 27, the 17th Airborne was deployed in a reserve position just behind the Main Line of Resistance (MLR) and west of the Meuse River. If they got this far, it was here the Germans had to be stopped. The 193rd Glider Regiment was located in the vicinity of Charleville, France. The snow was eight to ten inches deep and it was cold, foggy and damp. Visibility was limited to about 50 yards.

Two squads of our 1st Platoon, D Company, were detached and sent to guard a road intersection located about two hundred yards from the Franco-Belgian border. The clump of farm buildings where we set up, was about six miles east of the river. We were well aware that the river was to our backs. Although we were not close enough to hear small arms fire, we could hear the artillery booming away in the distance.

Second Lieutenant Bill Rudicel was in charge of this fire team. Staff Sergeant Roy McCaslin was the ranking non-com. In addition to our mortar, we had a light machine gun squad and a bazooka team attached to increase our firepower. But, we sure weren't equipped to stop a German Panzer column if they had come roaring down that road!

We did have one thing going for us. Some engineers had laid a minefield to either side of the road in the vicinity of the border crossing. Any tanks, if they did come this way, would be forced to keep to the road, thereby channeling the fire that could be brought to bear on them. With the snow several feet deep in the ditches, they probably would be forced to do that anyway.

A farmhouse close to our roadblock became our CP and the rest of us moved into a barn across the road. Lt. Rudicel took over one room of the house and the French family lived in the rest. There were about 28 or 30 of us enlisted men and we were content to nestle in the hay that filled the barn.

We dug in the machine gun and the bazooka so we could cover the road from our positions to the border. It wasn't bad duty as long as the Germans didn't come and we had a place to get in out of the cold. The barn was full of soft, warm hay and with the temperature hovering at zero and below, it was a welcome respite from being stuck on some wind-swept hillside.

Everyone pulled two different details; either as one of the roadblock crew or as a member of a two-man listening post at the border crossing. The first detail meant you had to be out in the open in a cold foxhole. The later was a much better deal. You walked up to the border where you served as a guard for the minefield and early-warning post.

There was a warm little guardhouse at the border crossing and a French border guard, or gendarme, was always on duty there. The guardhouse provided a nice place to get in from the cold. I also enjoyed conversing with the gendarme during the two hours I pulled this duty. I struggled with my French, aided by a small phrase book the army had given us, and the gendarme struggled with his English as we tried to talk.

I recall he was interested in what part of the United States was my home. Kentucky did not seem to ring a bell with him, but when I mentioned "cheval" or "horse," he caught on quickly! I had a small address book which I carried and it had a map of the United States in it. I showed him where Bowling Green was located. The small dot I made is still visible today.

I remember another incident that occurred during our two or three-day stay at that roadblock. We were given a couple of the new "10 in 1" rations. That means one meal for 10 men. They required some preparation so it meant we either learned how to prepare them or went hungry. We learned, but I still remember those powdered eggs were terrible.

Each night that we were there, "Bed-check Charlie" came over to snoop around. This was a German observation plane that flew low and slow over our area and so they said, was trying to pick out our defensive positions. I imagine he could spot only vehicles, but just the same, we always took cover and cursed him under our breaths. He never came around during the daylight hours as the sky belonged to the allies during the day!

Another problem arose while we were there. Someone noticed that on a high hilltop near us, flashing lights could be seen at night. As everyone was under a strict blackout rule, the lights were interpreted as signals by someone on the ground to Bed-check Charlie.

About this time a young Frenchman named Jean joined our group and he proved to be a great help to us. He was a member of the French "Maquis", the partisan organization that had continued to fight the Germans during the occupation. He wore a white armband with the letters "FFI" printed on it standing for "Free French of the Interior". Jean became our interpreter, our guide and practically a member of our company. He was really gung-ho to get at these saboteurs we felt were signaling from the hill, so Lt. Rudicel organized a patrol to go up and capture them.

On the first night the patrol climbed the hill, the lights abruptly stopped and there was no one in sight. The mystery remained until the second night when someone finally realized that the "lights" we had been seeing were actually reflections caused by "chaff". Chaff was made from small slivers of tinfoil and American bomber crews dropped it by the ton to foul-up German radar. The trees on the hills were sprinkled with it and when it waved in the wind it would reflect the light from the moon. That was the end of the saboteurs and the late-night patrols.

There were other advantages to being billeted in the barn. It wasn't long until some of the local belles were attracted there to talk to the handsome young Americans! They were also interested in some of the chocolate bars, cigarettes and chewing gum that the young Americans had! There was some interesting trading that took place in that barn, but of course, I was not involved in any of this!

There was one other interesting incident that took place while we were on this roadblock. Years after the war was over, I was reminded of it by S/Sgt Roy McCaslin, who said he will never forget it! Apparently, there had been an attempt by the Germans to infiltrate our lines and it had been successful. At least from our role in the incident, it was successful.

"Mac", as we called him, was on the guard post on the road in front of our weapons position when a jeep came through bearing the markings of a unit located on our flank. As the jeep did not come from the road leading to the border, but from a side road, it was not halted and did not arouse suspicion.

The two occupants, one an officer, stopped and talked to Mac for a minute asking directions to somewhere in the rear area. They even knew the password. Mac told them what they asked, they thanked him and drove away.

About an hour later, another jeep came up from the rear area. An officer in this jeep asked about the first jeep and wanted to know who passed them through our position. Mac readily admitted that he had and then they told him that the two soldiers in that jeep had been exposed in the rear area as being German infiltrators.

Mac was stunned, he said. But, as no damage had been done, nothing else was ever heard about the incident. I do remember about this time is when we were warned about German infiltrators in American uniforms and the importance of identifying all strangers. I was never put in the position of needing to identify someone, but now our guys resorted to the pratice of asking strangers such weird questions as "Who won the 1942 World Series?" or "Who is married to Harry James?"

Life on the roadblock was not bad. It's too bad we didn't get to stay longer. About January 2, a truck came and picked us up and we rejoined the rest of the company. The word was out: we were getting ready to move up for an attack. Our short introduction to the combat area was over. From now on it would be serious business. Our lives were about to change forever.

CHAPTER 49
SNIPER FIRE

A n event that remains quite memorable for a combat soldier is the first time he was fired on by the enemy. It's a rude awakening when you realize that there's someone out there that wants to kill you!

I guess the first time I was ever actually fired on was on December 26, when a German Me-l09 made a single pass and strafed our convoy. We heard the sound of gun fire, but in that weather no one expected an airplane to be up flying. The convoy never stopped and as none of the rounds hit near us, we never knew what was happening. However, division after-action reports record that one man was killed and he thus became the divison's first casualty. Maybe they were just letting us know we traveled the roads at great risk.

The time I'll always remember was when some German sniper had me in his sights, missed the first time and I gave him another shot before I wised up! The statistics say if you survive the first week or so in combat, your chances of surviving the war increases dramatically. I believe it.

I think this event occurred on January 4th. We were somewhere in that area southwest of Bastogne. The 194th was attacking, the l93rd was in a reserve role. Our company was advancing through some woods while up ahead the lead elements were making contact with delaying forces left by the enemy. There would be a few shots fired, we would all halt for awhile, there would be some more shooting and then we'd move on.

Although we could hear firing up ahead, it seemed quite safe on the narrow farm road where we were walking. I had just crossed another narrow road which intersected with ours when abruptly we were ordered to "hit the ground"! The word came down that the Jerries were firing up this cross road at our column as we moved by. I had been completely unaware of any fire, but I jumped into a ditch at the side of the road and waited.

I could hear firing in the nearby woods, so foolishly I peeped over the top of the ditch, trying to see if I could tell what was going on. Suddenly, about a foot to the right of my head, the snow fluffed up sending a small spray in my face. Dumb me, I wondered what caused that. I had heard nothing.

I did, however, heard the second shot which came about l0 seconds later. It was that pop sound that we had heard when we worked the targets in the pits on the firing range. It was an unforgettable sound and one we would hear many times later. When the bullet passed close by you, the air popped and then you knew it had missed, but not by much.

Green as I was, I did realize that I had given that unseen sniper a second shot at me. While the first shot had been to my right, he had corrected from his left to right, but fortunately for me, had been a little high and the round had snapped over my head. That was enough for me. I dropped down below the level of the ditch and made damn certain my head didn't stick up to give him a third chance.

About 10 minutes went by and we remained in our positions in the ditch. We had no idea what was going on up ahead. However, we were content to just sit tight and let the maneuvering elements clean up the trouble. Then we heard a machine gun firing and the dreaded sound of a powerful motor. Someone yelled, "Tank!"

I rolled over and stuck my head up over the lip of the ditch again. I was careful that I was several feet away from the spot where the sniper had been firing. There, down in the draw about 400 yards away, a Kraut tank had ventured forth from the woods and was firing toward our area. At the same time, the order came down for everyone to bring fire on it.

Our company machine guns rained fire on the tank. I doubt if it had much effect, but it must have sounded like the Fourth of July inside! We were then ordered to fire our mortar on it. We couldn't hope to penetrate the thick armor of the tank, but it was thought that the concentration of the fire would make the tank button up, turn tail and run.

When we went to ground I had been carrying the tube and baseplate of our mortar. Linrooth had been carrying the bipod and a load of ammunition. Now, I found that I was on one side of the intersecting road and he was on the other side. Neither of us wanted to cross that road junction as we knew we would be subject to sniper fire.

We solved the problem quickly. Linrooth rolled a couple of the shell canisters across the road to me and I set up the tube and baseplate on the hard, snow-packed road. Using "Kentucky windage", I began dropping the shells down the tube. Linrooth spotted for me and I got off three or four rounds.

This was the first time we had fired the mortar in combat and here I was doing it like John Wayne! Although any round within a radius of 25 yards was said to cause casualties to troops in the open, a direct hit by a .60 mm shell probably couldn't have knocked out the tank. Nevertheless, I know I did ding some metal off its sides!

The tank crew must have decided a bazooka was next, because as hoped, they turned tail and retreated into the woods and the threat was over. We lay huddled in the ditch for a few more minutes until the firing seemed to wane a bit. Then we got the order to move on.

As we moved up the road, I happened to pass my old friend, Paul Walker. Paul was a mortar squad leader in "F" Company. He was from Glasgow, Kentucky and we had played high school football against each other for at least three years before we entered service. After high school, Paul had gone to the University of Kentucky on a football scholarship. We had buddied around some during the time we had been in the 17th and we often exchanged news about home and mutual friends.

There were two other guys with Paul at the place where I saw him. We exchanged greetings but it wasn't the place to stand and chat. I moved on, telling him to be careful.

It wasn't until several years later back in Bowling Green that Paul and I discussed that day and what happened after I moved on. It seems a shell came in right on them about 5 minutes after I saw him. One of the three was killed and Paul and the other guy were badly injured.

Paul spent almost two years in military hospitals recovering from his wounds. They took 116 slivers of shrapnel out of his face, neck and shoulders. He lost most of his jaw on one side and had to have extensive reconstructive surgery. Even after all this, after his discharge, he walked on at the University of Louisville and earned a scholarship in basketball.

During the years I lived in Bowling Green before moving to Ashland, Paul was the City Recreation Director and we became even closer friends. He suffered a heart attack and died a few years before I moved back. I think about him quite often as the local municipal golf course is named for him and I often pass it traveling to and from my home.

Combat is like nothing else you'll ever do. To survive it, you have to remember everything you have been taught and be in the right place at the right time. You also have to have a lot of luck and I think you must have a close relationship with God.

CHAPTER 50
THE FIRST BIG ATTACK

T he first time a soldier goes into combat, his thoughts run rampant. Would he turn and run? Would he cry or scream and reveal a "yellow streak" that he had no idea he had? Would he give a good account of himself? Would he let his comrades down? Would he be wounded? Would it be only a flesh wound or would it be the loss of a limb or a gapping hole in his chest? And, lastly, would he be killed?

The prime concern, however, seems to be would he give a good account of himself. The fear of being less than a man seems to outweigh the thought of personal harm. I'm sure all of these thoughts were on the minds of all of us in Company D on the day we went into combat—real combat—on January 7, 1945.

We had left the comparative safety of our barracks at Mormelon-du-Grande early on Christmas morning and for the past ll days we had experienced only patrolling and guard duty. We had been in reserve a lot while other units had had some minor clashes. Our mission up until this time had been to defend the Meuse River in the event the German breakthrough reached that far. It didn't, so now we were ready to take the fight to them.

Early on January 6th, our company moved into the small Belgian village of Flamizoulle. It had been cleared only the day before by a unit of the 5l3th Parchute Infantry. They had moved straight on through and there were several German bodies around to testify to the battle that had raged here.

Our company was dispersed and our mortar squad moved into the area assigned to us. It was not an ideal fighting position, but one in which we could set our gun up and where there were some old foxholes which we could reclaim for individual protection. The snow was six to eight inches deep with drifts of two to four feet. The ground was frozen as hard as a rock and digging new holes posed a near-impossible problem.

No sooner had we started scooping the snow out of one of the old holes, when we discovered it contained the body of a dead German soldier. He had a tiny bullet hole in his head and that apparently was his only wound. It appeared he had died quietly and then frozen in a sitting position. He wore his soft cap and seemed perfectly at ease.

In a show of bravo, which I now realize was in an effort to buoy up our own nerve, we started calling him "Fritz"! We dusted the snow from his uniform, adjusted his cap, and set him on a nearby fallen tree. It seemed like he was "one of the boys" very much alive and just sitting there watching us settle in to our new positions!

We laughed and talked to "Fritz" like he could hear us and other company members nearby also laughed and joined in the sport! There was no disrespect meant, but already life had lost a lot of its meaning for us and in an environment where killing was commonplace, it didn't seem like what we were doing was a violation of the dead.

Someone finally opened one of the pockets on "Fritz's" blouse and took out his soldiers' paybook. The usual information was there including his name, rank, serial number and a stern, posed photo of "Fritz" in much better times. What stopped us, however, was another photograph which had been enclosed between the sheets of the book. It showed an attractive young lady standing in a flower garden holding the hands of two beautiful young girls.

Reality came back to us in a rush. There was little doubt in our minds that this photo was of "Fritz's" wife and two young daughters. Somewhere in Germany there was a family waiting for a soldier who was never to come home. Suddenly, we realized that what had happened to "Fritz" could happen to any one of us.

That was enough of the fun at "Fritz's" expense. We returned the photo and paybook to his blouse pocket, removed him from his perch on the fallen tree and carried him to the side of a nearby building. There we laid him carefully on the ground and jammed his rifle into the snow to mark the spot. The Graves Registration people would find him there and he would be given a proper burial.

Soon a jeep stopped at our roadside position and the driver asked some directions of the guys that gathered around the vehicle. The whole back end of the jeep was filled with cases of "C" rations. They looked pretty good to us at that point as we had been running on "K" rations, a considerable step or two down the nutrition ladder.

As Orville "Hungry" Linrooth and I stood toward the rear of the jeep, I nudged Hungry and pointed to one of the cases. He nodded and as the jeep pulled away, we reached inside the jeep and lifted up the case of rations. The jeep just drove out from under the case and it was ours!

Everyone in our squad and the third squad helped himself to a couple of cans and we knew we were going to eat well that day. Hungry and I then decided that it would be nice to have a little fresh meat to go with our meal. That's when we turned chicken thieves!

We had seen a couple of little banty hens and roosters pecking around one of the nearby houses and we decided to catch one of them. We cornered our prize inside a bedroom of the house. Then, falling over the furniture and each other, we finally caught the valiant little survivor.

Someone dug up some potatoes from the cellar of the house and someone else produced some green beans "canned" in a wine bottle. Hungry and I picked the little hen and roasted it over a spit. The meal we shared with the others in our squad wasn't the best, but it was a break from army rations.

Later, I went into the house and paused long enough to see a disgusting scene taking place in the main room. Two Germans were lying dead on the floor. They appeared to have set up their machine gun on the dining room table and had been firing it out of the window down the main road. When the troopers attacked the village, they had to be among the first to be killed..

Now, a skinny, malnourished cat was sitting on the chest of one of the Germans tearing at his upper lip. It was seeking to find a meal in this deserted, frozen land. I watched in horror for a minute and then shooed the cat away. I have no doubt the cat returned to its task after I left, but I couldn't bear to watch it happen, even to my enemy.

I walked up the road a little ways when I came upon Carl "Sonny" Gloor, a friend in our headquarters section. Sonny was our company mail orderly and there he was shaving like he was back in garrison! I rubbed my chin and it was pretty grubby. So, I asked for seconds on his razor! Then, using about a teacup of melted snow and a bar of soap, I hacked off almost two weeks' growth of whiskers!

Before it got completely dark that night, our kitchen truck brought up some hot chow. It really didn't matter what it was, just so it was hot and something besides "C" rations. We filed through the line with our messkits and they threw it all in there together in one big pile. Whatever it was, we ate every bit. All we cared about was that the coffee they served was both strong and hot!

As we scattered around the area to eat, I guess I tried to be a wise guy. There wasn't a good place left to eat, so I sauntered over to where a dead German lay flat on his back. He was frozen stiff and I sat down on him like he was a log. As I guess I had hoped, I got a few laughs.

After awhile I felt a lump where I was sitting and I rose to investigate. There was something in the German's pocket. I saw a chain attached to his belt and running into his pocket.

Although it could have been a booby trap, I pulled it and out came a great pocketknife. It had a corkscrew (a must for wine bottles) a screwdriver, bottle opener, leather punch and two cutting blades. It was a great find not only as a souvenir, but as a tool for living in the rough! I still have it today!

Soon it was night and we settled down to try and get some sleep. The squad leaders were called to meet with Captain Stuhrman and returned to give us the great news that we would make our first full scale attack the next morning. For security purposes we were sleeping two to a foxhole so that one would stay awake at all times. That night, however, no one slept very well.

Before dawn on Sunday, January 7th, we were up and getting ready to make our attack. We shed our cumbersome overcoats and many of the guys took off their heavy artics. I did leave the overcoat behind, but my fear of getting my feet wet and having them freeze, made me decide to keep the artics on.

Everyone was tense as we moved out down a narrow stock trail, but we were also excited at the impending action. This was it! No more training. No more maneuvers. No more problems. This was the real thing! Today it be a matter of life and death. When this day was over, some of us would be dead. I guess we all thought it would be the other guy— not us.

We moved out in fine style. No talking. No jingle of equipment. Everyone on the alert. Armed to the teeth. The five yard intervals were kept and there were no stragglers. No one wanted to go where we were going, but no one wanted to be left behind. We were all alert, but buried in our own thoughts.

This would be a full division attack. The 194th GIR would be on the left, the 513th PIR in the center, our 193rd GIR on the right and the 507th PIR in reserve. The big picture, unknown by the soldiers in the ranks at that time, had the 101st Airborne on our right flank and the 87th Infantry Division on our left.

Within the 193rd sector, the mission for our Second Battalion was to attack and clear fortified enemy positions in a wooded area. There would be a 15 minute artillery barrage on the woods once we got into position. D Company would attack with E Company on the left flank and F Company in reserve.

On that cold, foggy day with the mercury near zero and the visibility at only 25 to 30 yards, we had no idea what enemy units lay in wait for us. History has since revealed that the 17th Airborne would clash with elements of the Remmer Brigade. Opposing the 193rd was the 104th Panzer Grenadier Regiment with the 10th SS Panzer Division and the 11th Panzer Division in reserve. Also in the immediate area were the 26th Panzer Grenadier Regiment and the 8th Panzer Regiment. It would be a difficult day's work.

If everything had gone as planned, no doubt this story would have a different ending. Unfortunately, seldom does combat go as planned. Our approach to the IP—the jumping off point -was detected by the enemy and all hell broke loose. Some say someone stepped on a mine and alerted the Germans of our approach. Others adhere to the possibility that the enemy had an observer in a farmhouse some 200 yards in front of their main defensive line. Whatever the cause, they learned of our approach before we were in position.

Mortar and .88 fire started hitting us well before we got to our jumping off point, a ditch behind an elevated roadbed. Our platoon leader, Bill Rudicel, and his runner, Earl Keir, immediately went down badly wounded. Art Jastal, the third squad leader, and one of his riflemen, Ernie Stull, were badly wounded when a shell hit dead center on Sam Jordan.

The majority of us, however, made it to the ditch and hunkered down as our artillery sailed overhead. Then, it stopped prematurely. Later it was determined that our artillery observers had thought that our own fire was falling short and they ordered it lifted. Actually, it was the enemy's counterfire that was causing our casualties. In hindsight, it is easy to see that this is the sort of things that happens to green troops. That inexperience really hurt us that day.

With the lifting of the fire on their positions, the Germans came up from the bottom of their holes and began to concentrate small arms and automatic fire on Company D to their front. A machine gun to our left began raking the road and the entire company was quickly pinned to the ground with no one able to even raise his head. Our mortar squad was given the order to take this target under fire.

The range table included in every cloverleaf of mortar ammunition lists the elevation and number of charges for various distances starting at 200 yards. The machine gun bringing fire on us, however, was only about 100 yards to our front, so we had to guess at the range. Nevertheless, we were on the target in two rounds and fired "three for effect". Our training paid off as the hammering of the machine gun fell silent.

Just when our squad was feeling pretty good about the job we had done, another problem arose. Suddenly, we began taking small arms fire from our rear. We looked and across the snow-covered field we could see a skirmish line of troops advancing toward us firing as they came. Immediately we thought we had been surrounded and were now about to be chewed to pieces between two enemy forces!

We turned and leveled our rifles to the rear. Many began to return the fire. I swallowed hard. Shooting the mortar was one thing. You didn't see where those shells landed and you didn't see the people fall, but firing your rifle was something else. There would be no question here about whether you killed a man or not.

I watched one particular man as he plodded through the snow toward our position. I leveled my carbine and drew a bead on him. I just knew I couldn't miss, but I wanted to wait until he got just a little closer. Then, I realized that he didn't have on one of those coal bucket helmets. He was wearing an American helmet!

I started yelling, "cease firing!" and the same call began echoing up and down the line. Fortunately, everyone seemed to wise up at about the same time. The soldiers came on up to our line and it was then we found out they were E Company. They had taken enemy fire from their left flank and had wandered off line to their right and came up behind us. They thought they were attacking the Germans!

It was a tragic screw-up. We took two killed, including Sgt Carl Royce in the machine gun section, and four wounded. One of those wounded, Joe Chabowski, suffered a bad head wound and never fully recovered. E Company lost some men too—I don't know how many. In addition, while we were fighting each other, the Germans kept picking away at all of us.

Finally, someone got it straightened out and the word went up the line to get ready to assault the woods. Our mortar position was alongside the third squad and Robert "Red" Ewing was near us. Red was a good buddy of mine and had on at least one occasion come home with me while we were stationed at Camp Forrest.

"We'll never make it to those woods," Red cried out.

"Yes, you will!" I yelled back, although I hardly believed what I said. It looked like suicide to rush that woods head on. I was glad I was in a mortar squad and would not have to join that initial assault.

The signal to charge was to be a blast on the whistle by Sergeant Pierre and when he blew it, over the road bank the rifle squads went. Red took one or two steps and fell, a bullet through his temple. He was dead before he hit the ground. Even today I can still hear that sharp blast on the whistle that forever changed all our lives.

With no hesitation the men charged the woods, screaming and firing as they went. The troopers from both D and E Companies were mixed in together and although unit control was lost here for a time, the men lacked nothing in courage and willingness to close with the enemy. It was no place for the faint of heart.

Faced with the charge and wild screams of the troopers, the Germans either fled or surrendered. Those that managed to escape withdrew out of the woods back across an open field and into another clump of woods. There they set up there in some other prepared positions and began returning fire. D Company pressed on carrying the attack to them.

With the capture of the first woods, we were told to move our mortar up to a position just at the entrance to the woods and be ready to displace forward. As we moved up we saw Red lying there where he had fallen in the snow. His usual rosy complexion had turned waxy white. I couldn't bear to look at him and I turned away and followed Linrooth on up to the woods.

I walked on forward into the woods to see if I could find the location of the machine gun we had fired on. I found it all right. The gun lay in a shallow gun pit. Apparently, it had received a direct hit as it was bent out of shape and useless. One dead crewman was lying nearby and another one was lying about 10 yards away. We had done our job well.

There were several dead troopers near the edge of the woods. I looked at them and recognized them as being from E Company. I didn't see any of our guys lying dead in the woods. I later learned that Sgt. Pierre had suffered a mortal wound in this action and died in the hospital the next day. My buddy, Ray Crabtree, had also been wounded by shrapnel and evacuated, but he was not seriously injured.

Then I did a strange thing. While I was looking around the woods I happened to see a German messkit with food in it lying beside one of the foxholes. I picked it up and it was still warm. It contained noodles with big chunks of meat. We were always hungry, so I pulled a spoon from my pocket and began to eat some unknown German's breakfast! The noodles were great, but I made the comment that the meat was a little tough. That's when someone told me that was because it was horsemeat!

By this time the reserve, F Company, had been called up and committed to our right. E Company was now trying to reorganize to become the battalion reserve. This action seemed to leave our left flank unprotected and the Germans, taking full advantage of it, apparently began to infiltrate back into the woods. Some say the Germans in the left flank area, after causing E Company to swing into our rear, just laid low and held their fire while we overextended ourselves.

In any event, D Company, after pushing the Germans back, ran into trouble. We began to take fire from what appeared to be a tank or a self-propelled .88 in the other woods. It was firing point-blank into our ranks. Our attack immediately came to a grinding halt. Now getting fire from the flanks as well as to the front, there seemed to be no way to get across the open field to bring fire on the tank. A bazooka shell fired from the front would bounce harmlessly off the thick armor.

Captain Stuhrman called for artillery support but was informed none was available. The attack had bogged down and D Company and F Company were both taking casualties. Soon Stuhrman was told he should withdraw his company back to our original positions. E Company, badly shot up by this time as well, went out first, followed by D with F Company covering the withdrawal.

From the very beginning it didn't appear to me to be a very orderly withdrawal. Our new mortar position was beside another elevated road that led directly back from the woods. Apparntly, this was the Bastogne-Marche highway. We saw man after man leave the woods up ahead and run back down the road. There was the sense of panic in the air and you could see it in the faces of the men.

Then we saw several D Company men going back down the road and we began to realize maybe it was time we thought about leaving too. Still no one had given us any orders. Someone then yelled that the Germans had been reinforced and we had better get out fast. We could hear the unmistakable sound of the rapid-firing German machine guns and we realized once again that they were real close.

Finally, Henry Browning, our mortar squad leader, told us to pull out. We needed no urging at this point. As the French would say, it was time to "parti"! Despite the fact the road had many vehicle mines laid on the surface, we ran through them while heavy machine gun and small arms fire sprayed from our left and right flanks. We were caught in a murderous crossfire. There were dozens of guys running down the road and it had become a case of everyone for himself.

I could hear the bullets popping and snapping around me. There was no mistaking that sound. We had all heard it in the pits on the firing range. When you heard that popping noise it was because the rounds were coming right at you and they were real close. Then I realized that there were people all around me dropping on that road. I could also hear moans and screams over the shouting and firing.

I plowed on ahead as fast as I could run, but my lungs ached and soon I was winded. I had to stop. I dropped down on the road and lay on my stomach trying to get my breath. A few feet away lying on the edge of the road I saw Joe Weider, one of the guys in our headquarters section. Blood was seeping out from him and I saw the bright red color on the white, snow-packed road. Looking at his face, I realized he was dead.

I was still carrying the canvas saddlebag loaded with mortar ammunition. This meant

I was carrying about 36 extra pounds as well as a potential time bomb. I slipped out of the carrier and left it in the middle of the road. I also jettisoned my gas mask. Most of the guys had already done this, but I still had mine. I realized the number one thing here was to get back alive and I couldn't run as fast as I needed to burdened down with all that equipment.

As we were getting fire from both flanks, I also reasoned that if I got off the road, dropping down in the field on one side, I would be subject to just half the total amount of fire. The elevated road would shield me from one side and the machine guns would probably be more interested in multiple targets on the road rather than a single target in the field. The only bad thing was the field was covered in about a foot of snow. The going would be slower and lots tougher.

I decided to take the chance. I slid off the road into the field and began running across an open field toward a wooded area. I believe this is when I got headed in the wrong direction because nothing looked like the area where we had started from that morning and I didn't see any of the guys from my own company around me. I just followed the crowd.

The fire definitely was getting lighter now and despite the physical exertion of running through the deep snow drifts, I began to feel like I was going to make it. I stopped a couple of times to catch my breath and look around for a familiar face, but I continued on in what seemed to be a safe direction.

One of the times I stopped was by some trooper who had been hit and yelled to me for help. I quickly saw he had been "gut-shot" (a stomach wound) and I knew there was little hope for him. He was a big guy and I knew I couldn't carry him. Even if I could, we would probably draw enemy fire and both of us would be killed.

I told the poor guy I would try to send a medic for him, but down deep in my heart, I knew it was pointless and that I probably would never see a medic. The way I more or less abandoned this poor guy bothered me for years, long after the war was over. A few years ago I read where in that same action, two guys received medals for going out in a field and bringing in a seriously wounded guy. I have always hoped that it was the man I failed to help.

Finally, I seemed to find some protection from the grazing fire as I started down into a little draw. There was a wire stock fence running down the center of the draw and typically, there was a line of men waiting to get over a single low place in the fence. Although I had no rank to be giving orders, I realized what was happening. I yelled to spread out and get over the fence because there would be artillery fire coming in before long.

Almost on cue, we started getting .88s, mortar fire, and worst of all, Nebelwerfers, or as the GIs called them, "Screaming Mimies". These were the dreaded rocket artillery that made such a terrifying screech as they came in. Everyone scrambled over the fence and headed up the hill on the other side toward some more woods. There we could see some guys out in the open urging us on, so we knew these were friendly positions.

Several times we had to drop flat as incoming shells hit around us. I had almost reached the woods when I had to hit the ground as I heard a shell whistling in nearby. It caused no problem, but just as I was getting up, another shell apparently hit very close to me. I never heard it coming. Maybe it was timed that way—to catch a person getting up after the main barrage. In any event, it sure caught me unaware.

Although I have never been sure the blast actually threw me into the air, I had the feeling that I was hanging in black space and then slowly turning over and crashing back down to earth. The explosion seemed to crowd the whole world out of my mind and everything suddenly got real quiet and still. Later I recall lying on my back with the wind knocked out of me and gasping for air. Before I could get my breath, it seemed that it was getting dark and I felt a strange sense of peace.

Then I became aware of strange faces looking down at me as my brain swirled around. I struggled for words to tell them I was still alive, but nothing would come out. My body was tingling all over and my ears were ringing. I couldn't hear a thing.

Then these strange faces picked me up and dragged and carried me back into the woods to a small pup tent set up under some trees. There I slowly regained full consciousness. I tried hard to become aware of what was going on as the idea hit me that if I gave in to this desire I had to close my eyes and go to sleep, I might not wake up.

Soon a jeep arrived and I was helped aboard. I had, by that time, realized what had happened. An exploding shell had landed very near me and as a consequence, I was suffering from the concussion. My ears were ringing and I was nearly deaf, and I had taken a giant bite into my tongue. Outside of that, I didn't hurt anywhere else, so I figured I had not been hit.

When I got back in the hospital, I found I had two sizeable tears in the back of my jacket where shrapnel apparently had sprayed above me. I also had a small cut— and that's all it was—on my butt which must have been caused by one small piece of shrapnel that dug in my thick layers of clothing. It was a good thing I was lying down when that shell hit. I realized that I still had all of my parts, but it had been a very close call.

My new friends drove me to an aid station which was located in the basement of a farmhouse. A medic checked me out and told me I would be okay. Soon a chaplain came around to the litter where I lay and asked me if I would like for him to say a prayer for me. I knew I wasn't in any danger, but it had been a bad day and I was still quite shaken from my experience, so I agreed. From him I also learned that I had wandered back into the lines of the 327th Glider Infantry of the 101st Airborne and I was in their aid station.

Soon a medic knelt by me and said he was going to give me a sleeping pill so I could sleep it off. That sounded good to me. The last thing I remember was them loading me in an ambulance. It was at least 10 hours later when I woke up and found out I was in a hospital in Arlon, Belgium. For the next two days, I just ate and slept. Slowly my hearing came back and the tingling feeling began to leave. My tongue was swollen, but I could tell that it was healing fast.

The hospital was designated as the 101st Evacuation Hospital, however, that numerical designation had nothing to do with the 101st Airborne. The hospital was located in what had been an old monastery and the walls were of stone two feet thick. The chow was excellent and they even had a USO show one night while I was there.

Freddie Bartholomew and Mickey Rooney, two famous movie stars of that day, were GI members of the troupe. They visited the wards and I made a special effort to say something to Rooney. The first thing I thought of was to ask him did he know where the latrine was! I can't remember what he said, but he had some wise answer!

I got a V-Mail off to my parents as soon as I could as I knew they would be worried about me if they got a telegram from the War Department. As it developed, although

Captain Sturhman had returned all my mail from home marked "Missing in Action", my note explaining what had happened got there first, so there was no shock to my parents.

The guys in my ward seemed to have minor wounds or were sick. Out of the 15 or 20 guys in there, only about six or seven of them had wounds for which I could see they were being treated. I began to suspect at least some of the other ones that were sick were combat fatigue cases. The doctor told me the only problem I had was concussion and that sleep and rest was the only treatment I would need.

In two or three more days, I began to feel pretty good. My ears cleared up and my hearing returned to normal. Then I got a shower and some clean socks and underwear. This really boosted my morale! Although I was in no hurry to get back to combat, I did wish to get out of this ward and back to my buddies in the old company. I was not comfortable around these guys.

One morning, the orderly for our ward got about a dozen of us and announced that he was going to take us on a walk down through Arlon. We were all eager to get out and move around some. This must have been some kind of "test", and I guess I passed. After lunch, I was called in to the doctor's office for a "conference". The end result was he told me I was now recovered and that I would be heading back to my unit tomorrow.

I still remember how I felt when I was told I was to be sent back into combat. I wasn't overjoyed. There were a lot of cushy jobs back in the rear area. I wondered why my job had to be up front where people were getting killed and wounded? I was not the only GI to ponder this. After the war, I read where there had been an estimated 17,000 deserters in Paris alone, living off their wits and the black market.

But, however low I felt, I was not going to be a coward. I knew I had to think positively. I tried to remember that I just had a tougher job, that I was Airborne and there was a certain pride associated with being Airborne! But, does it really matter if you're dead? It was a meat-grinder up there and no one in his right mind would want to be there. The fact remained: I was stuck with it. It was my job and I had to go. Maybe God was testing me. I put it out of my mind. After all, I really had no choice.

Chapter 51

THE ROAD BACK TO THE FRONT

M y last day in the Evac Hospital in Arlon was January 13, at which time I started my trip back to the front. The trip actually took four days and nights en route. I spent the first night in a "repple depple" (replacement depot) and slept on a concrete floor. The next night was quite a change as I stayed in a beautiful resort, the Hotel Panarama in Bouillon, Belgium. The last two nights were spent in smelly, but safe, stock barns!

When I was moved to the repple depple, I began to worry that I would be sent to the first outfit that needed replacements. I damn sure didn't want to go to a line infantry division. If I had to go back into combat, and I realized that I did, I wanted it to be with 193D of the 17th Airborne! Everyone assured me that I would return to my outfit, but I was skeptical.

That repple depple was a real zoo. It was located in several above-ground buildings of the old French Maginot Line. I thought the decor rather strange in that many of the walls were painted in light pastel colors and giant, bright-colored flowers had been painted everywhere. It seemed a weird way to decorate the otherwise drab military surroundings.

The sleeping accommodations also left a lot to be desired. We had straw tick mattresses laid on the cold, concrete floor. The only thing we could hope for was that we would only be there for a short time. That wish was to come true sooner than I thought.

Like me, most of the guys seemed to be recovered enough to be returned to action. They generally just laid around, deep in their own thoughts and dreading the time when they had to leave for the front. The other guys there were fresh, young kids that had only landed in the theatre a few days before. Some of them were still joking and laughing and anticipating their first action while others were scared stiff of what they imagined lay ahead of them.

For those of us going back up front, this was our last opportunity to get any equipment that we might need. I had lost my helmet when the shell landed near me and I had a faint memory of leaving my carbine in the jeep when I was taken to the aid station. I had been given a helmet at the hospital in Arlon, but I did need to draw a new weapon.

Standing in a long line of guys at the supply room, I learned that some enterprising paratrooper in the line up ahead had convinced the issue clerk that all paratroopers were armed with a .45 automatic pistol in addition to their rifle. Several troopers ahead of me were able to obtain pistols this way, but as fate would have it, they had run out by the time I reached the issue point! I was told to come back in a day or so, but I knew that even tomorrow was too late for me.

I did pull one fast one on the supply guys. As my combat jacket had several tears in it, I cut it even more with my knife and salvaged it for a jeep driver's mackinaw. This type coat was lined with the same type of wool used in a GI blanket, had a wide shawl collar, slash pockets and was completely waterproof. It was many times as warm as the Airborne-style combat jacket.

I was issued a new carbine and told to take all the ball ammunition I wanted. I didn't know what the situation would be when I got back to the company, so I filled my pockets! The carbine was the M-1 type, not the M1-A1 (with the folding stock) that the Airborne used. At this point I didn't really care. With the jeep driver's coat, my artics and a new helmet, I was as well-prepared as anyone else for where I was going.

I took the carbine and walked down the road a couple of hundred yards to a little village. There were some old houses nearby that had been practically destroyed by artillery fire. I set up some old bottles among the ruins for targets and tried to zero-in my new carbine.

Then I saw a barber shop sign and as I hadn't had a haircut in about a month, I walked in. The barber, an old Belgian who had peaked out at me when he heard me firing the carbine, then proceeded to give me a shave and a haircut for only 5 francs, or about 16 cents! I think he was not too sure of me after seeing me doing the shooting and he seemed very glad to see I had some francs and intended to pay for his services!

Returning to the repple depple, I passed an old church that had been practically destroyed. The roof was gone as were most of the walls and the pews were tossed about in disarray. Snow had covered most of the inside of the church, but there on the altar was the pulpit and behind it, a ten-foot tall statue of the cross with our Lord Jesus looking down.

I stood there for a minute and began to choke up a bit. I had prayed to God to save me when I ran down that road and through that field. He did and I realized I had never even thanked Him. In fact, I don't think I had even prayed since that day. I knew I had to pray again right then. I knelt there in the snow at that altar and I prayed for my soul and for my salvation in the place where I was heading.

As a group of us, all from the 17th Airborne, waited for the truck that we were told would take us back to our old outfits, we were treated to a real aerial side show. Way, way up in the sky we could see literally hundreds of airplanes. Many were going east and many others were returning to the west. The sky was a patchwork of contrails for hours as the planes passed in a never-ending stream.

The word went around that the planes were staging a massive daylight bombing raid on the German city of Cologne. After the war that particular air raid was declared one of the largest of the war. It still boggles my mind to think of the number of planes and the thought of being on the receiving end of all that military might.

The hours ticked by and still we waited for the truck that was to take us back to our outfits. As we waited we slowly became aware of two disturbing developments. First, earlier on we had been able to hear artillery firing in the distance. Now, we realized that we were hearing machine gun fire! Soon we realized that some of the firing we were hearing was that made by the high cyclic rate of enemy machine guns!

There was no mistaking that sound once you ever heard it! It was like canvas ripping! The fire was so rapid, the bullets seemed to be only inches apart. Accordingly, the GIs had nick-named all German machine guns "burp" guns and everyone had the impression that the rounds poured out of the barrel like a long, steel rod. We wondered why they could ever miss.

If this wasn't scary enough, another development soon caught our attention. We noticed that the cooks at the repple depple didn't seem to be preparing the evening meal. Instead, they were packing the kitchen equipment into trucks! Obviously, they didn't plan on being here for the evening meal! It could be the same old bug-out hysteria building up that had accompanied the initial German breakthrough.

I wish I knew what happened to this volatile situation and how it worked out. You could see panic building up in the eyes of the repple depple troops and you just knew it wasn't going to be a pretty thing. But, just when it was getting interesting, our truck finally arrived and we loaded on. Quickly, in a swirl of snow, we were on our way. I was glad that our driver wanted to make tracks out of there!

We were delivered to the Hotel Panarama in Bouillon, Belgium. It was a beautiful resort hotel set on a high hill overlooking a deep valley and a picture-book Belgian village. The army had taken it over and it was being used as a stopover for troops being recycled to the front. The food was good and that night I slept in a real bed. That was the first time since England!

My roommate that night was a trooper from Nashville, Tennessee. We had a great time talking about our home area. I remember we tried for hours to think of the name of Francis Craig who had a popular orchestra that played around home in those days. Finally, after I had gone to sleep, he woke me up to tell me he had thought of the band leader's name!

We were also puzzled by the bidet which was in our bath. We had no idea what it was for! We were not very worldly in those early days! Years later, in 1984 on a trip I made back to Europe with some friends, we stayed a night in the Hotel Panarama. This time everything seemed smaller and not so plush as it had been that night back in 1945! And, strangely enough, our room had no bidet in the bath!

Slowly, our driver wound through the countyside on the snow-covered, one-lane roads, forced many times to put the truck's gear in "bulldog" to plow his way through. Our next stop was in a small village that we guessed was somewhere near Corp Headquarters. There were big 240 mm guns set up nearby, but not firing at that time. It was dark when we arrived and we were told to fan out and find shelter as we would spend the night here.

Several of us headed for a large barn nearby. Barns were like motels in those days. They offered shelter from the icy wind and snow, provided piles of warm straw for your sleeping comfort and, if you were lucky, maybe an egg or two and some warm milk for your breakfast!

It appeared this farmer had locked his barn tightly to keep out the soldiers. There were heavy doors on one end that we just couldn't seem to open. We pounded and I gave them a mighty tug, but to no avail. About that time one of the other guys yelled that they had gotten the doors on the other end open, so we ceased our efforts and walked to the other entrance.

Everyone found a cozy spot, opened up a can of C-rations and after eating we fell asleep for the night. With all the other troops occupying the area, we didn't bother with putting out our own security.

The next morning as we awakened and prepared to continue our journey, one of the guys who had been with me the night before when we had been trying to open that door, called to me. He walked me over to the door and pointed upward without saying a word.

There, wired to pull the pin if the door was opened, was a German "potato masher" hand grenade. It was a crude but effective booby trap just waiting for some dummy looking for a nice warm barn. The one thing its designer hadn't counted on was the fact the old warped door might not open easily. It sure made me glad I had stopped to pray in that church.

We told some nearby troops about the booby trap and they said they would tell their C.O. and get some engineers over there to clear it. Knowing the army chain of command, that grenade is probably still there!

Our route took us through Bastogne, a city of 5,500 people. I remember seeing a burned-out CG-4A glider in the field where they had flown in medical supplies. I also recall seeing a big Sherman tank, unable to negotiate a turn in the road due to the ice-covered cobblestones, spin its steel treads on the ice and slam sideways into a brick building. Then we stopped for about an hour at the parochial school that was General McAuliffe's command headquarters building. Devastation was everywhere.

Along the way we took a rest stop and a short distance from where we stopped was the remains of a German convoy. Apparently, allied planes had caught the convoy on the road and had a real turkey shoot. They had strafed and burned several dozen vehicles and horse-drawn wagons. The twisted wreckage and the battered bodies of horses and men frozen in death littered the road and ditches.

We knew the Germans were short on petrol and the dead horses proved that they had resorted to old-fashioned horsepower in an effort to get their equipment out of the Bulge. This was the worse scene of destruction I have ever seen, before or since.

We strolled down the length of the convoy, looking at the destruction and for any souvenirs we could find. I came to a small Volkswagon that had been caught in the carnage and had been burned out. For a moment I thought about opening the compartment in the dash. Then I thought about that booby-trapped barn door and decided to leave it alone.

A few moments later, after I had moved on, some guy opened the dash door and instead of a grenade blast, he was rewarded with finding a small Italian pistol. The handle grips had carvings of nude females! I groaned at my "near-find" of this choice war souvenir. Like they say, "War is Hell!"

Continuing on our way north, we stopped for supplies at the 17th Airborne's 411th Airborne Quartermaster Company. We were somewhere near the outskirts of the town of Houffalize which was about 10 miles north of Bastogne. The 17th was occupying the sector from Houffalize to Hardigney. I had a short visit with my friend, Jimmy Spencer, who was in the 411th.

We passed through Houffalize and finally reached a small clump of farm buildings where I was dropped off at the 193D rear eschelon—the kitchen and supply leg. It was getting late by now and the kitchen crew was busy preparing a hot meal to take up to the company that night. They would take another "hot" up before dawn.

I guess I was trying to put it off as long as I could. I told them I would sleep in the barn that night and go up with them when they took breakfast up before morning. It wouldn't hurt to get one more good night's sleep, I reasoned. I should have gone on that night. I realize now that it was my own unwillingness to face up to what I knew lay ahead.

CHAPTER 52
THE BATTLE OF THE OUR RIVER

I
t was in the still-dark, early morning hours of January 18 when I rejoined the company in their frontline positions. They were somewhere north of Houffalize occupying defensive positions in one of those dense, Ardennes pine forests. No one knew exactly where we were. All road signs that had not been destroyed in the fighting had been removed by one side or the other to confuse their enemy. As a result, both sides were often confused and everyone stayed lost most of the time.

If I thought I was going to be welcomed back with open arms, I was grossly mistaken. No one greeted me or appeared to notice that I had been gone for 11 days. They seemed to have retreated into themselves and didn't want to get too close. They were all unshaven, dirty, hunkered over and silent.

It was a change, I'm sure, that had come about from the days of combat that the company had seen and the losses they had taken. When the 193rd entered combat the regiment's strength was 1,964. One month later it would be 915, a loss of 47%. During the Bulge combat, no true replacements were ever received by any of the units, so all the companies were understrength.

Company D had entered combat with a strength of about 200. At the end of our attack on January 7, and the disastrous withdrawal that followed, only 64 troopers were present for duty that night. Others filtered in during the next two days, but after that day the company never exceeded 100 in strength.

As I had been a gunner on the first platoon mortar, I expected to return to that position. Then I learned that most of the squad had been evacuated with frozen feet and the mortar itself had been lost in the withdrawal. There was no first platoon mortar squad. I was told to report to S/Sgt Leroy McCaslin who was now leading the first platoon which consisted of about 25 troopers.

This is when I learned that T/Sgt Charles Pierre had been badly wounded on January 7 and had later died of his wounds. This was a terrible shock as I guess we all thought if anyone could get us through this war alive, it would be Pierre. We thought he was indestructible.

We also thought our platoon leader, Lt. Bill Rudicel had been killed. Rudicel had been badly wounded, but finally made it back to the company in France. I didn't learn of his surviving until 1990, just before he came to the 17th Airborne Reunion in Washington.

While I had been gone, the 193rd had been attached to the 11th Armored Division and organized into a special task force to clear Houffalize and the vicinity. By the time I rejoined the regiment, they had gone into defensive positions and the only action involved recon patrols sent out to maintain contact.

On January 18th, we were reattached to the 17th Airborne as it assumed responsibility for the area. For the next two days we patrolled and maintained contact as the Germans continued to pull back. On about January 20, the 193rd moved back near the town of Malompre where we were given a couple of days of rest and refitting. I added another set of long underwear!

We were then trucked back south and to the Wiltz area of Luxembourg. We hunkered down in the open bed of 2 1/2 ton GI trucks and tried to keep from freezing. After awhile we stopped in Eschweiler where we were told the 17th Airborne Division Headquarters was located, but we were too cold and miserable to care. We hardly looked up.

Then I heard someone say, "Sergeant McCaslin! How are you doing?"

I stared vacantly toward the tailgate where Mac was sitting and saw it was 1st Lt. John Van Sycle, our former platoon leader who had been transferred to Division Headquarters to become aide to General John Whitelaw, the Assistant Division Commander. I had had my problems with Van Sycle, mostly due to my own immaturity. If they had not transferred him to this new job, there's no telling what kind of trouble I would have gotten into.

"Hello, Lieutenant," Mac answered in a rather flat voice that I thought carried little emotion, "We're okay."

I looked at Van Sycle and I surprised myself. Instead of hating him, I felt kind of sorry for him. He had a .45 strapped to his leg, like the old cowboys used to do. He would never have to make a "quick draw" way back here in Division Headquarters. This was "rear echelon". He was safe back here!

"Where's the First Platoon, Sgt. McCaslin?" asked Van Sycle.

"They're right here, Lieutenant," Mac answered.

"I mean the rest of them," replied Van Sycle.

"Lieutenant, this is the rest of them," Mac replied, "The others are dead, wounded, evacuated with frozen feet or missing in action."

A look of shock and disbelief came over Van Sycle's face and I could see that this news shook him. He had led our platoon for some time and I know it hurt him to learn that we had been torn apart. I don't think he knew quite what to say after that. We began to move out about then so he just wished us luck and said to be careful.

I don't think he recognized me. At least he didn't appear to. I've often thought about him. No one seems to know what happened to him after the war. I'd like for him to know that the smart aleck kid he knew at Camp Mackall finally grew up. He'd probably have a hard time coming to grips with the fact that Uncle Sam eventually saw fit to commission me a lieutenant colonel in Special Forces!

The trucks moved on and we sensed we were getting close to our final destination. Finally our convoy came to a halt and we dismounted. We then moved into a wooded area where we occupied some old positions and waited. It was now January 22 and the mercury had dipped as low as 18 below zero and we still had a foot of snow on the ground.

Captain Stuhrman surprised me by telling me to join one of the machine gun squads of the third platoon. I'm sure the move was because they were short of people. I certainly knew nothing about machine guns. I hadn't even fired one! I wasn't too happy about the assignment as I knew they drew fire and were a prime target for the enemy.

We learned that the Second Battalion was going to attack Hautbellain and the high ground to the east the next day and that we would be the reserve for the battalion. Apparently everything went well because when we moved up there seemed very little for us to do. I heard a lot of small arms fire, but never felt that we came under fire ourselves. The reports say we "mopped up" but I never saw a live German anywhere!

It was now January 26, and we were told the division was going to relieve elements of the 80th and 26th Infantry Divisions that had been holding the area in the vicinity of Hosingen. We would relieve the 80th. The Germans held Hosingen and the west bank of the Our River. The river formed the border between Luxembourg and Germany. With their backs to the river and the Fatherland just beyond, the Krauts should be plenty tough to drive out.

Our first problem was the relief in place. A relief in place, especially at night, is a very delicate military maneuver. First, there is the possibility of the two units shooting up each other if recognition signals are not handled carefully. Second, during a relief is a terrible time to run into an enemy probing attack or a combat-strength patrol.

The night of January 26 was black dark. If there was any moon or stars out that night, they were masked entirely by the heavy pine trees that covered the hillsides. Soon we saw the 80th Division guys moving back. Everything was going good so far. Soon it was time for us to move up. We moved out cautiously knowing how vulnerable we were.

Many of us had the safety off on our weapons. We were trying to see through the darkness and trying to be as quiet as possible. We really didn't know what lay ahead. The only sound was the soft crunch of our boots in the crusty snow.

Suddenly, a shot rang out that shattered the silence and then there was the muffled cry of someone who had been hit. Everyone went to ground and there was a mad scramble for cover. As we lay wondering what had happened, there was a thrashing in the bushes and we heard whispering and talking and then it went completely quiet.

When the shot was fired, I was walking down a narrow road near an armored vehicle of some type, maybe a tank destroyer. I immediately dived under it for cover. As I lay there wondering what was happening, I heard the crew stirring inside the vehicle. Then I heard a low whine as one of the crew must have switched on the battery to "warm up" in the event they needed to move.

"My God, they're going to move the damn thing," I whispered to myself, "and I'm going to get run over by my own army!"

I threw snow in all directions as I scrambled out from under the vehicle and into the trees. There I lay panting from the excitement and fear. My heart was beating like mad!

Things soon quieted down and we found out what had happened. Mortar squad members have canvas carrying cases much like large pistol holsters for their folding stock carbines. These cases free up their hands to carry the mortar and/or ammunition. One of our company mortarmen, Casimir Stemkowski from McKees Rock, Pa., failed to put the safety on when he placed his carbine in the case. When he inadvertently jarred the piece, it fired and the round struck him in the lower leg.

It was a painful wound, but Stem was okay and after being treated by a medic, was evacuated. Things soon quieted down and the rest of the relief went without mishap. I thought to myself, I hope this isn't a forewarning of things to come.

I was still worried about my lack of know-how on the machine gun when T/Sgt Earl Peck, the MG Section Sergeant, held out some help for me. Peck said for me to share his hole with him and he would give me a crash course on how to load, aim and fire. We now had the new A-6 model with a bipod and I had never even touched this weapon.

During the early morning of January 27th, Peck showed me how to clear misfires and load the belts. We even covered how to deploy the gun and other facts I needed to know. I still wasn't happy to be in a machine gun squad, but I felt a whole lot better by the time we attacked at about 1000 hours.

After a preparatory barrage from our artillery, we left our holes and started toward the town. The terrain was mostly open and except for a few shell holes and a sunken roadbed to our front, it offered little protection. Hosingen was about 1000 yards away but it looked like it was a mile.

The first 200 yards we were not fired on, but although I detected no grazing fire, the mortar and 88s really began to rain down on us as we neared the first buildings of the town. The fire was mostly in battery and we moved forward rapidly during the brief lull between barrages. The whistle of the shells in the air was the signal to hit the ground!

Things seemed to me to be going well. If we were taking casualties I couldn't tell it. It was very difficult to run in the deep snow and I began to warm up and breath hard. Then I saw a roadbed to my right and I headed for it knowing the packed-down surface would make running easier.

The rest of our three-man machine gun squad was to my left and making slow progress through the snow. I veered right to hit the road. Then I heard another flight of shells coming in. I looked quickly for cover and saw a number of wooden crates just off the road in a clump of trees. I dived into an opening among the crates.

As the shells began exploding around me, I saw to my horror that the crates were filled with 88 ammunition! Nearby was the abandoned 88 artillery piece. I had picked a hell'uva spot to take cover. If one of those incoming shells hit the crates, they would go up like a Roman candle!

Rocks, dirt and some shrapnel slammed into the crates. I prayed that the shrapnel would not hit a detonator. Then I became aware of the fact a number of the shells whistling in were failing to detonate! They were duds! Maybe they had been sabotaged by forced labor in the German munitions plants or maybe the good Lord was still trying to get me through this war! I think it was more likely to have been the latter.

As soon as the last flight of shells came in, I got to my feet and ran as fast as I could down that road! I wanted to put as much distance between me and those 88 crates as I could! After about a 100 yard sprint, my lungs were bursting and I dived headlong into the ditch beside the road.

There were two other GIs in the ditch where I landed, but I quickly realized that they were both dead and frozen stiff. They wore the shoulder patch of the "Yankee" 26th Division and no doubt they had been there for several days. As I gasped for my breath, I looked into their faces.

One had his eyes wide open and they were glazed over with ice. He had a surprise look on his face as if to say, "Did this really happen to me?" The other had his head down on his arm. He seemed to be asleep. It occurred to me that he had not died quickly. I saw his wrist watch and it didn't seem to be ticking. Time had stopped forever for this mother's son.

I realized that I had to get into the houses of the town to find any real shelter, so I arose and ran to the nearest house. I was relieved to find the other members of my squad sprawled inside on the stone floor. The ground floor was actually the cellar and it served as a place of shelter for the family's livestock. The stone walls of the building were a foot thick and the cellar floor was covered with straw.

It was now about 1130 hours as I took a seat in a low window sill. I looked out and up the street where the sound of small arms fire told me the fighting was taking place. I realized that I was back in the swing of things once again. The fear that had gripped me during our big retreat January 7 was no longer there. The adrenalin was pumping, but I was in control. It felt good to be in control again at such a crazy time!

I looked around at my fellow squad members: Dale English from Arvada, Colorado and Alvin Miskavige of Minto, North Dakota. There were only three of us. They were both gasping for breath, unsmiling and haggard-looking. They seemed almost uninterested in what was going on. I guess it was fatigue, but it was like they felt doomed and had given up hope of ever getting out of this mess.

I asked if anyone knew if the upstairs had been checked out. When they shook their heads, I got up and climbed the stairs with my carbine at the ready. I sure didn't want some Kraut to roll a grenade down the stairs on us or to suddenly jump into the room and hose us down with his burp gun. I checked out the upper rooms and they were all empty. Inwardly proud of the fact that I had overcome my fear and done this necessary task, I returned to the cellar floor and resumed my seat in the window sill.

As we awaited orders to move up, mortar shells were hitting in the street outside and in the houses around us. I suddenly realized that sitting in the window sill might not be a good idea. If one of those mortar shells hit in the cobblestone street just outside, shrapnel could hit me. I moved from the window seat and joined the others on the floor.

It proved to be a very wise decision. Within a minute, a shell hit in the street just outside and shrapnel zinged in the window and buried itself in the thick wooden beams of the ceiling. I gulped as I realized I had just missed getting my head taken off. This was beginning to be a very exciting day.

We could hear fighting going on up the street but we received no orders to fire our weapon. Finally, we were ordered to displace forward and we moved out. We moved slowly at first and then we began moving quickly. I hoped that those ahead of us were doing a good job of clearing the buildings. It made me nervous to move so rapidly .

Many of the buildings had a wall or two knocked down and all of them had been badly damaged. As I passed in front of one of the buildings where the front wall was knocked out, I saw a large table facing the street and to my horror, there was a German lying across it with a rifle pointed straight ahead.

I whirled quickly toward him, brought my carbine up and fired about five or six rounds as fast as I could pull the trigger. I'm not sure if I hit the German, but I know I hit the table! Splinters flew and the German slowly slid off of the table onto the floor. Some guy ahead of me yelled, "Take it easy! He was already dead!"

I was highly excited. It was the first and only time I ever fired my personal weapon at the enemy and he turned out to be already dead! I felt a bit stupid, but no one laughed or said anything else, so I guess it was okay. I would have rather been wrong than sorry.

We continued on down the street until we reached the open contryside. As we started up a steep hill leading to some woods, the artillery started coming down on us again. We were forced to take shelter and during this time I believe most of the Germans made it back across the Our River into Germany.

We finally gained the woods and the high ground where we set up our MLR (Main Line of Resistance). I have since learned that our MLR was designated as line CHERRY and it was astride Skyline Drive, a high ridgeline in the Schnee Eifel (Snow Mountains). The ridge followed the course of the Our River for miles and this formed the German-Luxembourg border.

It was now late afternoon and we were exhausted. The Germans apparently were too and both sides seemed to be willing to call it a day and lick their wounds. We scooped out the snow from some old positions we found and collapsed. No sooner did we begin to get our breath, when the artillery started pounding us again. The 88 and mortar fire rained down on us for the next hour or more. The fire hit in the trees and the treebursts were hurting us bad. The Germans knew the area and the location of every hole where we were huddled. There was little we could to do about it, but hope they missed us.

CHAPTER 53
ANOTHER PURPLE HEART

We had taken Hosingen and the Germans had retreated out of Luxemborug back across the Our River and into Germany. Now, if we could only hold the ground we had taken! It might be a tough task, but we set about organizing our defensive line.

We knew it was not a good idea to occupy any old positions. In the first place, these were not deep enough. And, the Germans were bound to know where they were located and could zero in on them quickly. But, we had little choice. The ground was frozen like concrete and there was no way we could dig new positions. Besides, after the energy we had expended that day, we just didn't have the strength to dig new holes. So, when they started firing their artillery at us again, in a sense we were at their mercy.

We had set the machine gun up in an old weapons pit about five feet square and 1 1/2 feet deep. It had another eight to ten inches of snow-covered dirt piled around the forward edge and sides. Probably dug for a machine gun, it was located about 12 feet from the front edge of the thin woodline. Two shallow slit trenches lay nearby.

To our front was about 100 yards of gentle sloping, open ground. Beyond that it dropped off into the Our River Valley. Some 200 or 300 yards beyond lay the river. We could just barely see the outline of the river banks from our positions. Ice rimmed each bank and extended out some 20 yards toward the center, but there the river ran swift and angrily. It was still at flood stage and at least twice its normal width. We were right on the cutting edge of Skyline Drive and didn't even know it. Just beyond, out of our sight, was the Siegfried Line and with it, the famous "dragon's teeth".

To take cover from the mortar and artillery fire, Dale English and I had dived into the old weapons pit. Although the hole was large enough for two people, it had no overhead protection. I felt naked in it, but it was better than nothing. I pressed against the rear wall and really hunkered down. Most of the fire was landing behind us and I felt like I was trying to disappear inside my steel helmet!

The rounds were hitting in the trees and you could hear limbs and whole trees falling as the shrapnel zinged around like angry bees. Every now and then you would hear someone cry out when they had been hit. The cry, "Medic!" rang out from several directions. They were giving it to us good. This went on for over an hour, but I'm sure all of us would swear that it lasted twice that time.

Soldiers in the ETO had a saying about the German 88 artillery piece. They said the German 88 converted more people to Christianity than the Apostles John and Paul put together! I believe it. The weapon was extremely accurate. With a good crew and top grade ammunition, the gun could put a round in a barrel at 1,500 yards. It was, by far, the best artillery piece of World War II.

Sometime during this period, Captain Stuhrman was hit in the leg by shrapnel. The XO, lst Lt. Jim Logan, took over and soon he was also hit. Jerry Stuhrman later joked about the fact that Logan beat him to the aid station!

Second Lt. Henry Webb, leader of the second platoon, had to be sent over to E Company as they had lost all their officers. This meant lst Lt. John Bailey was the only officer left in D Company, and thus he became our Company Commander.

Finally, the shelling stopped. We were very thankful and to the man we hoped neither side would resume. It would only meant the other side would retaliate and the killing would start all over again. With the coming of darkness, we wanted to get something to eat and settle down and maybe catch some sleep. We were pretty well spent and we knew our friends across the river felt the same way!

As our machine gun outpost was about the farthest point of our defensive line, we were told to send one of our people out each hour as a connecting link to the rifle squad on our left flank. This might have been the way "the book" said to do it, but it seemed pure folly to us. We talked to the other squad and we agreed on the fact that stumbling around out there in the dark was just asking for someone to shoot you. We just wouldn't do it. That way, anyone out of his hole after dark was to be presumed to be enemy and you could open fire on him.

Once the last light of day faded away everyone stayed put in his hole. If you had to relieve yourself, you did it in your steel pot and emptied it as far as you could reach out of the hole. Get out of the hole yourself and more than likely, you would be dead. Fortunately, no enemy patrols probed our lines that night and just about everyone got at least a couple of hours of sleep.

The temperature that night dipped to near zero and up there on the ridge the wind chill must have lowered it to at least 10 degrees below. Someone told me it dipped to 20 degrees below zero. I dozed off several times, but after 30 or 45 minutes I would wake up with my feet numb. I would stomp around and clump my feet together until the circulation returned and then repeat the whole cycle over again. We were all playing "Russian Roulette" with getting frozen feet.

That night several guys in our company lost this cruel game with frostbite. The attack had left us all wet with perspiration and when the mercury tumbled that night, wet socks and clothes practically froze on our bodies. Al Miskavige could hardly breath the next morning. He probably had pneumonia. He was assisted back by one of our medics and that was the last we ever saw of him.

Later that day, Sunday, January 28, we received a replacement for Al. He was Lowell Kinnaman of Cedar Vale, Kansas. Kinny had been with the company since the very beginning, but had to be left behind in the hospital in England when we moved to the continent. He had not been able to walk due to large sores on his feet caused by breaking in a pair of those buckle-type combat boots! We were glad to see him, but having seen no combat up to this point, Kinny's eyes were wide with excitement!

Our squad still consisted of only three people: Dale English, Kinny and me. I really didn't know who was the squad leader, but I reckoned it was Dale. Both Dale and Kinny were trained machine gun squad members. I was the only odd ball in the squad. I still knew very little about the weapon or it's deployment and I found that fact very disturbing. I just hoped that it would not put my life and those of the others in danger.

The rest of the day passed quietly. We watched the Germans walking around their positions and they watched us doing the same. However, no one shot at the other and things were settling down. We sent out patrols and I guess they did too although none of them hit our outpost. That night I heard firing somewhere down the line and that was enough to keep us awake.

Early the next day, Monday, January 29, Lt. Bailey came around checking the company positions. I pointed out to him the Germans on the other side of the river whom we had been watching. They were only about 600 or 700 yards away. I even showed him the section of woods where we had figured out they had their mess area. I added that I hoped they would not shell them as the Germans would be sure to bring counterfire on us and I couldn't see how they could miss us, stuck out here practically in the open!

Lt. Bailey said he thought the regiment would be defending this line for a good while and he doubted if they would call up a fire mission at this time. Little did any of us realize that we would remain in these positions for only two more days. Then our regiment would be relieved by the 513th on Wednesday morning, January 31st, and we would be moved off the line and into Division Reserve.

What would have been even harder to imagine was that in 11 more days, on February 11, the entire 17th Airborne would be relieved from the line by the 6th Armored Division and we would be heading for a marshalling area at Chalons-Sur-Marne to prepare for our first and only Airborne assault. On that cold, icy morning I thought the war would go on forever and the 17th Airborne would be sloshing our way through the snow and mud until we pushed the Germans clear to Berlin—or beyond.

Before he left, Lt. Bailey, almost casually, said that I would now be the squad leader. I was dumb-founded! I was the only one of the three that wasn't trained as a machine gunner! Frankly, with my scant knowledge of machine gun squad tatics, I didn't want the responsibility.

"Lieutenant," I stammered, "I've been trained as a mortarman. I should be in a mortar squad. I don't know anything about machine guns!"

"Well, now's a damn good time to learn," he answered, "besides, you're a PFC and they're both privates. Just keep calm, you'll do okay."

With that he was gone. As I mulled over that illogical way of making a command decision, the others said nothing and got on with what they were doing. As it turned out, my tour of duty as a machine gun squad leader only lasted about six more hours, so I guess it didn't really matter.

It was late in the afternoon now and things were quiet on both sides of the river. I got to thinking about that shelling we had had and I suggested to the other guys that we gather some of the large limbs and tree trunks that had been felled and put them over the top of the gun pit. Then, if they shelled us again, all three of us could crowd in and have some degree of protection. Everyone agreed.

Dale moved the gun to one of the nearby slit trenches and kept watch across the river for any suspicious activity by the Germans. Meanwhile, Kinny and I shed our jackets and began dragging tree trunks and large limbs over the gun pit. I guess we were so into our work we really didn't see a patrol from one of the other companies that was approaching our outpost from the rear and preparing to head toward the enemy lines.

I was standing in the gun pit with my back to the river. Kinny was standing slightly to my left rear as he was passing logs to me. I can still hear that German M-42 machine gun as it was fired from across the river and the bullets ripped through the trees around us. It was too late to take cover. That first burst got me.

I don't know if I instinctively dropped down in the hole or if the shock from that .31 caliber bullet knocked me down, but the next thing I knew, I was in the bottom of that hole with my face in the dirt. I knew immediately that I had been hit. My left arm was bent awkwardly under me and when I tried to move it, I could feel the two ends of the upper left humerus bone scraping together. The whole arm had a dull, numb feeling, but there was no pain whatsoever.

"I'm hit, Kinny!" I shouted, "Yell for a medic!"

I heard Kinny yelling and in just a few minutes, a medic jumped in the hole. He helped roll me over and began cutting away my sleeve to get at the wound. I could feel the warm, wet blood as it trickled down my arm. My wool knit sweater was getting soaked with it. The medic applied some pressure above the wound, then sprinkled sulfur powder on it and wrapped it with a compress bandage. I could see that the bullet had entered from the rear, apparently had shattered the bone and then exited through the bicep in front. Thank God, it had not hit the artery or a large vein.

I realized that this wound was really not a threat to my life if I just didn't go into shock. In this bitter weather, people frequently died from shock, even from minor wounds. I gritted my teeth and willed myself that I would not go into shock! Another thing soon came to mind at this odd time. I knew that this was what we called a "million dollar wound". That is, I knew I would be going to a nice warm hospital, the arm would eventually heal and, best of all, the war might even be over for me!

Before this could happen, however, I had to get out of this touchy situation I found myself in! The enemy machine gun was still chopping away at our position. I lay on my side in the hole as the bullets chipped small limbs and bark off the trees above and showered them down into the gun pit on the medic and me. The patrol which had drawn the fire had gone to ground in the area around our position when the firing started, but now they were up and running and getting out of there.

As soon as the medic saw he had the bleeding stopped, he said he needed to move on with the patrol. He told me where I could find a medical evacuation jeep over behind a hill to our rear and off he went to catch up with the patrol. I lay there for another 10 or 15 minutes more while the machine gun continued to chop away at the trees over and around me. Finally, the fire lifted from our position as the gunner shifted to the direction the patrol had taken through the woods. I have never understood why that patrol showed themselves like that in broad daylight. They were asking for it.

I decided it was time to get out of there before I did go into shock. I still had no pain, so I tucked my limp arm underneath my belt in front of me and heaved myself over the back edge of the hole. Then I started crawling through the snow toward the shelter of the woods behind me. After about 30 yards I realized I was not drawing fire, so I stood up and began walking to the rear.

As I started to the rear, I saw Adrain Test and he yelled to ask did I have my mackinaw on when the medic cut my sleeve! It was obvious he was only interested in learning if the coat he had asked for was still in one piece! He wasn't really interested in the fact I had damn near lost my arm. That was the cold, uncaring way I guess we had all become. I assured him the coat was still intact and that I had left it hanging on a tree down near our hole. I have never learned if he was able to claim it!

We had started getting some mortar fire by now and the rounds were landing in the woods. They were searching for that patrol. I moved on quickly, thinking to myself wouldn't it be ironic after getting this million dollar wound and a ticket to safety, I would be killed by mortar fire on the way to the hospital!

Every time I would hear a round whistling in, I would stop and hit the ground. The medic had not given me a morphine shot as I had no pain and he wanted to avoid anything that might send me into shock. However, now the two shattered ends of that bone, jabbing around inside my arm each time I went down, was beginning to bring on the pain.

Finally I came out of the woods and there, across an open field, I saw the medic jeep parked alongside a fence. It had now been at least a half hour since I had been hit and that jeep represented relief from all this, so I said to myself, "To hell with the mortars," and holding my arm tightly, I ran without stopping to the jeep. Several rounds landed in the open field, but I was not touched.

The medic at the jeep helped me into the seat and after a short but bumpy ride, we were at the aid station which had been set up in a farmhouse. There, after awaiting my turn, I was given a morphine shot, some sulfur pills and lots of water. They also put a Johnson splint on my arm and that plus the morphine did the trick. I was uncomfortable thereafter, but I never had the severe pain that I expected to have.

Although I didn't know it for a fact, I began to think to myself perhaps the war in Europe was over for me. I guessed it would be four or five months before my arm would heal and I would be returned to duty. With a little luck, the war against Herr Schickelgruber might be over by then! But, there would still be the Japanese. I figured I'd cross that bridge when I got to it!

Years later at one of our reunions, Kinny and I talked about that day when I was hit. It seems he also received an whelp on his neck as apparently another round from that first burst burned past him. The German M-42 machine gun had a cyclic rate of about 1,000 rounds per minute. This meant the rounds were so close together, that if that gunner had fired two additional rounds, one at the beginning of his sweep and one at the end, he might have killed both of us! Kinny would have been hit through the neck and I would have taken one in the heart.

PART FIVE:
HOSPITALS AND HOME

CHAPTER 54
THE HOSPITAL TRAIL

The long trail back through the military hospitals was a boring seven months of my life. It was like marking time. But, it was also like being born again. Bored as I was, when I saw some of the other guys in those hospitals and the shape they were in, I learned all over again how to appreciate being alive.

It all started late in that day on January 29, 1945, when the German machine gun bullet found me on the cold, snowy slopes of the Our River in Luxembourg. The seven months that followed changed me from a physically-tough, mentally-ready member of a crack combat outfit into a soft, out-of-condition, rear-area commando. I didn't like the change I underwent and I desperately missed my friends of the past two years.

However, I tried to focus on the good things. I was out of the cold and misery of combat. There was a chance that I would be sent back to the States. And, later on when the Germans and Japanese surrendered, I realized that I was going to survive the war. In the end, it all worked out okay but, it was a bumpy road.

By the time I reached the battalion aid station—my first stop along the hospital trail— my arm had begun to hurt quite a bit. The medics finally gave me a morphine shot plus a handful of sulfur tablets, but I didn't get much pain relief until they put a Johnson splint on my arm. This appliance enabled them to pull my arm away from my shoulder and thus separate the jagged ends of the shattered bone. This helped a lot and with a couple of GI blankets wrapped around me, I began to feel better.

From Hosingen I was moved by ambulance to Luxembourg City and to a hospital they had set up in the city hall. They placed my stretcher down in the entrance hallway at the foot of a large stairway. I recognized the number designation of the hospital, the 58th Field Hospital, Unit #3, as being that to which a good friend of mine was assigned. He was Casim Olwan of Ashland, Kentucky and a former student at the Business University in Bowling Green. I had even been a guest at his home during a break in the school year.

One of the orderlies knew him, so I asked him if he would find him and tell him I was there. In a few minutes, Cas, or "Balls" as we called him, was kneeling beside my stretcher as I lay in the entrance hallway. It really helped my morale to see him. Later, he brought me some candy bars and all kinds of goodies that I hadn't seen for months! I think his being there was quite important for my morale.

I was moved to a large room with other American wounded to await medical attention. As it should be, the most seriously wounded were treated first. Waiting in the same room was a German prisoner. There was no guard on him, but he was not going anywhere. His feet were so badly frost-bitten that they were twice the normal size and the poor devil couldn't even stand up. He was not complaining, but I knew he was hurting.

Nevertheless, it was too soon for me in my condition to be placed that near one of the enemy. Even though I knew he was not the soldier that had wounded me, I cursed and defiled the guy. In some way I guess I was trying to get even with the whole German army. Naturally, I have been sorry since that I acted as I did, but I don't think he paid much attention to me or my ravings.

Finally, the doctors got to me. They put me to sleep while the bone in my arm was set, the entrance and exit wounds were sewed up and a cast applied. I was surprised when I awakened to find the cast covered my whole left arm and shoulder and wrapped around my body down to my waist. My wounded arm was folded in front of me and attached to the body portion of the cast by a short spike. Only my head and uninjured right arm was left free. I was really immobilized!

By noon of the next day, I had recovered somewhat from the operation and I spent much of the day talking with Balls as I waited for my cast to dry. I learned one reason he was so glad to see me was that Lt. Jim Logan had come through that hospital and Balls recognized from his records that he was from my outfit. Upon questioning Logan about me, Logan had reported that I had been killed! Even that he had seen my body! There was no reason for Logan to have said that as I don't remember even seeing Logan after we got into combat. He just spouted off about something about which he had no knowledge.

I had a great time talking with Balls about Bowling Green and the old B.U. days. I was sorry to learn that I would have to leave the following day. But, this was a busy hospital and the casualties were still pouring in from the Bulge. They had to make room for others by moving the patients along the trail.

My next stop was by ambulance to Verdun. This hospital was probably just a holding station as I don't recall getting any additional medical treatment there. In another day or so I was heading for Cherbourg and transportation to England. My spirits began to lift a little here as I had fond memories of England and I reasoned my recuperation there would be enjoyable.

The trip to Cherbourg was by hospital train. In a letter home to my parents some time later, I wrote that the First Sergeant of the unit that operated the hospital train was a fellow named Jim Purcell. Before the war, he had been a catcher for the Bowling Green Barons, the minor league baseball club we had in the Kitty League. Another connection with home!

I don't know how many railcars our train had, but it was a long, long train with dozens of wounded in each car. In my car, I was in the top stack of about five stretchers. I was so high up and close to the roof of the railcar, that with the big cast I had, I couldn't set up or even turn over on my side.

When we came into the railway station at Paris, I was especially upset. Here I was in Europe's number one "Fun City" and I couldn't even see out! I raised so much fuss, that two of the medical orderlies lifted my stretcher down from its high perch and helped me to stand on my feet! It was the first time I had stood up in days and it sure felt good!

After a hour or two delay, we wound out of Paris toward Cherbourg. Along the way I remember seeing groups of German POWs at work repairing the bombed-out railways. As we passed them, many of the patients (me included) would lean out and curse them. They just laughed and said nothing. I know they realized the war was over for them. As prisoners of the Americans, they had a good deal. But for us, the wounded, the war still went on.

Finally, we reached the dock area at Cherbourg. The Germans had virtually destroyed this port after they saw the D-Day invasion was succeeding. It was a truly remarkable engineering feat that the Allies had been able to completely rebuilt it and now it was in full operation only eight months later.

I crawled back onto my stretcher, which had been lowered to the floor of the railcar, and two German POWs came in and carried me outside. There we joined a long line of patients being carried along the dock, up the gangplank and onto a British hospital ship waiting at the pier. The line moved slowly and there were frequent stops. During these stops, all the stretcher bearers would put their loads down to wait until the line moved forward again.

This was okay for a couple of times, but the POWs then began to put me down rather roughly. They would lower me to within about six inches of the ground and then drop the stretcher the rest of the way. The resulting bump, especially when they let the head end fall first, was painful and I cursed at them.

A big—and I do mean big—black MP came up and asked what was the trouble. I told him these guys had been dropping me and without saying another word, he whacked one of the POWs with his billy club! He told me I need not worry any more, he would watch them and if they did it again he would knock them off the pier. I had no more problems!

After enjoying tea and crumpets with the Brits as soon as we got aboard, we had an easy trip across the channel to England. Landing in Plymouth, we were moved to a hospital somewhere in England not too far from London. An old letter I wrote from here records this date as February 5 and identifies my address as "Hospital Plant #4198, APO-514B". While I was here, my folks received post cards on February 9 and 24, reporting on my condition. These cards were marked as being sent from a "116th General Hospital", but I have no idea where that was.

About the first morning after I arrived at the new hospital I was surprised to awaken one morning to find my feet had "peeled" during the night! The sheet was covered with dead skin that had peeled off and my feet were as pink and tender as a baby's behind! The nurse explained that this was normal for a person exposed to wet and freezing weather for a length of time. She said I had come close to having frostbite, but that I should have no lasting effects.

The main nerve in my arm obviously had been torn by the bullet as I had no feeling in my hand and very little in the arm itself. I could clinch my fingers into a fist, but then I couldn't open my hand. I hadn't told my parents about this condition as yet and I decided to just keep this part of my injury a secret until I knew if it would be permanent. No need to worry them further.

Soon after I arrived, they operated on me again. This, they said, was to take out some bone chips which they said should help restore some feeling in my arm. I figured I'd only get another uncomfortable half-body cast. And, so I did.

Left unattended after the operation, as I began to wake up I felt nauseated. Instinctively turning my head to avoid throwing up in bed, I rolled out of the high hospital bed onto the tile floor. The fall cracked the plaster cast and my arm, mounted on the spike in front of my body, drove the spike back into my body nearly puncturing my sternum.

It was a couple of days before they could schedule me back into the operating room, check out the arm and put a new cast on me. Lying flat on my back in bed, sore all over, incased in a wet plaster cast during a cold, English February, was certainly miserable. However, every time I got to feeling sorry for myself, I just thought about how much better off I was here in a safe and warm hospital rather that being up on the line in some cold foxhole.

GIs will always find a fun side to every situation and I remember one during my stay in that hospital ward. A favorite passtime the guys had was racing down the length of the ward between the two rows of beds. What made it an interesting contest was the fact that the racers were all leg amputees. The rest of us would bet on them like they were racehorses!

I remember this one guy, Brekowski, a Polish kid that we called "Breezy". He would win almost every race! In between the giant leap he took with his crutches, he would make a one-legged broad jump that shot him out ahead of the others. I would be willing to bet that Breezy didn't have any problem in adjusting to a life with an artificial leg.

One great feature of this hospital was the fact that each cluster of four wards, or "spider" as they were called, had its own snack kitchen. They kept milk, juice, cokes, cookies, cake and all kinds of goodies on hand and all you had to do was help yourself! In fact, they encouraged it. All of us were underweight and this was one way they were encouraging us to gain weight. I guess this is were I started putting on the pounds as my cast soon got uncomfortably tight!

Twenty days later, on February 24, they moved several of us to the airport and we were loaded aboard a C-47 that had been rigged with stretchers. We were flown to a hospital somewhere in Wales. Once again, I never really knew where it was located. Old letters indicate only that I was now at "USA Hospital Plant 4204, APO 557". At this stage of the game, we were content to be shuttled around anywhere they wished just as long as there was no shooting going on there!

When I got to my ward in this new hospital, I realized that everyone there had suffered wounds where there was nerve damage. I was a bit shook up when I began to see some of the patients in this ward. Some had scars that were 10 to 16 inches long and others wore large, awkward appliances. I was not too encouraged by what I saw. My morale began to sag.

I was carefully examined by a couple of neuro-surgeons and I ended up literally begging them to give me a little more time before they operated. They said the sooner they cut, the better chance I had of full recovery. Finally, we agreed to try some theraphy and give my arm a couple more weeks to see how it responded.

To my cast, they taped a big metal ring which encircled my hand. Then they hung little rubber band slings from this ring to hold each finger. Thus, when I made a fist, then relaxed, my hand would open up again. Then they gave me a rubber ball and told me to squeeze the ball hard in my left hand, then open my hand, catch the ball in the other hand and then repeat. Over and over again all day, every day, I repeated this boring routine.

This seemed to be child's play and I tired of it in a day or so. But, when I looked at those horrible scars some of the guys had, I took heart and resolved to work hard and hopefully avoid any surgery. Finally, on February 29th, one month after I had been hit, I wrote my parents and to prepare them, told them the full extent of my injury. We were all quite relieved when the doctors eventually decided I was going to be okay without surgery. All I had needed was time.

I had always thought that one of these days I would be told that I was going to be sent back to my outfit. I really didn't know how bad a wound a person had to have before they wouldn't send you back into combat. My experience before, during the crunch of the

Bulge, led me to believe that you had to be half dead! But, even now as I really began to improve, I realized that in my present shape, I would have a hard time keeping up if I was sent back to a combat unit anytime soon.

At this time, I doubt any of us thought that the war was anywhere near over. It had almost become a way of life for us. I wrote home it should all be over in six months (which it was), but none of us really believed it would. We thought it would go on forever. We received the Stars and Stripes newspaper and we listened to the BBC and the AEF stations on the radio, but it was hard to be sure of what was the truth and what was really happening. We were really isolated.

One night early in March, we learned that the Luftwaffe had bombed London again. We were never told it was a small, 24-plane raid and a "last-fling" effort mainly intented to jack-up the German people's morale. Actually it was of no military importance, but we thought it was starting all over again and the Germans were coming back to haunt us.

My letters home from this hospital reeked with the boredom associated with recuperation. I joked about the bed pans calling them "flying forts" and the urinals as "P-38s". I mentioned reading "A Tree Grows In Brooklyn" and Bob Hope's "I Never Left Home" and that I had written some letters for other guys who couldn't write because of their wound. I remember that some of the letters were real personal and most everyone down-played the seriousness of his wound. Actually, they were all sad letters and I tried to keep mine on the light side.

The days dragged by slowly. I remember bending a wire coat hanger into a device which I could stick down the back of my cast and scratch my back! Boy, how I longed to really scratch those hard-to-reach places! Finally, they sawed off the top half of the cast covering my arm and replaced it with elastic wrap. This did wonders to eliminate the smell that had been coming up from the cast and at last, I could scratch my arm!

We were a sorry lot in our ward. Instead of being glad to be out of combat, we all had too many bad memories to be cheerful. I remember a wounded medic telling me that he had a young soldier die in his arms and his last words had been "What will my Momma say?" It continued to haunt him and he told the story over and over to anyone who would listen.

I recall a real downer that I experienced. We had one fellow in the ward who had lost his right arm, but had never informed his folks or his girlfriend as to the full extent of his injury. Official Army communications had stated only that he had been "severely injured". I had written several letters for him and finally he asked me to write to his parents and the girlfriend telling them the truth. I did the best I could and I can only hope I did an adequate job.

I figured I would be in the hospital another month or two and then be sent back to my outfit, wherever they were. Then, one day, out of a clear blue sky, I got the word that all the guys were waiting to hear: I had been "ZIed"! That meant I had been marked to be shipped to the Zone of the Interior— returned to the good old U.S.A.!

On March 21 I was moved to a holding facility at an airbase near Aires, Scotland. Here I was to await air transportation back to the States. As I left the hospital a stack of mail finally caught up with me. I received 145 letters from home including 23 from Georgeanna! What a morale booster this was!

All of the guys I saw at the airbase were in pretty bad shape. Many had suffered frozen feet and they were bedfast with their feet protruding from under the sheet. I had never seen feet like that—gun steel blue and some almost coal black with the toes nearly flat. Surely, these poor guys had to be facing amputation.

I remember seeing a familiar face from the 513th PIR while I was at the airbase. I never knew his name, but he was a small, thin trooper of Latin decent who had been one of our run instructors in jump school. We had admired the way he took class after class for their runs and seemed never to tire. He would run backwards much of the way, counting cadence as he went. He seemed like a running machine. He had been hit in one of his legs and now he needed a spring appliance attached to his boot to lift his foot when he stepped forward. It was all he could do to hobble along. It just didn't seem fair.

While we were there, we walked over to the area where some British fighter planes were parked. Several of the guys climbed up into the Spitfires and Mosquitos and got a close look! With my cast, I couldn't get in the Spitfire but I did climb up into the cockpit of one of the all-wood Mosquitos. It was easy to see why they said flying this plane was like going into combat already in your coffin!

I'll never forget one experience I had at this airbase. I was walking over to the mess hall one morning to eat breakfast. It was March 24, 1945. I saw a group of guys huddled around a radio listening to a special AEF news bulletin. I went over to find out what was the latest war news. What I heard brought my heart to my throat.

The announcer said that Airborne troops, the British 6th Airborne Division and the American 17th Airborne Division, had made an Airborne assault that morning across the Rhine River into Germany! No report was given on their progress, but they were said to be heavily engaged. As we later found out, 430 brave 17th Airborne troopers died on that first day.

It's hard to explain how I felt. I was happy that I had not needed a nerve operation and I was glad that I was going home to America. But, suddenly I felt terrible. My buddies had flown into battle as Airborne troops—what we had been training to do all these years—and I was not with them!

I was fully aware of the danger involved and that if I had been there I would have been in danger of being killed. I was also aware that in my present condition they would not have let me go. Yet, I felt like the dangers they had faced and were facing, I should have to face. I still felt like I was one of them and when I was needed, I should be there!

I was totally, totally frustrated at the situation. I didn't care who saw me or what they thought, the tears came and I began to cry. No one spoke. I guess they understood.

After about a week's wait, our ride back to the States was ready. It was a C-54 transport plane rigged with stretchers and complete with a physician and several flight nurses aboard. I remember there was a big cheer that went up from all the patients when we lifted off! I don't know the number of patients it carried, but it was a full load, probably 40 or 50. Few of us had ever thought we would live to see this day.

On a stretcher opposite mine, there was a black soldier and I could tell he was in bad shape. I learned that he had been a tanker, his tank had been hit and he had lost a leg. The amputation was near the hip and there were several tubes in his hip and body. He was a very sick man and one of the nurses was at his side constantly. Then the doctor began working on him and I could tell things were getting critical. Finally, just before we reached Iceland, our first stop on the way home, they lost him and they quietly pulled the blanket over his head.

We landed at Iceland and an ambulance came out and they off-loaded the body. I was glad they had another way to send it home rather than with us. We were quiet for awhile, but then some GIs in a jeep came out with several five-gallon containers of real American ice cream! That really put a smile on our faces as many of us—including me—hadn't even seen any real ice cream since we left the States!

We also had an interesting visitor to our plane while they were refueling. It was Col. Phillip Cochran who was with the Air Force and currently stationed in Iceland. Cochran had been the inspiration for Col. Flip Corkin, hero of Milton Caniff's popular comic strip of that time, "Terry and the Pirates".

The next leg of our trip brought us to Newfoundland where we landed for refueling. It was in the middle of the night so we really saw nothing of the place. I stirred awake and then went back to sleep. Then, it was on to Long Island, New York and we landed just as dawn was breaking. We were home at last! I had never cared much for New York, but it sure looked good that morning!

They took us to a hospital ward and we had a great breakfast (in bed) of ham and eggs—real eggs! Then, a lady from the Red Cross came around with a cart carrying a portable telephone. She plugged it in to a jack located by each bed and told the patient he could have a free telephone call to anywhere in the United States!

I selected Mother and Dad for my free call, but I also asked the lady to call Georgeanna's home as long as she had the Kentucky line! I offered to pay for it, but she said to forget it. Georgeanna and I had "broken up" about a year before, but we had continued to write to each other occasionally and I guess I always knew that I still loved her. She was the one I was most anxious see when I got home. I could tell by the sound of our conversation that things looked encouraging!

Later that morning they came around the ward asking who would like to go in a van and enjoy a sight-seeing tour of New York City, topped off with a free live show at the Paramount Theater. Despite my cast and the fact I would have to wear pajamas and a bath robe, I quickly "volunteered". That was about the smartest thing I ever did! What a live show that was! Ella Fitzgerald singing on stage with the Cootie Williams' orchestra! It was a great welcome home.

Once again, however, I failed to outsmart the army when it came to selecting my assignment to a general hospital here in the States. We were instructed to list our preferences in order, 1-2-3. They said they would try to locate us as near our homes as possible. I listed Kentucky, Tennessee and Ohio in that order. Naturally, they sent me to Mississippi. So, the best I could do was to look out of the C-47 hospital plane when it flew over Bowling Green on its way to Jackson, Mississippi, my home-to-be for the next three or four months.

CHAPTER 55
HOME AT LAST!

I arrived at Foster General Hospital in Jackson, Mississippi on March 28, 1945 and was assigned to Ward 22. Two days later on March 30, my large body cast was removed and a small cast encasing only my left arm, was applied. Oh, it was Heaven to be able to scratch my back and stomach again! It was already turning hot in Mississippi and the arm cast was much cooler and so much more comfortable.

Another great thing about my new cast was the fact I could now wear my uniform again. Shedding those hospital "jump suits" and the pajamas and robe was a pleasure! And, because I could now wear clothes, I was given a 30-day furlough and got to go home! With a wad of emergency pay in my pocket, I caught the train for Bowling Green.

What followed was the longest train ride in history! It took about seven or eight hours and it seemed like we were creeping along. When the Bowling Green train station came into sight, I was estatic! That old station was later abandoned and fell into poor repair, but recently when I visited the site, and saw the efforts underway to restore it to all its glory, all the old memories of the war years came rushing back. I recalled when the troops trains passed through here and when many of my friends left for the service from that station. Most of all, however, I remembered this wonderful homecoming day of mine!

My Dad was working on this day when I returned, but Mother met the train and it was great to see her again. I had been here on pass from Camp Forrest in July of 1944, and here I was home again in only about nine months! A lot of water had gone under the bridge in that short time. I'm sure I was not the same person I had been before.

Also meeting the train was Evelyn, Georgeanna's sister. Although Georgeanna was at home, she deliberately stayed away from the "homecoming" scene! I guess that was the right thing for her to do as she didn't want to seem too eager to renew our relationship. Of course, I guess she was a bit uncertain about whether she wanted to or not. I couldn't blame her.

We stopped at the post office and I went in the back door to see Dad. We embraced and Dad teared up. Today, as a parent myself, I can well understand how he felt to have me back out of the hell where I had been. I don't know if I could have handled it if my two sons had been called to service during Vietnam. It's one thing if you have never been to war, but if you have, and survived, you know the danger involved.

I can't recall how it came to pass that Georgeanna and I made up. I just know that in a short time everything was okay again with us and I was very happy. Now, over 52 years later after our marriage, I still consider myself a very lucky guy!

Just before my 30-day furlough was up, I learned that my old buddy, "Butter" Williams, was due to come in on leave from the navy. We had been inseparable before we both went in service and I wanted very much to see him again. I thought it was hopeless, but I went to the Red Cross and they wired for a five-day extension for me. To my surprise, I got it! I'll never forget those days Butter and I had together that summer.

Those beautiful 35 Spring days of April and early May at home passed quickly and by May 10 I had returned to the hospital at Jackson. I remember one of the big bands, Frankie Masters, played at the hospital on May 16. I still had my arm in the cast, but that night I jitterbugged with his female vocalist while everyone cleared a circle and cheered! I was getting my legs back even if the old arm was still a bit shaky!

Another night at the hospital I saw Egar Kennedy in a Red Cross show. He's the actor who had the bad temper in movie short features that were popular in those days. Helen Keller, the blind writer, was another notable that I saw and attended her lecture at the hospital that May in 1944.

I saw several guys from our division that I recognized and one who had been in our company and with us on the attack at Hosingen. Then, one day in the PX I ran into Jimmy Wilson, a friend from pre-war Bowling Green who had lived only two houses from me! He had been in the Seventh Army and had been evacuated with rheumatic fever.

I received a letter from Robert Ryan while I was in the hospital. He had been in my mortar squad and we had packed some of our gear together when we left England for combat. The letter had been written in March before the Rhine operation. He said he was now in B Company of the 194th. He also said he would try to send various personal items to me, but I never received anything or heard from him again. I understand he did survive the war, however.

Finally, on May 14, the cast was removed and I began a program to rehabilitate my arm. I recall we played croquet for hours! The numbness had greatly diminished and most of my fingers had begun to work again, but the elbow had been in the bent position for so long, I couldn't straighten it out. However, for the first time, I began to think that my arm was going to be as good as before.

Foster General was a big hospital and we got good care there. I had my teeth checked and for the first time in my life, they found some cavities. Three of them! I had these filled and then they pulled my two upper wisdom teeth! This was quite an experience for me, but I had no problems and very little pain. I do remember that the lieutenant colonel dentist that pulled them practically climbed up in my lap to get them out!

On June 9, I heard from my old squad leader, Sgt Henry Clay Browning from Seikston, MO. Brownie had left the company about mid-January with frozen feet and was now at Camp Carlson, Colorado. He told me Hungry had also had frozen feet and after getting out of the hospital, had been reclassified and was now in the Air Corps and a cashier in a PX in France! My old friend from home, T. H. Posey, was at Camp Carlson and I got him together with Brownie. I guess they discussed me at length!

After a few weeks of the tiring rehabilitation program, the whole arm really began to improve. When I was able to get it almost straight and the muscle had begun to strengthen, they transferred me to Wakeman Convalescent Hospital at Camp Atterbury, Indiana. This wasn't too far from Bowling Green, so I was looking forward to getting home some more from there.

I arrived at the hospital at Camp Atterbury at 3 a.m. on June 12. I was assigned a bed and promptly decided to "get lost"! I ignored an early morning wake-up call and slept in.

A few months in the hospitals sure got a person out of the habit of soldiering! I had been half-starved when I was hospitalized and after stuffing myself for several months, I also was getting fat and lazy. I weighed 180 pounds and was no longer trim.

I was billeted in the upstairs of a double-deck troop barracks and I soon learned no one ever came up there all day. So, the next day, I slept in again and again no one bothered me or came to check on me. It was a pretty good deal and I resolved I would keep it up as long as it lasted!

By questioning the other guys and being a bit observant, I began to see where their system was flawed! Unless you reported in for reveille, you were not scheduled for any rehab classes. As long as the NCO who had been appointed barracks chief saw you were there, he didn't turn you in as AWOL. Therefore, as long as you were there, and didn't report in for a rehab assignment, you fell through the crack!

To determine if I wanted to set up a rehab schedule, I went around to check on what the other guys were doing. One activity class was being taught by an ex-professional wrestler, popularly know in those days as "Man Mountain Dean". I knew I didn't want any part of his pulling and stretching class!

Another class played basketball all day, another played volleyball and another touch football. These guys all returned to the barracks in the afternoon, hot, sweaty and worn out. I decided this type of exercise was not for me.

From this violent routine, it went on down to woodworking, making bead belts and leather whatnots to painting and calisthenics. I came to the conclusion their entire program wasn't suited for me and that I would rather walk around the PX and read magazines in the service club. And, so I did and my arm healed just fine!

On June 27, I went over to Fort Ben Harrison to see Art Jastal who was a patient in the hospital there. Jastal had been badly wounded on January 7 in our first big attack. He had a big plug out of the thigh of one leg where a chunk of shrapnel hit him that day. The same shell had wounded Ernie Stull and resulted in his transfer to the Air Corps. Jastal was lucky not to have lost his leg. Years later when I saw him he still had a decided limp.

On July 9, the night before I left the Camp Atterbury facility, another soldier and I went into Indianapolis. You can't believe how many big bands were playing there that night! We went to a theater for a stage performance by Vaughn Monroe's orchestra, and then to a hotel where we listened to Frankie Carl's band.

Later, we topped off the evening by going to another hotel to hear Blue Baron's orchestra. Blue Baron—or whatever his real name was—had been assigned to the Airborne back when we were at Camp Mackall. How he got out of the service I don't know or remember, but there he was. He invited us to sit at his private table with his wife and during the band's breaks he sat with us and we talked about the old Camp Mackall days. It was some night and I'll always remember it fondly.

Someone finally caught up with me and I guess it was determined that it was time for me to leave the Convalescent Hospital at Camp Atterbury. So, on July 10, I was given another furlough! This was a 60-day delay enroute with orders to report to a hotel on Miami Beach! The army had taken over a number of the hotels and were operating them like a rest area. It was a good deal. So good in fact, I thought sure there must be a catch in it somewhere, but as it turned out, there wasn't!

The 60 days in Bowling Green, coming just shortly after the previous 30-day furlough, wasn't all that great a deal. Most of my friends were still somewhere in the service and Georgeanna was going to Western all day. After a few days, I really didn't know what to do with my time.

All the action seemed to be at Western, so I decided I'd just go to college myself and I signed up for the six-week summer session. This way I would be with Georgeanna some of the time and at least, around other young people. It beat hanging around the pool room!

I signed up for an art course because I enjoyed drawing and because I liked Dr. Ivan Wilson so much. I really enjoyed this class and I will always have a special place in my heart for this kind, gentle man. Then, for no other reason except the fact that Georgeanna was in the class, I signed up for trigonometry with Dr. Johnson. This decision proved to be a nightmare.

To begin with, I was always slow in math and trig was way over my head. In addition, I realize now I was not really adjusted to college life after what I had been through and I found it impossible to study properly. Georgeanna tried to help me, but I could not concentrate and in no time, I was flunking the course.

I remember going in to take our first test which was after about two weeks of classwork. There were five problems on the blackboard for us to solve. I couldn't even make a stab at working any of them. I only knew I had to get out of that class fast, so I wrote "I quit" on my paper, handed it in and walked out!

Three years later, on the eve of my graduation from Western with an A.B. degree, I was informed that I had an "F" in trig and all failing grades had to be made up before you could graduate. I was frantic! Would I have to stay on for another whole semester just to repeat that stupid trig class that I didn't even need to graduate?

I went to see Dr. Johnson and because trig was not required for a degree in English, he graciously agreed to waive the failing grade so that I could graduate. I remember him saying I should have applied myself better and that I hadn't had the proper attitude! I don't think he had any idea of the quantum leap I had made coming from the battlefield to the classroom.

CHAPTER 56
THE WAR IS OVER!

People like to recall where they were and what they did on VE-Day. For some unexplained reason, I don't remember anything about what I did on VE-Day, May 8, 1945. From a letter written to Georgeanna on May 9, I have learned that I spent the better part of the day in Bowling Green as I wound up a 35-day furlough. I caught a train late that evening and headed back to Foster General Hospital in Jackson, Mississippi. In the letter I said that the conductor (who saw that I was a wounded veteran) found me a double seat in a special coach and I curled up and slept from Memphis to Jackson. It was certainly an uneventful day for me.

I also can't remember any celebrating at the hospital. All the guys there were acutely aware that Japan was still in the fight and the job was far from completed. By that time, almost everyone had expected Germany to fold. The war news had been so encouraging we realized it had to end soon.

Hovering over everything, however, was the dread that maybe we would be sent to the Pacific and it would be the same old meat grinder all over again. You must remember at that time no one knew anything about an atomic bomb. Everyone was planning on a foot-by-foot fight for the Japanese islands. It was a real feeling of relief when the bombs were dropped and Japan was forced to surrender.

Only with Japan's surrender could any serviceman dare to think about a future. Only then could a young man begin to think about the possibility of a life after the military. I was surprised to realize how I had put my life "on hold" and had no idea what I was going to do when I got out of the service.

The only two things I was certain of was that I wanted to marry Georgeanna and that I wanted to return and finish college. I just hoped that everything else would soon fall into place. I was just so darn glad to have survived, that I really didn't worry too much about the future.

I was home on leave again from the hospital on 6 August 1945, when they dropped the bomb on Hiroshima. I had never heard of the place, but I knew many had died that day. Still the Japanese would not surrender. Then on 9 August, another bomb was dropped on Nagasaki and more died. I had no regrets as I reasoned they had started this thing in the first place and it served them right.

Today, I am saddened by the carnage that took place those days. My heart goes out to the thousands of men, women and children who perished. Although dropping the bombs no doubt saved the lives of thousands of GIs who would have died in a conventional invasion, it was still a horrible way to end what had been such a bloody conflict.

What is often forgotten is the fact that the bombs saved a lot of Japanese lives too. If we had invaded—and we certainly would have—they would have defended every inch of their homeland to the death. There was just no easy way to end it.

When Emperor Hirohito surrendered on 15 August 1945, I found it hard to comprehend what was happening. I was stunned. I could hardly believe this day that we had all been waiting for was actually here! I had survived! I would have to make new plans. The old ones no longer held true.

Early in the evening on that historic day I remember walking down State Street in downtown Bowling Green. Bells had been ringing all day and the horns of automobiles were being sounded continuously. There was a constant din in the air of people laughing and singing. Bowling Green's downtown was turning into a wild, happy carnival.

The streets around the "square" were packed with people. I'm sure a lot of alcohol was flowing, but there was little need for spirits as people were genuinely happy and not shy about showing it. It was a day like I had never seen before and have not seen since.

If you were in uniform, and I was, people stopped you, shook your hand and thanked you for serving. Some of the more daring young ladies even kissed you—an act not common in conservative Bowling Green of 1945!

I walked along in a daze and I felt very uncomfortable. I didn't feel like a hero or anyone who deserved all the attention I was getting. I made for Hurt's Poolroom, a place where Butter and I used to loaf, meet our buddies and shoot some pool. There it would be normal, I hoped.

Before I could reach the poolroom, I was stopped by two Military Policemen. They were from Fort (then Camp) Campbell and as many of the Campbell soldiers visited Bowling Green in their off-duty hours, the MPs helped the local police keep order. It was very warm in Bowling Green that evening and I was not wearing a tie. Suddenly, I was in trouble.

Although wearing a tie was required by the Camp Campbell regulations, I somehow felt I was not subject to their regulations. I wasn't stationed at Campbell and I must admit, as a combat veteran, I regarded the regulation as pure "chicken".

On the other hand, the MPs were determined to enforce their orders and I feel sure, they relished the idea of showing a cocky paratrooper and a combat veteran that in this city, their word was law. Threatened with being locked up in my own home town on such a day of celebration, I agreed to return to my car, get my tie and put it on.

As soon as I was out of their sight, I continued on my way, sans tie, and hopefully, got lost in the crowd of people that was now collecting in downtown. And, it was a crowd! At that time there were no malls and no shopping centers in the suburbs. Everyone came downtown! The sidewalks were crowded!

Soon a big rally was started over in the courthouse yard. There was a large speaker's stand—left over from some political rally—and it became the center of activity. It was the American Legion that got things going and my soon-to-be father-in-law, Charlie Banks, who was one of the Legion's local officials, was directly involved.

They had a band playing patriotic music and all the politicians and Legionnaires were on the platform vying for speaking time. The people were cheering and laughing and it was a great day! After all the years of war, it was finally over and everyone was just letting go!

Charlie spotted me in the crowd and yelled for me to come up and say a few words. Well, you couldn't refuse a suggestion like that, especially if you hoped to marry his daughter! I was a bit embarrassed, but I went to the microphone and said something, God only knows what! I later saw a newspaper account of the rally and it said that "Sergeant" Bartley Hagerman spoke! I apparently was a huge success!

My time on the speaker's stand nearly became my downfall, however. The two MPs who had jumped me for no tie and then had let me go with a warning, were in the audience. Needless to say, they came after me as soon as I left the platform. I eluded them for the moment as I beat a hasty retreat. About a block away they finally caught up with me. They then loaded me into the back of their jeep and set out around the square heading for the Police Department and their lockup.

By this time the streets around the square were filled with people all celebrating VJ-Day. I felt like a fool perched back there on the rear seat of the jeep with two MPs up front and heading for the jail! The wounded veteran, back to his hometown on leave from the hospital, thrown in the slammer because he wouldn't wear a necktie! A hell of a note.

The jeep slowed due to people crowding into the street and when it did, I vaulted over the side and ran as fast as I could! In no time, I was lost in the crowd and the MPs were history. I ran to where I had parked the family car and left the downtown area as quickly as I could.

I remember a number of us went out to Hill's cabin on Barren River Road that night. I don't remember who was in the group but there were 10 or 12 of us who had gone to school together before the war. Included in the group was Mitchell Leichhardt who was then a captain in the Army Air Corps. Mitch was a navigator who had completed his 25 missions in the European Theater and was also home on leave. We had been friends since childhood and our parents had also been close friends.

About midnight, we came back into town and about six or seven of us decided to get something to eat before going home. The Greyhound Bus Station was about the only place open at that time so we all filed in and occupied one of the circular booths.

I had just ordered my food when up walked the two MPs and ordered me to get out of the booth. No amount of begging would change their tone and I slowly got up. My friends had all heard my tale of jumping from the jeep and escaping from the MPs before but now they were silent as little mice, waiting to see if the MPs were going to handcuff me and haul me off to jail, or just shoot me on the spot.

Thank the Lord, Mitchell came to my rescue. Normally the mildest-mannered person you ever saw, slow of speech and ever the diplomat, Mitchell saved me from the slammer that night. We all went outside and in the privacy of the parking lot, Mitchell negotiated my release. Speaking softly at times, then at other times raising his voice and using his status as an officer, he soon had the MPs feeling ashamed of themselves as to the way they were treating this brave combat veteran!

Mitch assumed full responsibility for my conduct and promised the MPs that he would see that I put on my tie and that I would immediately leave for my home. Someway, he convinced them that locking me up would not be necessary and I am to this day indebted to him. That would have been a tough one to explain: how I spent VJ-night in jail.

With the surrender of Japan, my thoughts, like the millions of other GIs, quickly turned to things not associated with the military. The military became just a necessary delay until you could start up your life again. "When will you get out?" became the words on everyone's lips.

My memory of VJ-Day will always remain crystal clear with me. But, for the life of me, I can't remember a thing about what I did on VE-Day! I know, however, I had to have been very, very happy!

Chapter 57
VACATION ON THE GOVERNMENT

W hen I left Camp Atterbury, they told me I was going to be sent to the Army
Ground & Service Forces Redistribution Station (A.G. & S.F.D.S.) at Miami
Beach. I liked the sound of Miami Beach as that was the premier vacation spot
in the United States at that time. But, the words, "Redistribution Station" sounded very
much like reassignment to the Pacific Theater of Operations.

At that time, no one had any idea of what an atomic bomb was, much least how it
would change everyone's lives in the future. The key information was that my assignment
to Miami Beach would involve another delay-enroute set of orders. Little did I know that
the next 30 days would rewrite the history books and my life with it.

Enroute to Miami Beach, and the so-called Army Redistribution Station, I did
something I have never been too proud of. Fearing that Florida might be "dry", I got off
the train briefly in Atlanta and purchased two fifths of Canadian Club whiskey. I put them
in a little canvas carry-on bag I had and stored them in the overhead rack above my seat.

Another soldier got on in Atlanta and sat down with me and we struck up a
conversation. Also getting on the train at Atlanta—and filling all the remaining vacant
seats—were a number of Baptist preachers. They had been to some sort of meeting and
they were chattering away about the soul-saving new ideas they had picked up at their
meeting.

As the train began to move, the two bottles in the bag overhead began to jiggle and
bang together. Slowly the conversation among the preachers subsided and one after
another, their eyes shifted up toward the bag wondering what the noise was. Maybe they
guessed! The soldier beside me caught on quickly and we began to smile at each other.

After awhile, the soldier said to me that he sure wished he had a drink! With that, I
thought what the hell, let's have one! I opened one of the bottles, we got some paper cups
and laughing, the two of us had several drinks! We even offered the preachers some, but
they all declined! From there on to Florida, everyone on that railcar was quiet as a
mouse—except the other soldier and me!

The two weeks I spent in Miami Beach were really something. I still can't get over
what the Army did. It was completely out of character. It was as if they suddenly realized
that we had been through Hell and were trying to compensate or award us for what we had
done. It was like they were trying to say they realized how terrible they had treated us all
these years and that they were sorry! I was afraid I would wake up and find it was all a
dream!

As my orders stated, on September 1, I reported in to the Albion Hotel and was sent
over to the Sands Hotel. It was right on the ocean and at that time one of the finest hotels
on the beach. The rooms were the best I had ever seen. There was a beautiful swimming

pool at the rear and lots of white sand and the ocean beyond. I remember the hotel provided me with my first experience with a guest-operated elevator!

I shared a oceanview room with another soldier, Earl "Ham" Hamilton of Harlan, Kentucky who had been in the 14th Armored Division. There were no set hours. We slept late, ate when we wished to and could have stayed out all night if we had wanted. We were our own bosses for the first and only time while I was in the service!

All the hotels on the beach had been taken over by the military and they had turned it into one big resort area. We were given an identification card and to eat we just went into a place called the Hoffman Cafeteria and showed the card. Movies were also free to us and the Army had set up a number of ice cream stands where all you had to do was show your ID. You didn't need money...except in the bars!

After a couple of days, I ran into James Bruton who was from Bowling Green. Bruton had been in the 82nd Airborne and had become a POW in Holland. We knocked around together while we were there on the beach and I ran into him again the next month in Columbus, Georgia when we were both stationed at Fort Benning. It wasn't until December 20, 1996—fifty-one years later—that I saw Bruton again. He thought he recognized me at a party and came over to check me out. When he mentioned "Airborne", I immediately came up with his name. "Airborne" is the common denominator that seems to link us old troopers together!

One evening I decided to go see the movie, "Anchors Aweight" starring Gene Kelley and Frank Sinatra. I had also met a WAC as we were going in the theater, so I sat with her. The GIs were very noisy and the soldiers (me included) began yelling insulting remarks at the sailors on the screen! We were really just having fun and meant no harm.

All of a sudden, this sailor sitting in front of me turns around and throws a cup of coke all over me and calls me a few choice names. Well, what could I do? I naturally took a swing at him. In nothing flat, here was this big, mean, 250-pound usher grabbing me and hustling me out the door!

Before I really knew what was happening, I was on the sidewalk and on my way! Oh well, I didn't care much for the movie and that WAC wasn't much better! Quite a few years later, I watched the rest of that movie on television. It wasn't too hot either!

For one whole day we were processed through a number of offices where they reconstructed 201 files for us. Mostly it was a series of interviews. One surprising thing that I found out was that apparently, I had never been authorized the Purple Heart for that first time I was hospitalized after our January 7th attack. The only Purple Heart officially awarded to me was for the January 29th wound.

Back in January I could have cared less about medals, but in the last month or so a special new point system had been announced. In addition to your months of service and time served overseas, this new system awarded a serviceman five points for each combat award he received. And, the higher your point total the sooner you would be discharged!

So, I decided I would be smart to try to get those five extra points for my total. I was told to prepare an affidavit and I even had to drop my pants to show a medic the small scar I had on my behind where I was nicked by that little piece of shrapnel! There was no way I could show them the big bite I had taken out of my tongue as a result of that concussion!

The necessary papers were drawn up, signed and I was told it had been approved. This was September 6, and I was informed they were authorizing a cluster to the Purple Heart for what actually should have been the initial award. It made no difference to me how they worked it—I was only interested in getting the five points! Leaving the office, I glanced at the entry they had made in my file and saw that the award had been made for a bayonet wound!

Like an idiot, I went back and called this mistake to the clerk's attention. No one had even mentioned anything about a bayonet! I have no idea where this came from. He said he would correct the error and take care of it. Leaving the file with him was another mistake I made. When I saw it next—on the train to Fort Benning—the reference to a bayonet wound had been deleted and it stated I had been treated for a shrapnel wound by the Germans while I was a POW!

That was enough for me. All I was interested in was the five points, so I let it go at that. I had had enough of army red tape. I'm not sure this was ever properly straightened out as I never received any official documentation for a Purple Heart Cluster from the army. However, I did receive the five extra points for my service record and the Army mailed me another Purple Heart medal! I'm left to assume I received the award.

Finally, after 11 days of this vacation on the government, I was among a group of some 25 or 30 paratroopers who were put on orders for September 12 to Fort Benning, Georgia and assignment to The Parachute School (TPS). I was pleased but a bit concerned if I would be up to it physically. I had hurt my knee when I slipped and fell coming from the hotel swimming pool. I hoped they weren't planning on me becoming a jogging instructor!

A trooper I had met from the 513th named Pittman, also was on the orders to go to Benning. We had done some bar-hopping together one night while we were in Florida, so we sat together on the train. Our trip to Benning was another real adventure!

We stopped at some station while en route and a couple of the guys decided they would get off and run over to make a purchase at a nearby liquor store. The train was pulling out when they came running back through the station. For some unknown reason, they elected not to come back through the main gate, but to take a short cut and catch our coach at the end of the platform. Unfortunately, there was no opening down there. The last we saw of them they were looking through the bars of a 10-foot-high steel fence as our train disappeared down the track!

We lost another trooper on that trip. This guy had brought his own booze and when we arrived at Columbus, he had had way too much to drink and was passed out cold on one of the seats. We couldn't get him to stand up, so rather than carry him, we just pulled the backs of the seats together over him and left him on the train. I don't know what ever happened to him!

The three months I spent at Fort Benning before I was discharged were good ones. It was especially good to be back among Airborne people! What I'll always remember about Benning, however, was not the Airborne, but the fact that when Georgeanna and I were finally married in October, Columbus and Fort Benning is where we first lived together as man and wife. Starting then, life took on a whole new meaning for me.

Chapter 58
LIFE AT FORT BENNING

Fort Benning was a great army post with super facilities. As a permanent post, it was much better than the other two where I had been stationed. But, it was hard to really feel comfortable there. Everyone, including myself, wanted out of the service and the sooner the better. We had put our lives on hold, but now we had begun to realize we had survived the war and we wanted to get our lives started again.

When I arrived there on September 12, 1945, I had two main objectives at the time: to get back on jump status and to find an easy job until I could get discharged. After any paratrooper is hospitalized six months, he is automatically taken off jump status and that means he no longer receives that extra $50 jump pay. To get back on jump status involved passing a physical and then returning to a schedule of making a jump every three months.

I thought my arm was now strong enough to pass the physical, but while at Miami Beach I had slipped while running to catch the elevator from the swimming pool and hit my knee against the door facing. My knee really bothered me and I was afraid it wouldn't pass a medical examination and maybe not even support me if I did make another jump.

All my worry was for no avail, however, as in true army fashion, the medic that examined me just asked if I was okay to jump. I said yes, and he stamped me back on jump status effective September 20. I was told that jumpers would be notified to report to Lawson Field when there were jump slots available. Each day a list was posted and it was obvious there was a big back-log.

My other objective, finding an easy job, came a little harder. When I was processed in, I made the mistake of saying that I could type. I was looking for some type of easy, inside job. I was not looking for a job drilling troops going through jump school! I gave little or no thought to the fact I hadn't touched a typewriter since I was in high school. I just wanted an easy job until I could get out!

I was assigned to an office that had been set up in the upstairs of an old wooden troop barracks. Here they were updating and recreating service files for the many former Airborne troops like myself that had automatically been returned to Benning. This was before air conditioning and it was hot as the devil and the work was the most boring I ever did.

I struggled with the job a couple of days and I was going nuts. I was no longer able to sit at a desk all day and type some dumb record form. I was surrounded by dozens of other typewriters and the noise had me ready to bolt out of there. I couldn't concentrate and I had no patience. The whole job was making me a nervous wreck. I was about ready to blow my top and I knew I had to do something fast.

I went to the lieutenant who was in charge and told him I couldn't take it any longer and he had to get me another assignment. He tried to talk me out of it, but I was at the end of my patience and was about ready to flip. I got right up in his face and told him calmly I was going to throw that typewriter out the window and then I screamed that I also might kill that sergeant in charge who was bugging me! This lieutenant had not been in combat, was not Airborne and was very young. I think I finally got his attention as his eyes got as big as saucers!

He told me to take the rest of the day off and he would see what he could do. As I stormed out, I told him he had better work something out or there would be hell to pay! I don't know what got into me! I had never talked to anyone, much least an officer, like I did that day. I just boiled over and without any real provocation.

When I came in the next morning ready to apologize, he told me he had worked it out that I would move over to another building and into a low-key, no-pressure job. I believe in those days when a combat veteran said he was going to kill someone, they were afraid not to take you at your word!

My new job, which I started on September 18, turned out to be a good one. We assembled 201 files for people who were to be sent to Separation Centers. We interviewed them, determined what awards they were entitled to and then added up their points. We even made them new dog tags if they needed them. There were actually too many of us in the office, but that meant we just didn't have to work very hard!

Our unit designation was 1st Headquarters Company, The Parachute School, and our quarters were not more that 75 yards from the main TPS building. My new work station was in a smaller building a little distance away and just next door to the company day room. During slack time in the day, we would go over to the day room and shoot pool. If they got busy in the office, one of the guys would just come and get us. It was a pretty good deal and at last I was able to relax.

I was surprised to find that Col. Coutts was the Parachute School Commandant. When I had been wounded and left the division, Col. Coutts was the Regimental Commander of the 513 PIR of the 17th Airborne. One day he came through our office and when I saw him I called attention and really popped to. He ate it up. He asked my regiment and said he was glad I had made it. I told him I was glad he had too and he smiled!

The Army also did a good job providing various forms of wholesome entertainment to occupy our off-duty time. Of course, this was to keep us from getting into trouble. The movie theater at the main post was a fine facility and they got all the newest movies well before they played at the civilian theaters. Camp buses provided transportation from the barracks areas to the main post, so getting around was easy.

The Broadway cast of "Oklahoma" also came to Benning and I went to see their live performance. It was one of the highlights of my stay there. I really enjoyed it. There were some other stage shows that came, but they paled as compared to "Oklahoma" and I have long since forgotten them.

As Georgeanna and I were married in October, we were both there during the later part of the '45 football season, so we went to several of the post games. There was a former All-American at the University of Kentucky named Clyde Johnson who was on the Fort Benning team and I enjoyed seeing him play.

My best friend in my company at Benning was a young trooper from the 82nd Airborne. I can't remember his full name, but his first name was Danny and he was from Albany, New York. He was three days older than me, had played high school football as a guard and had attended Villanova for a year before the war. He and I took in several games before Georgeanna and I were married. I especially remember we went to see several of the Columbus High School games.

One cool September night Danny and I went to one of these high school games and as both teams looked pretty bad that night, we became rather bored watching them. We had bought a half pint of whiskey before going to the game to "insulate us from the cold". It must have been pretty cold that night because we soon polished off the booze and ended up paying very little attention to the game.

Danny said we ought to do something to liven up the place and asked me if I would do anything he would do. It was a dare and I knew it, but like a fool I agreed. I guess it was part of being a paratrooper in those days. We were noted for being wild and crazy guys! However, I never guessed what was ahead.

The first thing Danny did was vault over the stadium railing onto the cinder track below. It was about a 12 foot drop and of course we both crashed onto the cinders in our clean suntan uniforms. Then he ran to where the cheerleaders were leading cheers for the fans up in the stands. He joined right in and started leaping and screaming. And, like a fool again, I added my version of cheerleading to this wild scene!

Amid boos and laughter from the fans, off we went again. This time Danny ducked under the wire and ran down behind one of the team benches. I followed, but I was beginning to loose my enthusiasm for this crazy game we were playing. However, I didn't want to be one to "chicken" out.

Our grand finale was coming up. There was a time-out on the field and while play was stopped, Danny cut and headed out on the playing field. I was only a few yards behind him. Across the field we went. We circled a bewildered home team and headed for the goal line. I felt certain there would be a couple of MPs waiting there for us!

Amazingly, we made it without being arrested. Danny then ran straight out of the stadium with me on his coattails! In fact, we ran at least a half block down the street just to make sure we weren't being followed. We certainly made fools out of ourselves, but we laughed about that night and our performance for weeks!

I guess this was our way of "letting off steam" and maybe an unconscious way of readjusting to civilian life! It became obvious to me that if Georgeanna didn't hurry up and set the date for us to get married, I was a cinch to end up in Fort Leavenworth Military Prison or the local nut house!

Sometime during the last of September in a telephone conversation, Georgeanna and I agreed that we should go ahead and get married now instead of waiting until my discharge. I was all for that, so I paid a visit to the Post Chaplain and he got me a 10-day furlough starting October 17, to go home and get married. The bulk of the planning was left to the folks back in Bowling Green!

The big event went off like clockwork. Several of my friends served as groomsmen and my old buddy, Butter Williams, got special leave and came home to serve as my best man. All the men wore their uniforms. Never have I had a better shine on my jump boots!

After the big event we went to Gatlinburg, Tennessee for our honeymoon and then Georgeanna and I packed and headed by train to Fort Benning. We stayed in a guest house for a few days until we found a room in a house in Columbus. The address was 816 2nd

Avenue and our landlady was a Miss Thelma Smith. We shared the house (and a refrigerator) with two other couples and paid Miss Smith $32 per month!

The house was in a nice area and very conveniently located. It was around the corner from the bus station and across the street from the USO. I would come to town each night, arriving at about 6:00 p.m. and then leave at 7:30 each morning for the post. Our Headquarters Company even ran a GI truck as a free shuttle for the married men living in town.

Much of our time together in the evenings was spent walking around town or preparing letters to various colleges seeking admission for me to their January term. I was interested in going to a journalism school and was accepted at Ohio State and the University of Georgia. A couple of others said they were filled up to the following September, so great was the flood of veterans returning home.

One day we saw Bob Cochran in Columbus and learned he was in Officer's Candidate School at the Infantry School which is also located at Fort Benning. We had known Bob at Western. When he graduated in a few weeks, Georgeanna went to the ceremony and pinned his second lieutenant bars on him.

Nearly every day our office would gather the 201 files for a shipment of men who were to be discharged. The men with the highest number of points were being separated first. These points were awarded for time in the service, time overseas, number of campaigns participated in and decorations received.

Twice a week we would notify a group to report to our office the next morning where we would have a bus waiting. We would check their names off and then a couple of us would accompany them either to the separation center there on the post, or to a train where they would be taken to a separation center nearer their homes.

We also knew this was the same system through which each of us eventually would be separated, so we all had our own personal files in tip-top shape just waiting for our time to go! Up until November 26, 1945, the point total to qualify for separation was 55. I had 51 points and I knew the next drop in points would take it to 50 and I would qualify!

When I arrived at the office at about 8:00 a.m. on the morning of November 27, they had just received the official notification that the points had dropped to 50. Outside in the yard beside our office were about 40 troopers waiting to be taken to the Separation Center there on the post. They had been notified the day before to report that morning. All of these guys had at least 55 points.

I got my own file, shut my eyes and pulled some poor unsuspecting trooper's file out of the box and substituted my own. The unlucky trooper who was left standing there when the bus had been loaded was told there had been a mix-up, but he would be number one on the list for our next shipment. He departed somewhat disappointed, but happy that he definitely would be leaving in another two or three days!

This was not the first time the guys in our office had pulled this trick. It was a dirty thing to do, but that's the way it is in the Army! You take care of your own first! I never gave it a second thought. I was on the bus and on my way to the Fort Benning Separation Center!

I was out of the Army by the time the work day was over and when I went into town as usual to meet Georgeanna that night, I had my discharge and the discharge insignia (called "The Ruptured Duck" by the GIs) sewed on my uniform. I decided to see how long it took her to notice it and she never did! We went out to dinner and after returning to our room I finally had to call her attention to it.

We packed our bags the next day and began making plans to return home immediately. An old Bowling Green friend, Jimmie Lively who happened to be in town that week, offered to drive us to Atlanta where we could catch a fast train home. We readily accepted his offer and we were out of there!

My first problem on arriving home was where could I find some civilian clothes to buy? Our children may find that hard to believe, but civilian clothes, especially quality civilian clothes, were hard to come by in those post-war months and nothing I had fitted me any more. I finally heard about some suits that were available in Franklin, Kentucky, about 20 miles from Bowling Green, so I went there and bought some things. It really felt strange after almost three years, but it sure felt good!

CHAPTER 59
THE CIVILIAN SOLDIER

A fter my discharge from the army November 27, 1945, I returned to college and sought to pick up my life where I had left it April 13, 1943. With a new wife and a new mindset after all I had been through, I had no doubt that college would be a bit different than it had been before. I was right on that score.

Knowing that I would soon be getting out of the army, while I was at Fort Benning I sent letters to several colleges and universities seeking admission for the January term. I was accepted at Ohio State and the University of Georgia. All the others said they were filled up with all the veterans returning from service.

I decided on Ohio State as it was nearer home and had a great journalism school. I declined at Georgia and rented an apartment in Columbus and paid rent on it for December to hold it for our arrival in January. After all, I had been away from home for the last four Christmases and this year I planned to be home!

Just before Christmas and about two weeks before I was due to leave for school, I got a letter from Ohio State saying they were sorry, but they would have to deny me admission due to the large number of Ohio veterans that had requested admission. I thought this was a cheap thing to do and I was quite angry with them. I still haven't forgiven them!

I immediately fired off a telegram to the University of Georgia saying my plans had changed and could I still be admitted. They replied the same day saying they would be happy to have me at Georgia. Ever since then, I have had a soft spot in my heart for Georgia!

On New Year's Day of 1946, Georgeanna and I arrived by train in Athens, Georgia. I remember we listened to the radio that day in our hotel room as Georgia, led by Charlie Trippi, beat some school in the Sugar Bowl. The next day I enrolled at the University of Georgia in their School of Journalism.

Those were good days we spent at Georgia and I enjoyed my journalism studies there. I like to think that my career in the field of advertising and public relations was fueled by the early training I had at the University of Georgia.

I also enrolled in Advanced ROTC at Georgia and was doing well. I was selected as one of the student battalion's staff officers and made the rifle team. I was on track to win a letter in that sport. Then, one day I received notice that I had been awarded a 30% disability rating by the Veterans Administration. This meant additional subsistence allowance, but also it meant I would have to resign from ROTC.

Later that year our first daughter, Kem, was born and we made the decision to return to Bowling Green. There I would continue my education at Western Kentucky State College, later to become Western Kentucky University. In the back of my mind, I planned to return to Georgia to graduate.

As I became involved in life at Western and daughter Julie was born, I gradually gave up the idea of returning to Georgia. I stayed at Western for my undergraduate degree and then for my master's degree. The plan to return to Georgia got side tracked. It was nice being home after all this time.

Just before I received my master's degree, I got a letter from the War Department offering me the opportunity to apply for a reserve commission. The offer was completely unexpected. I decided to go for it, so I filed all the necessary papers and went to Fort Campbell for an interview.

Apparently all went well as in 1949, I was commissioned a second lieutenant in the Army Reserve. The reserve drills offered me the opportunity to pick up some extra money and every little bit was needed at that time with my growing family. During the drill weekends I had to waive my disability compensation but it was a good trade-off.

After graduation from college, I took a job at Elizabethtown High School in Elizabethtown, Kentucky as teacher and assistant athletic coach. I was also transferred into the Inactive Reserve which received no drill pay. Soon I was contacted about starting a line company in Elizabethtown for the Army Reserve's 100th Division. It had just been designated as an Airborne division and they were eager to recruit all former Airborne troopers that were located in the area.

I went through the necessary hoops for organizing the unit, but they failed to get enough people so the plans for the unit folded. I was not put back on jump status, but this brief contact with the Airborne, sharpened my desire to once again be a part of the military.

During the summer of 1950, needing some type of employment during the summer months while school was out, I applied for a short tour of duty at Fort Knox as supervisor of the post swimming pools. I received a 30-day tour to start about the first of June and a week after I reported, the Korean War broke out. Immediately they "froze" all of us that were on TDY (Temporary Active Duty) and we found ourselves back on active duty with a very uncertain future.

I was assigned as the Special Services Officer for all the reserve and national guard units that trained at Fort Knox that summer. My duties consisted of issuing softball, volleyball and other sports equipment to the troops. I was also responsible for issuing the chrome and foam rubber furniture for their respective dayrooms. My contribution to the war effort was not proving to be very essential and my morale tumbled to an all-time low!

I began to think about how I could get a release from the Army and return to my job at Elizabethtown. First, I had to get a letter from the school board and then fill out a bunch of forms. Finally, under a hardship regulation and the fact that I had the 30% disability, I was released from active duty after about three months. I was late in returning to school and football practice had already started, but it worked out.

In 1952, after Tom's birth, realizing that coaching was a dead end job for me, we returned to Bowling Green and I took a job as News Director for WLBJ radio. Once again, to add to my income I joined an active reserve unit in the city. It was called the 8830th Military Police Replacement Training Battalion. As much as I didn't like being an MP, I needed the drill pay, so I set myself to being a good MP officer.

Promotions were slow in those days as there was no "time in-grade" regulation. Only a unit vacancy in the next rank would get you a promotion. After four years, I finally made first lieutenant and then was stuck in that rank for seven years. I joined Ashland Oil in 1958, and in 1960, was transferred to Louisville, Kentucky where I joined another battalion of the same MP unit. Almost immediately, I was promoted to Captain. During the time I had worked off the required correspondence courses and had become branch qualified.

In 1961, I was transferred to Ashland, Kentucky where the only reserve unit available was an engineer battalion. It was okay, but I knew very little about engineer units and it was a drag just putting in time and drawing my check. In 1963, in one of the many reorganizations the reserve components underwent in those days, that unit was dissolved and I was again without a pay slot. I needed that extra cash as Kem was now ready for college.

Checking around, I found that there was a pay slot available across the Ohio River in Huntington, West Virginia, with a National Guard unit of the newly-organized Army Special Forces. It meant being back in a unit with people who thought more like I did and it meant jumping out of airplanes again! I was excited about it, but I wondered if after all these years I could still propel myself out of a perfectly good airplane!

Well, the rest is history. I joined Company "A" of the 16th Special Forces Group, West Virginia Army National Guard in Huntington and I started jumping again. I wasn't surprised to find out that I still loved it!

During our summer training period in 1964, I had a great experience as an "A" Team commander. I took 12 men and we made a night jump into the wild and wonderful hills of Preston County, West Virginia and for two weeks we really went native. It really taught us how Special Forces troops operated in a combat situation and it was great fun.

There were four teams in the field that year, but my team was rated the best and we proudly carried away a special trophy that was awarded. I really took to the idea of working as Special Forces and operating in the hills and woods of the rough Preston County area. I got a great feeling of accomplishment from working with these most capable Special Forces troopers.

The next year, 1965, I served as a guerilla chief for a band of some 30 troops. We linked up with an SF team out of Rhode Island and operated in the hills for two weeks. The Rhode Island team wasn't a very good team, but for me, operating as a guerilla and living in the wild, it was a great learning experience. I called my guerilla soldiers "Black Bart's Band"!

Another reorganization came later that year and West Virginia became part of the 19th Special Forces Group. The West Virginia element was divided between Huntington, Charleston and Bluefield with an Augmentation Detachment in Kingwood, West Virginia. I had made major by this time and was named to command the Huntington element. It was composed of two "B" teams and four "A" teams consisting of about 50 troops.

In August-September of 1965, I was placed in command of about 25 troopers from West Virginia and 20 troopers from North Carolina and we flew to Alaska. There, for two weeks we attended the Northern Warfare Training Center at Fort Greely.

The training we had there, the Summer Mountain Operation Course, was excellent. I would never have believed we would ever have become so skilled as to pull off the mountain climbing feats that we did! We went up sheer stone faces with petons and climbing ropes and crossed deep ravines with rope bridges.

We also made a jump from a helicopter and everyone went up to their ankles in the soft tundra. We even staged a night infiltration of one of the DEW system radar stations, and were successful! I'll never forget that night walking along a pitch dark road and coming nose to nose with a huge bull buffalo!

I was surprised to see a lot of buffalo all around the post. There were herds of them. There were also moose, caribou and longhorn sheep. We could see them jumping around on the mountainsides! I did manage to bring home a moose rack and a caribou rack. The moose rack we found and I bought the caribou rack from one of the soldiers stationed up there. They now adorn my office wall and serve to remind me of a wonderful trip to Alaska!

Fishing was also outstanding in the area where we trained. One day we went on a problem paddling longboats up a river where graylings were practically jumping out of the water! For our evening meal that night, we had grayling cooked over an open fire and they were wonderful! This place is a hunter's paradise!

I took a risk I shouldn't have when it came time to come home. I allowed one of my sergeants to catch a ride with the Air Force to California instead of returning with us. He wanted to see his sister (?) out there and I decided to take the chance he would get home safely. He did, but I sweated it out something would happen to him or that someone would find out that I left one of my people in Alaska! I resolved right there that I would never bend that far again just to be a "nice guy".

Another great trip we had with Special Forces was a two-week exercise in Utah in 1966. We jumped a couple of times out there and found that the thinner air really gave us a rough landing. I hit so hard it jarred one of my contacts out! The country was beautiful, however, and we visited Salt Lake City and among other sights, the Mormon Tabernacle and the Great Salt Lake.

Although we jumped at least once during each three-month quarter, I really didn't get many jumps until I transferred to the Augmentation Detachment at Camp Dawson near Kingwood, West Virginia. The state's Assistant Adjutant General and commander of the unit was Colonel Bill Miller who had been a tech sergeant in Headquarters of the 17th Airborne Division. Just like everywhere, it helped to have connections in high places! This transfer meant driving quite a distance to attend the monthly weekend drills, but it was well worth it.

We were the only Airborne element at Dawson and our unit supplied the parachutes and other special equipment for all the other units of the 19th SFG located in the Eastern United States. This included companies in North Carolina, Rhode Island, Pennsylvania, Maryland and West Virginia. I was the Adjutant of the 12-man detachment and we essentially were the controlling element at Camp Dawson during the two-week summer training cycle.

Included in our detachment TO&E was an A-6 airplane and a pilot. Consequently, we jumped at least once during every monthly drill. We also had easy access to the helicopters that flew in and out of Camp Dawson each day, so we had ample air support. I recall one day I jumped five times.

Rapidly I advanced to Senior Parachutist and then after attending the Jumpmaster School at Fort Bragg, I was rated as a Master Parachutist. In addition to our trips to Alaska and Utah, the 19th SFG also sent troops on training trips to Germany, Okinawa and Taiwan. Unfortunately, my job with Ashland Oil prevented me from making these interesting "fly-out" trips.

At Camp Dawson we often staged regular army Special Forces troops prior to their departure for Vietnam. The wilds of West Virginia proved to be good training terrain for what they would see when they got in country. SF personnel who had been to Vietnam said our training was quite realistic.

We also provided helicopter rapeling and STABO training at Dawson. In STABO training the SF trooper, sans parachute, would be secured in a harness and dangled at the end of a line some 50-60 feet below a chopper. It was a technique used for inserting or extracting a person in hostile jungle terrain where there was a heavy overhead bush canopy and jumping was not practical. This proved a big thrill for me as one day I was towed over the town of Kingwood, West Virginia at about 1,000 feet! Then, on the way back to the camp, the pilot lowered me to within six feet of the lake surface. Wow!

Jumping was great fun and when I finally got out of Special Forces in 1973, I had made 117 jumps and had been promoted to lieutenant colonel. There was no doubt about it; this was the best assignment I had during my military career which spanned 31 years. I had enjoyed every minute of it.

I did not want to get out of Special Forces when I did, but the politics of being a resident of Kentucky and needing a hard-to-get slot as a lieutenant colonel in the West Virginia Army National Guard finally forced me out. I even waived my promotion from major for two years when the Assistant Adjutant General of West Virginia promised me that in that period of time he would find a lieutenant colonel's slot for me. The lost of one of those two extra years in grade would later keep me from being able to retire as a full colonel.

In 1973, West Virginia transferred me to the Inactive Reserve to make room for an officer who lived and, incidentally, voted in West Virginia. He was a nice fellow, but was not even Airborne qualified or Airborne trained. The only thing he did have working for him was the right political connections! I had learned the hard way, (1) don't ever believe that the word of a general is gospel, and (2) the National Guard system is steeped in favoritism.

I thought this was the end of my jumping, but in 1984, I decided to take a trip to Israel with a veteran's group. Georgeanna went with me and we had a great time. We toured the Holy Land like the rest of the tourists, but our trip was highlighted by visiting the Israel Defense Forces and making a jump with them from a C-130 near Tel Aviv.

That last jump made my total 118. Not bad for an old glider rider! Maybe I would still be jumping had it not been for a neck operation I had in early 1986. After that problem I realized that jumping was a risk that I should not take.

I spent the last two years of my military career in the Army Reserve in Louisville assigned to the Maneuver Training Command of the 100th Division. We traveled all over the Eastern United States training brigade and division staffs via computerized tabletop maneuvers. It was interesting work, but nothing compared to parachute jumping!

Then in 1975, having had 26 years of commissioned service, but lacking that one more year in grade, I was forced to go on the retired list as a Lieutenant Colonel. As a reserve officer, my actual retirement became effective November 4, 1984. Maybe there had been a few pitfalls along the way and a few disappointments here and there, but I have always regarded my military career as a good ride and I can truly say I enjoyed my time in service.

Today, those memories of when I was jumping, wearing the Green Beret and serving my country in the Airborne are among my most cherished moments. I loved the thrill of jumping from that "big iron bird" and I can truthfully say I never had any real fear of it. As the old Airborne saying goes, "I loved to jump and I loved being with people who did!"

PART VI:
REFLECTIONS

CHAPTER 60
THE FIGHTS!

If you join the army—especially the Airborne—you had better be ready to defend yourself in a few fist fights. Maybe it's the intensity of the training, maybe it's the type of people the Airborne attracts, or maybe it's just the close contact in which you live. Something always seemed to trigger frequent misunderstandings and that resulted in a fist fight most every day!

Earlier in this book I told about the fight that Don Wonderly and I had back in basic training and how we became good friends thereafter. I also told about my scrap with John Barnes while we were in England. That fight helped "clear the air" between Barnes and I. It seems like there was nothing like a good fight to get all your frustrations out and restore harmony!

I remember a couple of more fights I had while in the military. One was while we were at Camp Forrest and the last one was while I was stationed at Fort Benning. Both of these also had positive results and restored normal relations.

At Camp Forrest we were billeted by squads. As such, I slept next to Alfred Lee Barclay, an ammo bearer in our first platoon mortar squad. We had been working pretty hard at that time and I think we had just seen too much of each other. We had always gotten along okay, but Al—or "Fatty"—as we called him, was a bit lazy and we were always on him for something. I guess he just got enough of our taunts one night.

The lights were out in the barracks that night and we were all lying in bed, but still awake and talking amongst ourselves. I have no idea now what was said, but something Fatty said tipped me over the edge. I jumped out of my bed and pounced on him while he lay in bed. I rained down blows on him until someone pulled me off!

I regret doing this now, whatever our disagreement might have been. Old Barclay was not a bad guy and we still correspond today. At that time our tempers were made even shorter by the tough, hard training we were undergoing prior to shipping overseas and none of us were really responsible for many of our actions.

At Fort Benning in late 1945, there were other pressures that were eating at us. We all felt like we were stuck in "do-nothing", unimportant jobs, just passing the time until we were discharged. We couldn't understand why they didn't just turn us loose and let us go home! Nevertheless, there we were working a few hours each day and goofing off the rest of the time and no one even seemed to care.

I have forgotten his name, but there was a young trooper in our barracks who had joined the 82nd Airborne Division in the last days of the war. I don't think he had seen much combat, but he was as cocky as if he had been with them from the very beginning. The only reason he was here and not still in Berlin, was the fact that he had been captured. Once liberated they usually shipped all former POWs home.

This fellow was a guy about my size, but with a terrible attitude and not a nice word for anyone. I didn't like him from the git-go and neither did anyone else. Somehow, from the very beginning I knew we were going to have trouble. He just kept nipping at me and we kept jawing at each other. I avoided trouble with him for several weeks, but it had to happen.

Once again, one night in our barracks after everyone had gone to bed, he got to jawing back at me until I couldn't take it any longer. I leaped out of bed, pulled him, mattress and all down from a top bunk, and gave him a good pounding! I don't think he got in a blow and I made short work of him. I guess I had learned that it was easy to whip a guy that was in bed and partially held down by blankets and sheets!

In any event, he "gave up" and agreed to get off my back. After that he did and we got along fine. I never had much to do with him in the future, but he was no longer a problem for me. I think he just realized who he could bluff and whom he couldn't. Some guys are like that.

However, I must admit, he did manage to get in the last lick at me after all. Not in the fight, but afterwards he out-smarted me! It was a case of how I learned another valuable lesson in the military!

When I got married, I bought a custom-made Ike jacket to wear at the ceremony. It was of beautiful worsted wool, satin lined and the finest made and tailored garment you ever saw. That fact can be documented by examining our wedding photos as it is easy to see that the jacket I had on was finer than any GI issue!

Well, about the time I was getting discharged, my 82nd friend was also set to get married at Fort Benning. He asked to try on the jacket and like a fool, I let him. It fit him perfectly and he begged me to let him borrow it to wear when he got married. He promised he would then ship it to my home in Bowling Green. Like a fool, I agreed. Naturally, that was the last I ever saw of my beautifully tailored Ike jacket!

As I later joined the Army Reserve, I could have used that jacket. I had no idea where his home was or I would have gone after him! I had to go out and buy a GI model and it was not nearly so fine. It wasn't long after that, however, until the Army went to the green uniform and it no longer mattered. I did hate to think he had pulled that dirty trick on me.

I guess that was the last fight I have had. They all seemed to have been necessary at the time. After each fight, I got along great with the other guy. In the Army it seemed that the guys just tested you to see if you were all words and mouth and no guts. I didn't particularly enjoy fighting, but I did have a sense of personal pride and I was determined no one was going to push me around. And they didn't.

CHAPTER 61
WHEN THINGS GO WRONG

Parachute jumping is great fun, except when things go wrong. Fortunately, that is a very rare occasion. I was blessed in that I never had to deal with a situation where I, or one of the men under my command was seriously injured while parachuting. However, there were a few scary moments!

The only incident that I was involved in had a happy ending. We were making a "Hollywood" jump at Camp Dawson on July 4, 1967. A "Hollywood" jump was usually one made just for fun, or for pay purposes only. It was never tactical, always under ideal weather conditions and often it drew a crowd of local sightseers from the nearby town of Kingwood, West Virginia.

We were jumping the fixed wing A-2 aircraft that was assigned to pilot Bud Merritt, a member of our 12-man Augmentation Detachment. The chute I wore was the T-10 which deployed in a sleeve and then opened, thus reducing by far the opening shock the jumper received.

The T-10, however, did not have toggles or "slip-through" risers with which the jumper could adequately guide his decent. All he could do was pull hard on the correct risers and the parachute would respond by slipping gently in that directions. To put it bluntly, control was only slight at best.

I made a good exit from the aircraft and was in perfect position. The chute deployed smoothly and I had a full canopy over my head. I reached up for the risers and found that the two on my left were crossed!

The chute could not have inverted as the other two risers also would have been crossed. The error could only have been in the packing of the chute. Immediately I knew that the rigger who had packed it had made a mistake and the rigger who had checked his work also had failed to pick up the error.

I guess all this flashed through my mind, but at the moment, all I was concerned with was what kind of decent I was making. I checked the other jumpers in the air with me and my decent rate was normal. However, I was slowly rotating and slipping toward the main gate to Camp Dawson and dangerously close to some power lines and the creek that ran alongside the road into the camp.

The power lines were the main lines that carried all the power for the camp so I knew they carried a heavy electric load and were to be avoided at all costs. I began climbing those risers, trying to offset the "built-in" slip the crossed risers were giving me. I swung my legs and my body with the hope that I could land in one of the trees just in front of the power lines.

At the last second, seeing that I couldn't make the trees and hoping to miss the top power line, I pulled my legs up as far as I could. It was hardly the proper position to make a parachute landing, but it was all I could think of to do. I let go of the risers and grabbed the two Capewell releases. I reasoned if I hit the lines, I would cut away from the canopy before I could "ground" myself.

I hit the top power line with my rear end and the insulated, quarter-inch copper line snapped. I landed on the blacktop road leading into the camp and almost immediately pulled the Capewells. I tumbled in to make the world's fastest PLF (Parachute Landing Fall) and was on my feet, free of the canopy before it touched the ground!

Meanwhile, the power line snapped and cracked nearby and white hot sparks flew in the grass and in the air! I moved away and the spectators in the area scrambled away to give it plenty of room. In a minute or so, it seemed to burn itself out and lay smothering and smoking in the grass.

One of the first troopers to reach me was Sgt. Joe Smiddle, who later turned out to be the rigger who had packed my chute. Once he determined that I was okay, he asked me what had happened. I replied that the risers on my left were crossed and I was in an uncontrollable slip. Unfortunately, when I cut away from the canopy with the Capewells, that also disconnected the risers so there was no evidence to support the fact that they had been crossed.

Later, when I filed my after-action report and made this statement, Joe became quite upset. I guess it was professional pride, because I certainly have never held it against him and he suffered no reprimand for his part in this matter.

That power line had other repercussions in addition to knocking out electric service to Camp Dawson for the remainder of the day. About half of Preston County, West Virginia also suffered a power interruption and several businesses experienced power surges that had interesting consequences.

A sawmill in nearby Kingwood reported that two electric motors were burned out and I understand the state had to pay them damages of several thousand dollars. I was subpoenaed on this case and had to make a deposition as to what had happened.

The most interesting case was that of a nearby business that operated a turkey farm. The farmer-owner of the business reported that when the power went out, his incubator also went off and several hundred of his squabs—baby turkey chicks—died of exposure. Although Assistant Adjutant General, Colonel Bill Miller, told the farmer in his own unique way to "get lost", I understand the state also had to pay the farmer for the squabs to avoid another lawsuit.

After the jump the adrenalin was pumping through my veins and it took awhile for me to "cool down". I went back to the BOQ, had a beer and then reported back to the chute issue point. As was the custom in the "old days", when a jumper had a malfunction, they always sent him back up to jump so as to keep him from loosing his nerve. Mostly, I think it was just a macho thing they started in the paratroops!

In any event, I drew another chute and hopped aboard the plane again. Up we went and out I went! This one was a good jump, right on the DZ, near the panels and no twisted risers! It did make me feel good and I guess I did feel kind of macho!

That evening I went back to the DZ and watched as the men from the power company were busy stringing a new line. I broke off the end of the old burned-out line with its melted end and I have kept it for a souvenir. I resolved right then that I never wanted to see another power line.

On another jump at Camp Dawson, I was unable to avoid hitting on the roof of one of the buildings. It was the latrine! I was mainly interested in missing the metal stovepipe that reached up from the stove that supplied hot water for the showers.

I saw at the last second that I couldn't miss it, so I put my boots together and hit it full blast! The whole stovepipe went sailing and I crashed on the shingled roof. I bounced once and then plunged off the roof onto the ground.

Except for a sand-papered hole in the seat of my pants and a few minor scratches, I was unhurt. Once more it was that adrenalin and the excitement of jumping; it was hard to feel any hurt under those conditions!

Although the jumps in the thin air of Utah were rough, there was one other time that I had a rough landing. We were jumping at Camp Dawson and the wind was near maximum or above. Probably we should have aborted the jump, but we were eager to jump while we had an available aircraft.

I came in with a good landing attitude, but I was really traveling! When I hit, I made a good PLF, but I guess my head slammed on the ground as I immediately blacked out for a few seconds. Some troopers on the ground collapsed my chute so I was not dragged very far. I remember my football-type jump helmet was turned sideways so I was almost looking out one of the ear holes!

My wrist watch band snapped and it was only after a lengthy search that we were able to find the watch in the grass. We also found some change that had been jarred from my pockets! I was a bit dopey and it was several minutes before I was able to talk rationally.

One other time I had a scary jump. We were making a night jump near Charleston, West Virginia. The DZ was in a valley and although flat, it was not long enough for more than six jumpers when jumping the Air Guard's C-ll9s. This night I was to be the jumpmaster for a plane load of 12 which would be six jumpers out of each of the two side doors.

All went well as we approached the DZ. I had five jumpers set for the left door and six for the right door. I would stand with my back to the tail of the aircraft, give the jump commands and seeing the last man in the right stick exit, would turn and follow the fifth man out the left door.

When the green light came on I yelled "Go!" and the men tumbled out. As I saw that last man exit the right door, I turned into the left door and ran into the backpack of the last jumper who was still standing there! I bounced back as I realized he had "frozen in the door"!

I screamed "Go!", then added a few expletives and drove my forearms into the back of his main chute and propelled him out the open door. I was right on his back as I cleared the aircraft. I knew that DZ was short and any hesitation on the part of any of the jumpers could put the last man into the trees or the barn located at the end of the field.

It was pitch dark and only the faint glow of a few stars lit the earth below. At 1,000 feet, you had little margin for error and scant time for decisions. All I could see below were trees and the biggest, widest barn I had ever seen! I couldn't see much open field, but I began slipping away from that barn as fast as I could.

I came down in the barnyard, missing the roof of the barn by a scant 10 to 15 feet. The barn was a monster, some 30 feet or more in height with a sharp, sloped roof. If I had landed on that roof I might have gotten away with that, but I would have shot right off onto the ground below. A out-of-control fall from that height with a collapsed parachute could have been very unhealthy.

I never was much for "chewing tail" as an officer, but I couldn't wait to get my teeth into that young trooper that had frozen in the door and put me in such a bind. He was a cook in the Charleston unit. Luckily it was for him that he was not a member of my Huntington detachment.

I gave it to him full blast. By freezing he put both our lives in jeopardy and I wanted to make sure he knew it and would never do it again. I guess I got my point over as he later quit the unit. That night was the last jump he ever made. And, I took comfort in that fact.

Those were the jumps I made when something went wrong. But before you get the idea they were bad jumps, let me correct you! These were only four jumps out of the ones I made that turned out to be a bit hairy. For me there were really no bad jumps because I walked away uninjured from every one of them. Those other 114 were pure joy and beauties to behold!

CHAPTER 62
COMBAT CHANGED US ALL

B asic training in the Airborne was tough. There were good days and there were bad days, but no one really enjoyed it. We just hung in there and made the best of it. One of the things that kept us going was the little touches of humor that we were able to find along the way.

We came up with various nicknames like "Hungry" and "Rabbit" and "Mary" and we played pranks on each other. One of the pranks we played—described elsewhere in this book—got me "busted" from PFC to PVT, but I have always felt it was well worth it! Some way, we had to break up the drudgery of the intense training.

Slowly, but surely, we rounded into top physical and mental condition. Home sickness was soon behind us, our confidence in ourselves soared and we were growing impatient to get about the job that lay ahead. We were even cocky about it saying that once we hit the enemy, the war would soon be over.

Some of this might have been just bravado, but we were an elite fighting unit and it was hard to be humble! Even when we sailed overseas and during our stay in England, we kept up the spirit we had. Few would have transferred out of the Airborne if the chance had been afforded them.

I think the first big change I noted occurred when we were finally alerted during the Bulge to fly to the continent. It came so suddenly and it was no leisurely move. Once alerted, we were rushed to the marshalling area in hours. There had been a break in the harsh December weather and the planes were flying again.

The seriousness of the situation seemed to effect every one of us. We seemed to realize the fun was over and it was going to be a serious matter from here on. No more pranks, no more kidding, it would be serious business now. I can't remember hearing anyone laugh from this time on.

We were still green as far as combat went, but this actually helped us to be alert as to what was happening. There was no joking around, no "goofing off" and no shirking of duty. We knew who our friends were and we were anxious to be near them! We took strength from each other.

At first we thought there was a German behind every tree. Gradually, we calmed down and although we stayed alert, we were able to catch a few hours of sleep when it was possible and the lump in our throats gradually began to ease. We still talked among ourselves and we realized that we were at last, in harm's way. Soon, we knew, we were going to be called on to kill a human being and we all secretly wondered if we were up to the task.

The big attack our battalion made on January 7, which is described earlier, answered many questions. When confronted with the choice of kill or be killed, most of us did not give it a second thought. We did what we had to do to survive. Our greatest fear turned out to be peer approval. No one wanted to appear to be a coward and no one wanted to let a buddy or the company down.

After that horrid day, some of us may have thought hard about what we had done, but most of us had other things to worry about that seemed more important. Like staying alive. When I was back in the hospital in Arlon, Belgium, I had plenty of time to think about the terror of combat. I lay on my cot and thought over the events of that fateful day. Was every day in combat going to be like that?

I had not pulled the trigger of my carbine, but I had dropped the shells in our mortar that had killed two of my enemy. I had no regrets, but it was not a pleasant thought. They were firing a machine gun at us and we could hear the rounds popping a foot or so above our heads. Snow and dirt was being showered down on us as the rapid fire of the machine gun searched for us in the ditch in which we had taken shelter. It was either them or us.

After a few days in the hospital and a couple of more on the road, I returned to my company. I had missed my buddies badly. The company had become your family by this time and you wanted to be back where your friends were. I fully expected to be welcomed with open arms. I expected the guys to say they were glad to see I was okay and welcome back!

No such welcome awaited me. Everyone seemed to have retreated deep within themselves. No one smiled and there was very little talking among the men. One fellow said he had heard I had been killed. I learned that Lt. Logan had told a friend of mine that he had seen my body.

To make it even worse, when I learned that Captain Stuhrman had returned my mail and marked it "Missing In Action", it sort of gave me the feeling of being "written off" and forgotten. Fortunately, I was able to get a V-Mail home before all those letters were returned, otherwise my parents would have really been torn up. Then, I thought, no one up here would have cared.

I soon realized that all this was no indication that I was no longer liked by my comrades. It was a change that had seemed to come over everyone during the week or so that I had been gone. The honeymoon was over. Everyone had finally realized that we were playing a game where the guy you were talking to one minute could be dead the next. Life had come to be very cheap.

Unconsciously, I think everyone was kind of pulling back. There seemed to be a feeling if you got too close to someone, you could be hurt, both physically and emotionally. We cooperated and worked with each other, but there was no more of the fun-loving camaraderie that we had known before. Everyone seemed to realize that for now, everything was for keeps.

During the Bulge, we never received any replacements or I am sure they would have led a very lonely life. I know the people we received in England were placed in that situation to some degree. These were people we didn't know too well and we couldn't be too sure of their abilities and knowledge. As time went on and these people had a chance to prove themselves, this feeling disappeared. The very fact they remained alive proved they knew something.

After the Bulge, replacements did come into the different units and I am told that this feeling of distrust did exist for a time. However, with the strain of combat it soon vanished and today some of the best and most loyal of our division association members are fellows that joined the 17th Airborne before the Rhine operation.

Whenever we had any "down time", that is, time we could call our own, we put it to different use than we had before. You saw men digging deeper and improving their foxholes, cleaning their weapon, writing a letter home or just staring off into space. The accuracy of the German .88 artillery had put new meaning to the phrase, "don't bunch up", so you saw the men sitting alone and not engaging in the bull sessions like before.

They even looked different. Few had shaved and no one, except me, had taken a bath since we left England. Faces were blackened by the smoke from huddling around wood fires. Scarfs and knitted caps had appeared to fight the cold and the men no longer looked as uniform as before. Those that did not have artics had wrapped strips of blankets around their boots and they looked strangely awkward. We looked like Willie and Joe in Bill Mauldin's popular cartoon, "Up Front"!

During the time I was back in the hospital I was issued some clothing and equipment not normally issued to Airborne troops. I had lost my helmet and weapon so I was given a "leg" helmet (one without the chin strap and web net covering) and a regular stock carbine. I also received a warm jeep driver's mackinaw in place of my torn combat jacket. This was a great addition as it was light, very warm and water repellent.

Everyone admired the coat and was eager to hear how I got it. One fellow, Adrian Test, a machine gunner in the Third Platoon, asked me if something happened to me, could he have the coat. I readily agreed as I thought I had had my wound and would be wearing that coat for a long, long time!

Later on, when I was wounded in the arm and the medic had to cut my sleeve away to the shoulder, Test saw me heading for the rear and suddenly he became really concerned. For a minute I thought he was concerned about me, but finally he blurted out, "I hope you didn't have my coat on when you were hit!"

Everyone was interested in one thing: something to eat. The kitchen truck got up when they could and the hot food (mostly beans and corn cakes) and coffee they brought was much appreciated. When the situation prevented providing hot meals, we lived on cold C's or K-rations and by now these seemed barely adequate to keep us going. There was a continual foraging for food in the houses we passed along the way. A few bottles of wine appeared, but I don't recall drinking being a problem on the front lines. Everyone wanted to be sober and at their best.

What little talking the men did, frequently turned to the experiences they had had since entering combat. They spoke of close calls they had survived, a scary patrol they had been on, or a "Jerry" patrol they had ambushed, or the number of bodies they had found when they moved into a certain area. But the prime subject of their conversation was of the misery of their living conditions, the bitter cold and their ever-present hunger.

We seemed to always be going somewhere. As we walked we often saw dead bodies lying beside the road or in the fields. The bodies were both those of the enemy and other Americans. Most of the time, the men hardly seemed to give them a glance. They were ignored, but they were seen. It was as if they looked at the bodies too closely they might see a friend or, worse still, it could be themselves.

Some of the dead were badly torn up and I found it hard not to look. The lower half of an American soldier lying alongside a road is a sight I will always remember. His belt was still buckled intact and it seemed to hold his lower half remains as if in a neat bag. I even saw this scene in my dreams a few times after I returned to civilian life, but with time, it long ago ceased to haunt me. There was a mental armor you had to put on; the dead were like broken equipment, they were not real people at all, they were just part of the debris left behind by the war.

There was always some talk about getting that "million dollar" wound. That was a wound that was not life-threatening and one that you would recover from in time. But, it was a ticket to the hospital and at least for a while, out of the hell of combat. We envied the men who received them because we knew they were headed for a nice safe place, a warm bed with clean, white sheets and all the food they could eat. Maybe they would even survive the war.

Every combat soldier has heard tales about self-inflicted wounds. It's the ultimate sin among front line troops, but I can understand how it happens. Despair finally overcomes a person and in a desperate last-ditch effort to save his life, he can be easily driven to this "out".

We had one guy in our company who was said to have shot himself in the foot. I never really knew if he did. After the war, he regularly made donations to our Memorial Fund, but no one could ever get him to come to a reunion. This naturally says nothing, but we have always wondered if he was living with this shame.

As I reflect now on those days, I can fully understand the reaction we experienced and the self-imposed loneliness we adopted. It was a kind of insulation against the horror all around us. Some of the fellows have never shook it, but the majority of us have put our lives back together again and returned to the ways of civilian life. Somehow, it all seems like a bad dream—a bad dream that came true.

Chapter 63
GAYS IN THE MILITARY?

For the last few years the military has been trying to deal with the question of whether admitted gays should be allowed to serve in the military. The press has taken up the issue and Congress has debated it and it is still a mess. The courts even ruled some admitted gays must be returned to active duty on the grounds that their human rights were violated.

One news story reported that some 17,000 military personnel had been discharged in the last decade due to their confession that they were gay. The policy within the military has now come to a "don't ask, don't tell" situation. And, it isn't working all that well.

I don't want to debate this issue here, but it does make me think about my days in the service and how it was in the 17th Airborne. Maybe the parachute regiments didn't have a problem of this sort but, in the glider regiments where we were not volunteers, we got all kinds of individuals and the law of averages points to the fact that some of them were gay.

At my early age and lack of experience with these type of people, I doubt if I was a very good judge of who might have been gay and who wasn't. Nevertheless, thinking I knew everything about everything at that age, I thought we had a gay in our platoon. Everyone else seemed to agree. His name was Robert Ryan.

All the members of the platoon quickly picked up on the fact that Ryan somehow "different" from the rest of us. He made no overtures to anyone, minded his own business and carried his share of the load. He was a good soldier, but he was different and we all knew it.

It is hard to know whether a person is gay, or just a bit "sissy". Ryan was certainly feminine so it was not long before we started calling him "Mary"! Soon everyone called him that. I'm sure Ryan didn't like it, but he never complained and eventually he ignored what started out as an insult and even answered to that name!

In the army, your platoon became your family. We got to be a pretty close unit. We shared duties equally and soon learned to look after each other. We trained together, ate together and were billeted together. I can truthfully say that never at any time did Ryan shirk any of his duties or fail to do his part. In fact, he didn't gripe and complain near as much as the rest of us did! All in all, he was a good soldier.

Ryan didn't seem to have any close friends in or out of the company. He went to the movies alone, he ate alone and quietly moved around without joining in any of the barracks bull sessions. He would sit on his bunk writing letters until everyone went to bed. Then he would go down by himself and shower and shave while the latrine was empty.

While most of us were nervously chattering as we took our first glider ride, Ryan was silent. He was sweating and plainly concerned, but made no comment before, during or after. Later, when we were given the opportunity to volunteer for parachute training, Ryan quietly declined. He never held back, however, when we were ordered to make glider flights.

During maneuvers and on field problems it was necessary for us to pair up for sleeping arrangements. It took two men to join their shelter halves and make a tent and in bitter cold weather it was almost necessary that two sleep together in order to share body heat and blankets. No one ever had any problem with Ryan in these cases.

Upon entering combat, Ryan reacted in much the same way that all of us did. He was afraid just as we all were, but he performed his duties and as before, carried his share of the load. There was nothing in his performance under this stress that could be faulted. You couldn't have asked for anyone to have done more.

Our first attack on January 7, 1945, which ended in a hasty and tragic withdrawal, left our company in complete disarray by nightfall. I was injured during the withdrawal, so it was several days before I returned from the hospital to the company. Ryan had been transferred to another platoon just as had several others. Most of the members of my old squad, had been evacuated with frozen feet.

I don't remember seeing Ryan after January 7, but I know he made it okay. After I was wounded again on January 29, I wrote to the company seeking information about where they were, etc. I received a letter from, of all people, Bob Ryan who wrote to me apparently while the division was in the rest camp before the Rhine invasion. He said he would try to send me my personal items in my barracks bags. However, I never heard from him again or did I receive any of the said items.

Apparently, Ryan made the invasion and came through the rest of the war okay. Other friends told me that he did, but no one could add much to the story. His nature of keeping to himself resulted in that no one could remember much about him being around. It was like he was invisible.

Years later, I made another effort to get in touch with Ryan by sending a letter through the Veterans Administration, but because of the Privacy Act, they will not give out current addresses. You must write your letter and send it to them and they will forward it on to the addressee. However, if the letter is returned, they will advise you of that fact.

I never received a reply from Ryan and I never received word that my letter had been returned. So, I believe that he received it and just decided not to renew any friendships he had had in the Army. It really doesn't surprise me and I really don't blame him. After the way all of us treated him, if I were him, I would want to put my military service behind me and forget it.

Of course, all this still doesn't shed any light on whether Ryan was or was not gay. We were all young and wild in those days and I'm afraid we totally ignored anyone's personal feelings. We really didn't care at that time if we did falsely accuse him. It was a dangerous time in which we lived and we were in a rough outfit. We had no time for niceties.

So, Bob Ryan, if you're out there somewhere and read this, my humble apologies go out to you. I am truly sorry for the way the platoon and especially myself may have treated you. We couldn't have asked for a better soldier or a nicer human being than you. Your sexual preference—whatever it may have been—matters not one iota to me!

CHAPTER 64
THE FRIENDS WHO FELL

I have put off writing this chapter. It will not be easy to recall the circumstances where members of our company were killed. But, this work would not be complete without some sort of tribute to them. They were the losers in this obscene lottery of determining who would live and who would die.

The Bulge was not a pretty event. Over one million men were locked in mortal combat there. There were 600,000 Americans involved. This included three armies and six corps, the equivalent of 31 divisions. It was more than the combined Union and Confederate forces at Gettysburg. These troops took approximately 81,000 casualties including 19,000 killed in action. There were also 15,000 captured.

The Brits had 55,000 troops involved with three divisions and three brigades. Also, there were various contingents of Belgian, Canadian and French troops. The British had 1,400 casualties including over 200 killed.

The Germans are the ones who really paid the price. They had 500,000 troops involved, being assigned to three German Armies and 10 Corps, the equivalent of 29 divisions. Over 100,000 ended up as casualties.

The losses in equipment was crucial to the outcome of the war. Each side lost over 800 tanks and in addition the Germans lost 1,000 aircraft.

My regiment, the 193rd, suffered 53.4 percent casualties (this includes wounded, killed and captured) receiving no replacements during the period December 31, 1944 until relieved on February 1, 1945. That's a total of 1,049 men. It breaks down into 36 officers, one warrant officer and 1012 enlisted men. During the 21-day period January 4 through 25, the Division itself recorded 41% casualties including 519 KIAs.

The strength of Company D, 193rd Glider Infantry was somewhere in the neighborhood of 200 officers and men when we entered combat in December, 1944. Like the rest of the division, we received no replacements while we were engaged in combat during the Bulge. All the companies came out of the Bulge way below strength. Some had almost ceased to exist.

Two days after I was hit, on February 1, our company was pulled off the line and went into reserve. Later the division was pulled back to a rest area. At that time we were down to about 60 men and officers reporting for duty. We were hardly a force to be reckoned with.

Officially, the division was relieved on February 10th and moved back to Chalons-Sur-Marne in France to refit and prepare for the coming Airborne operation over the Rhine River. One of the first acts of preparation for this was the changing of the T.O.& E. (Table of Organization and Equipment). The 193rd GIR was deactivated and the survivors actually became replacements for the 194th GIR. The 194th GIR was then organized into the l94th Regimental Combat Team with the assignment of the 550th Airborne Infantry as a third battalion. Even then, it was necessary to draw upon fresh replacements from the States to fill out the ranks.

The best I can determine, during the war we had 20 people from the original Company D roster killed in action or died of their wounds. Of this number, I believe thirteen were lost during the Bulge including eleven on that fateful day of January 7, 1945, and two more before we were relieved on January 31st. On January 7th, the 193rd alone suffered 65 killed.

On March 24, l945, the day of the Rhine crossing and after the l93rd had been asorbed into the l94th, we lost six more. Only two more died during the operation on into Germany.

Jerry Stuhrman, who was our Company Commander for Company D of the l93rd during the Bulge and later for Company A of the l94th for the Rhine and after, puts the total loss of men under his command at 24. I can account for only 21, so the other three must be new men who joined Company A before "Operation Varsity".

One of the first to die was Robert F. "Red" Ewing from Shippingport, PA. Red died right near me and the account of his death is recorded elsewhere in this book. He was a close buddy and his death, with a bullet through his head, was a traumatic experience for me, especially on that first day when we were getting our baptism of fire and were all scared to death.

When I was home on leave from the hospital, Georgeanna urged me to write his parents and tell them how it happened, but I couldn't do it. Finally, on the last day of my leave, with her urging, I did write them. Without prior notice, his mother and father got on a train and came to Bowling Green to meet me.

With my leave over, I had returned to the hospital by then and never got to see them. However, my mother and dad, and Georgeanna, spent time with them and they seemed satisfied. I never got around to visiting them, a fact of life that I'll always regret. I hope additional letters I later wrote helped to answer their questions.

Red was killed on January 7, 1945 in our first big attack. That day also accounted for several other members of our company; William Brown, Charles E. Gilbert, Sam Jordan, Frank Krohn, Louis Thomas, Garold Tidball, Carl Royce and Joseph G. Weider all died that day. Charles R. Pierre died the next day of wounds he received.

Sgt. Royce was a victim of "friendly fire". When E Company swung wide coming on line for our attack, they mistook us for the enemy and opened up on us from the rear. Before the situation was determined and corrected, several were wounded and Sgt Royce was killed by machine gun fire.

When Sgt. Pierre went down we all mourned his loss. As we charged point-blank into the German-held woods, he was hit by artillery fire. Fatally wounded, he died the next day in a hospital. To loose Pierre was probably the worst thing that ever happened to D Company. I firmly believe he was the best non-com in the division and there is no telling how his loss diminished our overall abilities.

Later on that day, as we raced back to avoid being surrounded by the Germans, Joe Wilder was hit by grazing fire and died on the elevated Bastogne-Marche road. I'll always remember my dash down that road that day and when I dropped to the surface for a moment to catch my breath. I looked over three or four feet from where I lay and saw Joe lying in a pool of blood.

It was the sight of Joe that made me decide to crawl off the highly exposed road and make my way back through the open field. Although running through the deep snow in the fields slowed you down considerably, one man was not as inviting a target as a road full of fleeing soldiers. It proved to be a wise decision for me. For Joe it was too late.

Bob Kepler, our First Sergeant, later had the sad task of volunteering for a detail to go back to the site of the battle to recover the bodies of Ewing, Royce, Weider and others. Both Pierre and Weider are still buried in the U.S. Cemetery near Luxembourg City. When I visited their graves in 1984, I was deeply moved.

Things are a bit blurred as to the order of when these fine troopers met their death. Some occurred while I was back in the hospital and there are some I just don't recall when they happened. I think it has something to do with the way we seemed to get used to death. Someone would say they heard so and so had been killed and often no one would even reply or ask how it had happened.

Samuel E. Jordan, a scout in the third squad, never knew what hit him on January 7th. He got a direct hit from what must have been an .88 and he literally disappeared. In discussing it one day I remember someone saying it was the only thing Sam never saw. His night vision ability was a well-known talent throughout the company. Everyone said at night Sam had the eyes of a cat.

Harlan Jung was one of those who was killed on January 7th. The thing I remember about Jung was when we were at Camp Mackall and he was the victim of a "GI party". For those of you unfamiliar with what that means, it was a scrubbing with GI soap and GI brushes for someone who didn't bath frequently enough. It sure got the dirt off, but it also took a bit of skin.

It was usually done by five or six people who ganged up and surprised the victim and dragged him into the shower. Also, usually a knock-down, drag-out fight resulted and in this case that was the case. Jung just didn't bath frequently enough and his undershirt was always dirty. Consequently, he caused the whole platoon to be restricted several times. The "GI party" cured Jung and from then on he was a good soldier.

We lost a good one in Franklin R. Krohn. He was the squad leader for the second platoon mortar squad. Krohn was a highly intelligent soldier, well-liked by all the men in the company. I don't know how he was hit, but he died the next day of his wounds.

William A. Brown, Louis M. Thomas, and Garold D. Tidball, were others in the company who died in the Bulge action. Thomas had a twin brother in the 194th and I know it must have taken a lot of guts for the brother to board his glider and fly into Operation Varsity after Louis was killed. The story of the close call he experienced is recorded in my earlier book, "War Stories: The Men of the Airborne."

Three troopers who died and I can't remember were William A. Brown, Charles E. Gilbert and Walter F. Hodges. I believe I might remember that Hodges and Brown were with us from Mackall, but I am inclined to believe Gilbert was one of the additional people we received while we were in England. We received about 15 or 20 men from the replacement depots as we added bazooka teams to the each of the rifle squads. We never had time to get to know these guys too well.

At a recent 17th Airborne Reunion we honored Hodges by having his sister attend as a "Gold Star Sister". Although his face was familiar, I cannot really say I remember him. Being honored at our reunion was a fitting recognition as far too many joined the division and were killed without anyone really getting to know them. It is sad that this happens, but it does.

The operation across the Rhine and the campaign on into Germany accounted for our other seven KIAs. These were Phillip L. Mynarzyk, Austin A. Ernst, Albert W. Johnson, Alexander Poulson, John C. Sutton, Chester D. Wonderly and Chester G. Quick. These men, therefore, are listed as being with Company A of the 194th.

I do not know the circumstances of the deaths of Ernst, Johnson, Mynarzyk and Sutton, but the other three all died together in the Airborne invasion and a tragic train of events thereafter. The details never came to light until 1983, years after the war was over.

While we were at our annual reunion—this time in Memphis, Tennessee—I was approached by a man who introduced himself as Charles Bonner Ruff. He said he taught music at nearby Arkansas State University and this was the first reunion he had ever attended. He said he had been in Company A of the 194th and he would like to talk to Jerry Stuhrman.

I don't think any of us, including Jerry, was ready for what came next. In a private conversation with Jerry he broke down and cried, saying he was responsible for the deaths of Gerry Quick, Don Wonderly and Al Poulson. He said it was a burden that he had carried all these years and that he had to "confess" to someone for his own peace of mind.

He then told Stuhrman the story of events as they occurred that day back in 1945 as his glider landed in Germany over the Rhine River. He was a green replacement in Gerry Quick's rifle squad and admitted to being scared to death as their glider careened down through the smoke and anti-aircraft fire.

The glider pilot had missed his LZ and the glider landed far out of the area and deep into enemy territory. They were immediately brought under fire and the squad scrambled into a ditch to take cover.

For awhile they returned the fire directed at them by the Germans from a nearby woods. After a fire fight of several minutes, a number of the squad had been wounded. Gerry realized that it was hopeless to resist further and when the Germans cried out for them to surrender, he decided to do so. He threw his helmet out as a signal of surrender and yelled to the men to hold their fire.

As the Germans cautiously advanced from their positions, Ruff said he peeped over the rim of the ditch and saw a German advancing toward him completely exposed. As he had failed to hear Gerry's order to cease fire, he raised his M1 and dropped the German. He said he was wild with excitement and fear and really didn't know what he was doing.

With that breach of the surrender truce, the Germans opened up on the troopers in the ditch. When the firing stopped only five of the 13 troopers were left living. Quick, Poulson and Wonderly were among those that died and most of those surviving, including Ruff, were wounded and captured.

Ruff was eventually liberated when the German hospital where he was a patient was overrun by British forces. He received a medical discharge and had picked up his life and tried to forget about his fateful decision that day in March. However, it had troubled him continuously and by his confession that day to Jerry Stuhrman, he hoped to ease his conscience.

It was a tragic blunder, but of course, Jerry Stuhrman told him that we all forgave him and told him to put the whole incident behind him and forget it. He assured him it was only another incident of the stupidity of war and that no one can predict what they'll do when confronted with such a life and death situation.

I noticed that sometime in the early 1990's, Bonner Ruff died. I hope he went to his maker with a clear conscience of that terrible day in 1945. I feel sure my good buddy, Gerry Quick, had long ago forgiven him.

AUTHOR'S NOTES

In telling this story of my life in the military, I felt that it was important to use the actual names of the individuals that shared this time with me. I have tried to do this throughout the book. However, in a few cases where we thought the incident might prove embarrassing if that person ever read our book, we took the liberty of substituting a false name in the text. The events depicted, however, are 100% true. They really happened!

Chapter 31, "The War Of The Floors"; chapter 41, "I Remember Lilly"; and chapter 52, "The Battle Of The Our River", first appeared in my earlier book, WAR STORIES: THE MEN OF THE AIRBORNE. Since then, additional details regarding these incidents have been learned and those chapters are repeated here in an updated version. The title of chapter 52 also was changed from "The Second Time Around" to be more descriptive of this combat action.

The incident described in chapter 50, "The First Big Attack", first appeared in my book, HISTORY OF THE 17TH AIRBORNE DIVISION, as a short story entitled "Dog Company's Baptism Of Fire". The narrative of that action also has been revised and expanded and includes additional information that has since become known.

In writing this account some 50 years after it all took place, I have had to rely heavily on my fading memory! Many of the dates, events, places and names included herein have been confirmed through personal letters, interviews, other historical works and the U.S. Archives files. I feel this finished effort is 99% accurate, but I must ask your indulgence if something doesn't quite check out. I've wished a million times I could have kept a diary in order to match dates with events. But, in a line Airborne outfit, such would not have been possible.

EPILOGUE

It doesn't snow often in our area of South Central Kentucky. In fact, it had been 1969 since we last had a genuine "White Christmas". However, Christmas morning of 1992 found our little corner of the world wrapped in a beautiful, white blanket of soft, cushiony snow that by afternoon had reached a depth of nearly four inches.

My two young grandsons, visiting us for the holidays, thought it was wonderful and couldn't wait to open their Christmas presents and then get out in the yard to romp and play. My wife and daughter-in-law "oohed" and "aahed" about the beauty the snow brought to everything. Even my son waxed poetic about the "peace and calm" that the snow seemed to bestow on the neighborhood.

All of a sudden I felt strangely alone in this happy gathering of loved ones. As I looked out of the window and saw the snow and hazy fog, I was transported back in time to the Ardennes and that fateful Christmas season of 1944. A shiver went up my back and I gritted my teeth with the bitter memories this icy wonderland brought back. Must the memory of those horrible days of the Battle of the Bulge haunt me forever? After all these years must I still suffer the memory of the worst days of my life?

I found myself peering through the hazy-white fog trying to pick out any threatening movement among the snow-decked pine trees. Was that only a neighbor's car parked down the street or was it the blackened hull of a knocked-out tank? Was that just a rounded hump of snow on that distant fencepost or was it the snow-camouflaged helmet of an enemy soldier lying motionless while he plotted the range of my position?

Thinking like this was foolish, I told myself. This was Christmas 1992 and the need for those kind of fears were long past. I was no longer the scared, barely-20-year-old that I was in 1944. I was warm and safe and it angered me that I would even remember any of this. I knew I should be enjoying these precious moments with my loved ones. But, it is hard to keep those kind of memories in check, even after all these years.

In my mind I could see the blue-white lips of "Red" Ewing as he lay in the snow, a bullet through his temple. I could hear the screams of "Medic!" coming from all directions, the ripping sound of tearing canvas as the German machine guns took their toll and I could see the crimson blood of my comrades lying stark on the white snow.

I have come to understand the problems soldiers from the Vietnam War era have had with "flashbacks" and many the inability to readjust to civilian life. Theirs is not a cry for sympathy, but a lonely cry for help. Unless you yourself have journeyed to the gates of Hell, you'll never know what mortal combat is really like. And, when you see your friends fall while you survive, you'll always wonder why it was them and not you.

There's one thing I do know for sure. Those days during the Battle of the Bulge have helped me to appreciate life more today. Every day that I live is both a challenge and a joy. I am aware that I'm here only through the grace of God and I am determined to make good use of every minute of my time.

I have no idea of what God had in mind when He let us march headlong into that inferno. Maybe He did it to test us. Then maybe, just maybe, He saved each one of us for some special purpose in life. Then again, maybe it was so that many years later we would be able to see and enjoy the crystal-clean snow and the majestic, fog-shrouded pine forests as what they really are—nature's wonderland. Only then will we be able to fully appreciate the beauty of His work.

Index

Hospitals

– A –

– B –

– C –

GRANDDADDY WAS AIRBORNE!

As an 18 year-old, Bart Hagerman volunteered for military service in April, 1943. With the activation of the 17th Airborne Division, he became a glider trooper in "D" Company of the 193rd Glider Infantry. Following months of rugged Airborne training and Tennessee Maneuvers, plus qualification as a paratrooper, he went overseas with the Division.

From England, the 17th Airborne was flown to France and committed to combat on Christmas Day during the Battle of the Bulge. Hagerman was wounded in action and hospitalized, then returned to the States and eventually to civilian life.

After graduation from college, he accepted a direct commission and was recalled briefly during the Korean conflict. As a civilian he held various advertising and public relations positions while remaining active in the Army Reserve and the Army National Guard Special Forces. He retired from the Army in 1978 as a lieutenant colonel and a master parachutist.

Hagerman resides with his wife in their hometown of Bowling Green, Kentucky.

Other Turner Publishing Company books by Bart Hagerman.

17th Airborne Division History
50th Anniversary of the U.S.A. Airborne
War Stories: The Men of the Airborne
17th Airborne Division History, Vol. II

TURNER
PUBLISHING COMPANY
424 CHURCH STREET, SUITE 2240
NASHVILLE, TENNESSEE 37219
WWW.TURNERPUBLISHING.COM